D1104079

The Fullness of Christ
Unfolded in the History of Joseph

The Fullness of Christ
Unfolded in the History of Joseph

by
OCTAVIUS WINSLOW

REFORMATION HERITAGE BOOKS
Grand Rapids, Michigan

REFORMATION HERITAGE BOOKS
2965 Leonard St., NE
Grand Rapids, MI 49525
616-977-0599 / Fax 616-285-3246
e-mail: orders@heritagebooks.org
website: www.heritagebooks.org

10 digit ISBN #1-892777-74-6
13 digit ISBN #978-1-892777-74-4

Originally published
LONDON: JOHN F. SHAW & CO., 1863

The text has been lightly updated, edited, and prepared for press by Grace Gems — www.gracegems.org.

Scripture references are in KJV.

For additional Reformed literature, both new and used, request a free book list from Reformation Heritage Books at the above address.

PREFACE

THE somewhat familiar style in which the teaching of the present volume is presented, may require an explanation and apology. The simple fact is, these pages are rather the impromptu utterances of the pulpit, than the premeditated compositions of the study. The substance of the book formed a series of extemporary expositions primarily delivered by the Author in the course of his usual weekday ministrations. Rescued by the skill of stenography from the oblivion to which, perhaps, it were well for his literary reputation they had been consigned, they are now reproduced in a new and more permanent form, with the hope that a wider diffusion of the Christ-illustrating truths they unfold, may be but a greater extension of the Divine blessing with which they were originally spoken. The Author has not included all the subjects treated in the progress of the exposition, for the obvious reason that the volume would have exceeded its proper limit.

Several able and valuable works have appeared on the history of Joseph and his brethren, presenting the interesting narrative in different lights, and with varied talents, but by no means exhaustive. As far as he can ascertain, however, the plan of illustration that the Author has adopted will not bring his work into collision with other and abler treatises on the same subject. His one aim has been to present CHRIST as the central object of the picture, grouping around Him—as the Saviour ever delights to be portrayed—the Church that He has redeemed by His precious blood, and taken into personal and inseparable union by the Spirit. Great and frequent stress is laid in this volume upon the fact that the believer has to do with a LIVING CHRIST—a truth but faintly received by many of the Lord's people. And yet, what vital and precious blessings are involved in this doctrine! We are subjects of spiritual life only as a living Christ dwells in us; and we live in the daily battle only as the life of Christ is manifest in our mortal bodies. All is life—life in the soul, life in duty, life in service, life in trial, life in death—as faith closely and firmly entwines around a risen, living, and enthroned Redeemer. It is not we who live,—it is Christ who lives in us. The central fact of the entrancing story illustrated in this volume was that—Joseph lived; around that one fact all its charm, beauty, and vitality gathered. The central fact of Christianity is—A LIVING CHRIST; and faith dealing with this truth in all the circumstances, trivial and great, of the believer's daily history, will bring tides of blessing into the soul in this life, and unveil to faith's eye bright visions of glory in the life that is to come.

With the appropriate lines of a Christian poet, who flourished above two centuries ago, the Author takes his leave of the reader, commending both him and the book to the blessing of Israel's covenant Triune God, and praying that, like Joseph, he may be "a fruitful bough, even a fruitful bough by a well, whose branches run over the wall." Amen.

"Jesus lives! no longer now
  Can thy terrors, Death, appall us;
Jesus lives! by this we know
  Thou, O Grave, canst not enthrall us!

"Jesus lives! henceforth is death
  But the gate of life immortal;
This shall calm our trembling breath
  When we pass its gloomy portal.

"Jesus lives! for us He died;
  Then, alone to Jesus living,
Pure in heart may we abide,
  Glory to our Saviour giving.

"Jesus lives! our hearts know well
  Nought from us His love shall sever;
Life, nor death, nor powers of hell,
  Tear us from His keeping ever.

"Jesus lives! to Him the throne
  Over all the world is given;
May we go where He is gone!
  Rest and reign with Him in heaven.

"Praise the Father! praise the Son,
  Who to us new life hath given!
Praise the Spirit! Three in One,
  All in earth, and all in heaven."

—*Louisa Henrietta*, Electress of Brandenburg, 1696

CONTENTS

The Famished Egyptians Sent to Joseph for Bread 3

Joseph Recognizes His Brethren 27

The Sacks Filled with Corn 47

Jacob's Lament 66

Joseph Making Himself Known to His Brethren 86

Joseph Making Himself Known to His Brethren as Their
    Brother, and Comforting Them 109

Joseph's Exaltation in Egypt 135

The Patriarch's Emigration to Egypt 152

Joseph's Exhortation to Unity 171

Joseph Alive 191

The Patriarch's Contentment and Resolve 206

The Patriarch's Solemn Sacrifice 214

Jacob Sees Joseph and Desires to Die 230

Joseph's Introduction of His Brethren to Pharaoh 241

Jacob's Pilgrimage 250

The Famished Egyptians Sent to Joseph for Bread

GO TO JESUS

And when all the land of Egypt was famished, the people cried to Pharaoh for bread: and Pharaoh said unto all the Egyptians, Go unto Joseph; what he saith to you, do. GENESIS 41:55

THE Word of God is as a garden of fruit and flowers—luscious with the sweetness, penciled with the beauty, and fragrant with the perfume of—CHRIST. All its shadows, types, and prophecies, all its doctrines, precepts, and promises testify of HIM. Search the Scriptures in whatever part, or view them from whatever standpoint you may, of CHRIST they speak, and to CHRIST they lead. The star of the east pendent over the lowly manger of Bethlehem pointed not more truly, conducted not more surely the wise men to the spot where the infant Savior lay, than does this "more sure word of prophecy, which is as a light that shineth in a dark place," lead the mind inquiring for truth, the sinner in search of the Savior, the disciple in quest of his Lord, to Christ, the way, the truth, the life. Let us, dear reader, often walk within this Divine enclosure, this sacred garden, where the north wind and the south wind blows—the *law* humbling and condemning, the *gospel* comforting and saving—and eat the pleasant fruits, and inhale the perfume of Sharon's Rose.

Committing ourselves to the teaching of God's Word, we are about to search for CHRIST among patriarchal shadows. JOSEPH, by general agreement, and fitted to be, in the most essential incidents of his history, is a personal and remarkable type of the Lord Jesus Christ. It is true we have no express declaration of this in Scripture; nevertheless, if the history of Joseph, as recorded by Moses in Genesis, be compared with the history of the Lord Jesus Christ, as recorded by the evangelists in the gospels, the analogy will be found complete. Indeed, it would seem impossible to take the most cursory survey of his eventful and chequered life, and not see *the Lord Jesus foreshadowed in each circumstance as it passes in review before the spiritual and reflective mind.*

In this patriarchal study of Christ, we are also necessarily led to study important things in relation to the Church of Christ. It is a beautiful and consolatory arrangement that we cannot study the person and work of Christ—His Headship, beauty, and salvation—without at the same time being enchanted into a study of the history, the relation, privileges, and glory of the Church of God. All that Jesus did in His mediatorial character, He did as a *representative* person. He represented God, on the one hand, and He represented His Church, on the other.

Oh, how faintly do the saints of God realize the position of dignity, exaltation, wealth, and power, to which they are raised in virtue of their union with the Lord Jesus! In consequence of this federal, close, and inseparable union, believers are *crucified* with Christ, are *raised* with Christ, *ascend* with Christ, will *come* with Christ, and with Christ will *reign* in glory, wherever the seat of His government may be, as "kings and priests unto God" forever!

The hallowed and soothing influence of this truth upon the mind must be of the happiest character. Realize that Christ and you are *one*—closely, tenderly, indissolubly one—and this reciprocity of affection, this identity of interests, this ever-present source of all supply, will unclasp many a burden, quell many a fear, tinge with golden light many a dark cloud, and constrain you by love to run the way of your Lord's commands with a cheerful, unquestioning, unreserved obedience.

Let us now humbly and devoutly bend our thoughts to the spiritual contemplation of Christ, as shadowed forth in this chapter of patriarchal history. May the Divine Spirit, the Revealer and Interpreter of Christ and His truth, impart to our minds that anointing which gives to the *type* its meaning, to the *shadow* its substance, to the *prophecy* its solution, that our meditations on the present theme may be scriptural and sober, spiritual and sanctifying—abasing self, exalting Christ, to the glory of God the Father!

To reach the present important period of the patriarch's history, we necessarily pass by unnoticed many striking and instructive events, tracing his transition from suffering and humiliation, to that dignity and aggrandizement which we make our starting-point in the present series of subjects. Some of those events, however, not essentially relevant to the gospel truths we are about to illustrate, will incidentally appear in the process of our discussion, and will be interwoven with these shadows of Christ and His Church.

We commence, then, at an epoch of Joseph's history which finds him exalted to the prime-minister of Pharaoh's kingdom, the governor of all Egypt, the greatest man in the land, second only to the Pharaoh himself; to whose custody and administration were confided the government and treasures of the kingdom. "And Pharaoh said unto Joseph, Forasmuch as God hath shewed thee all this, there is none so discreet and wise as thou art: Thou shalt be over my house, and according unto thy word shall all my people be ruled: only in the throne will I be greater than thou. And Pharaoh said unto Joseph, See, I have set thee over all the land of Egypt."

Having said thus much, let us again remind the reader what our specific object is in bringing before him these typical shadows. It is not our intention so much to unfold the history of the patriarch, as *to illustrate the Lord Jesus Christ in the relation in which He stands to His Church, to unveil His glory, beauty, and fullness, to define the close bond of union that unites to Him all His brethren, and to bring you into a more personal realization of what Christ is to you, and of what you are to Christ.*

The points for our meditation in the present chapter are—the FAMINE,—the CRY FOR BREAD,—and the COMMAND, *"Go to Joseph."*

The land of Egypt was now smitten with a grievous and widespread famine. The seven years of plenty had expired. The people having lived upon the old stock of corn until their resources were wholly exhausted, their granaries were emptied, their supplies consumed, a gnawing and crushing famine had succeeded. All this came to pass exactly and literally as Joseph had predicted; for Joseph was a man of God, and spoke as the Spirit of God moved him. It was by the Spirit of God that he interpreted the dreams of Pharaoh; and, consequently, as he spoke by the inspiration of the Spirit, so all that he said literally came to pass.

Allow us to throw in one remark here. Let your faith in, and your reverence for, the Divine inspiration of the Scriptures of truth become firmer and deeper; for, be assured, "holy men of God spake as they were moved by the Holy Ghost," and all that they have said, both of mercy and judgment, shall literally and surely come to pass!

We turn now from this event of national history, to contemplate *the spiritual gospel instruction* with which it is so deeply and richly fraught.

A greater famine than that which now prevailed in Egypt is raging throughout this fallen and apostate world! The years of spiritual plenty in which the world in its original state of righteousness, rectitude, and holiness, enjoyed every blessing that God could give, or man experience, have passed away. Man lived upon his own righteousness, stood in his own holiness, walked in fellowship with Jehovah, up to the moment that he broke from his allegiance to God, and became a fugitive from the garden of Eden. They were years of richness, of abundance, of plenty, to our race.

What imagination can depict, what thought conceive, what tongue describe the blessedness, the fullness of all blessing which our nature experienced and enjoyed during those years when righteousness, holiness, and peace reigned supreme and paramount in this now sinful and accursed world of ours! But those *years of plenty* have passed away forever; and the *years of spiritual famine* have succeeded. Study what age of the world you may, travel into what climate you may, look into the face of what human being you may, and there confronts you a *moral* famine, a *spiritual* destitution of the soul—every man exhibiting in his life, the existence of a raging, gnawing destitution, which no created object can supply.

The whole scheme of our salvation, the redemption of man by the Lord Jesus Christ, the revelation of the "glorious gospel of the blessed God," all the provisions that God has made in the Son of His love, are based on the one momentous fact—that our nature, spiritual and intellectual, is a famished, starving, destitute nature, there being nothing in the vast storehouse, the universal granary of the world's goods, that can meet and satisfy a single need or craving of the human soul.

Why this air of restlessness which pervades our nature? Why this look of dissatisfaction imprinted on every countenance? Why those deep furrows on every brow? Why this universal cry of our humanity, "Who will shew us *any* good?" What! can you find *no* good in this vast universe that God has formed? Ah, no! Man finds all *created good* to be but a broken cistern. He hews out cistern after cistern, sets on foot enterprise after enterprise, devises new plans for happiness, each one more promising than the other, and still his soul is filled with one vast, aching void—the heart restless, the spirit anxious, the mind dissatisfied; and so our poor, famished, craving, destitute nature travels round the circle of all *created* blessing, and terminates the journey by reiterating the plaintive cry, "Who will shew us any good?"

We pass from this part of the subject to consider—*the cry for bread.* "And when all the land of Egypt was famished, the people cried to Pharaoh for bread."

In the first place, listen to the *appeal*—"The people *cried* to Pharaoh." Here was something like sensibility, life, a deep, intense conviction of the prevailing famine. It is not *merely* the existence of the fact, but the deep-felt, agonizing conviction of the fact. They not only knew that they were starving, that their granaries were empty, that their resources were entirely exhausted, but they were a people who rose as one man, under the crushing weight of their necessity, and made their appeal. They felt the biting famine, were conscious of the gnawing hunger, that the wolf was feeding at their vitals, and they rose as one people and uttered their cry, "Give us bread."

Look at the spiritual teaching of this. There is a universal existence in our race of a need—that need is *happiness;* a need for something that will meet the intense yearning and craving of our spiritual, moral, and intellectual being. Some seek it in the gay world, some in the sensual world, others in the intellectual world, others more in the political world, and there are not a few who are seeking it in what is termed conventionally the *religious world.*

These have little or no taste for the world's gaieties, less for intellectual pursuits, and still less ambition to climb the steep of human distinction and carve their name on some lofty column; but they seek to meet the yearning, the panting, and the craving of their nature in a religion of their own; and religious duties, religious engagements, religious excitement, and religious rites and ceremonies, are eagerly sought and sedulously cultivated, with a view of meeting this moral craving for that which will give repose and satisfaction to the soul.

But we pass from these to another class, more circumscribed, but decidedly more spiritual and blessed. We refer to those from whom the cry for bread issues under the teaching, quickening influence of God the Eternal Spirit. *The hungering and thirsting after righteousness, after holiness, after Christ, after God, which marks a gracious soul,* is not the breathing of the unregenerate, unawakened, and carnal mind. Ah, no! The blessed and Eternal Spirit is the author of all spiritual feelings, convictions, desires, and breathings in the quickened and renewed man. Are you breathing after Christ? Are you hungering for Christ, the bread of life? Are you thirsting for Christ, the wellspring of life? Is your soul panting for God in a dry and thirsty land where there is no water? Then, beloved, you are the subject of *spiritual thirst and spiritual hunger, wrought in your soul by the Holy Spirit.*

It is the Spirit convincing you of your lost, self-ruined and undone condition. It is the Spirit opening your eyes to see your sinfulness, vileness, and nothingness. It is the Spirit showing you the entire loss of all your original righteousness, and bringing you to see that you are a poor, starving, famishing sinner, lying at the feet of Jesus, realizing that none but Jesus can meet your case. Oh, we beseech you, keep your eye on the fine line of distinction between a soul only thirsting for natural good and for worldly happiness, and a soul spiritually hungering and thirsting for Christ.

If, my dear reader, you were at one time seeking to satisfy this craving of your spiritual nature in religious rites, ceremonies, and duties, going to your sacraments, to your church, to your district, and returning to your chamber still with the crushing weight of sin, still with the gnawing hunger, no peace with God, no sense of pardon, no clear view of your interest in Christ, no star of hope twinkling in the dark clouds overshadowing you, no consciousness of adoption; but now if the blessed Spirit has opened your eyes to see that your own works and doings will avail you nothing, and has brought you, empty and sinful, to the Savior's feet, craving the bread that comes from God, thankful even for the crumbs that fall from His table, then we wish you joy of your new-born feelings!

It may be but a sigh, but a tear, but a desire bursting from your full, penitent heart; nevertheless, the Spirit is its author and will be its finisher. It came from God, to God it will rise, and in God it will terminate and eternally rest. Thus much for the cry.

Now, for a moment, let us advert to the *object* of that cry. What was the cry for? There was but *one thing* that could meet the needs of the nation. Offer them the most precious jewels, domains the most extensive, tell them of rank the highest, of wealth countless as the sands, they would turn from you and say, "Cruel mockers are you of our misery! We are starving, we are famishing, we are hungry; give us *bread*, or we die!"

Now, what is the one grand requirement of the soul? What will meet this deep, intense craving? Is it *wealth?* It has been tried to its utmost, and found lacking. Ask the millionaire, and he will tell you that the toil of obtaining it, the risk of investing it, the fear of losing it, and the thought of leaving it, robs him of all comfort in the possession of it, and that thus riches are utterly incompetent to make their possessor happy.

Is it the *world?* Ah, no! It has been searched and ransacked through and through, and can scarcely afford a single new source of pleasure or enjoyment. One could sometimes smile, were the spectacle not too awful, at the puerile, childish expedients to which the worldling resorts to meet this intense craving of the mind. See the bubbles he blows, the baubles he chases, the straws he gathers, while the Son of God holds out a jeweled crown to the aspirant for true glory, honor, and immortality.

Will the *creature* supply it? Ask him who has found the noblest, the dearest that earth ever afforded, if that angel of intellect and beauty, before whom the soul burns the incense of adoration, has filled this deep and aching void. What a hallucination, what a fantasy, what a mockery is all this!— the mirage of the desert not more deceptive. In the striking and solemn language of the prophet—"It shall even be as when an hungry man dreameth, and, behold, he eateth; but he awaketh, and his soul is empty: or as when a thirsty man dreameth, and behold, he drinketh; but he awaketh, and, behold, he is faint, and his soul hath appetite."

We ask again, what will meet the craving of the soul? Bread, and *bread* only! We might learn much instruction from this fact in our efforts to evangelize the world. Why all this discussion about *Education?* Will Education meet the craving of the soul of man? Why all this excitement about *Social Science?* Will Social Science meet the moral famine of our nature? How do our legislators, our philosophers, our political economists, and many of the moral reformers, lose sight of this great truth!

The soul of man needs the Gospel, and *nothing but the gospel of Christ* will meet its spiritual and deep necessities— *nothing but the Gospel* will uplift, ennoble, sanctify, and save our fallen, famishing, and crushed race. The world is asking for bread, and in giving it education, and science, and moral reform, while withholding the Gospel of Christ, we are offering it—a *stone!* Oh, keep the eye firmly fixed on this truth, and you will be wiser than the wisest of the worldly wise, a more profound philosopher than the most learned, that nothing short of the glorious Gospel of the blessed God will regenerate, sanctify, and save the soul of man.

How impressively and emphatically did our Lord embody this truth in the great commission with which He clothed His apostles, before He left the scene of His toil and suffering,—"Go ye into all the world and PREACH THE GOSPEL to every creature!" As though He had said, "The world is famishing—man is perishing; I give to you the bread of life—go forth and distribute it fully and freely to every creature under heaven. The extent of man's neediness and misery shall be the only limit to your mission."

But let us circumscribe this train of thought. *What is the one specific cry of a truly spiritually regenerated and awakened soul?* Is it not for JESUS, the bread of life? Most assuredly! Go to the sinner bowed beneath the weight of the law, to the man awakened to a conviction of his sinful and lost condition, who has been brought to know the nothingness of his own righteousness, and ask him, 'What will make you happy?' Bid him go to his religious duties, to his sacraments, to his church, to his minister. Oh, how bitter will be his reproof—"I asked you, as a starving man, for bread, and you give me husks. I need Christ—I need to know that my sins are pardoned—that my transgressions are blotted out—that I am an accepted, forgiven child of God. And nothing short of this will meet my case. I have tried every other expedient, have come to the end of all my own doings, and I perish with hunger. I have been feeding upon ashes. I have sought to meet the cravings of my spirit with the chaff. I have been drinking in the wind. Give me Christ, or I die! None but Christ! None but Christ! Place me upon a pinnacle, and give me the world. I survey from there, still, without Christ I am undone—I starve—I perish! Lord, I fall at Your feet. You only have the bread of eternal life. Here will I lie, here will I cling; and if I perish in my hunger, it shall be asking You, imploring You, crying to You for bread!"

Oh, thank God if the blessed Spirit has brought you to see the difference between the bread of life and the husks with which man would seek to meet your spiritual craving! Fall on your knees, and thank God if you have been taught that none but Christ—a crucified, atoning, and full Savior—a Savior whose blood blots out the deepest stain of guilt, and whose flowing robe of righteousness justifies the believing soul from all sin—can meet your soul's necessity!

That *Jesus is the bread of the spiritual soul*, how clear and impressive is His own teaching—"And Jesus said unto them, I am the bread of life: he that cometh to me shall never hunger; and he that believeth on me shall never thirst." "I am the living bread which came down from heaven; if any man eat of this bread, he shall live for ever: and the bread that I will give is my flesh, which I will give for the life of the world." "Verily, verily, I say unto you, Except ye eat the flesh of the Son of man, and drink his blood, ye have no life in you." "He that eateth my flesh and drinketh my blood, dwelleth in me and I in him." "He that eateth of this bread shall live for ever." Shall we not exclaim, in view of this marvelous statement, "Lord, evermore give us *this* bread!"

But let us view this general truth in some of its particulars. Bread is composed of a variety of constituent parts. There are *various views of Christ*, each one precious to those who know and love Him. And in the sovereignty of the Spirit one view of the Lord Jesus may be unfolded and applied with more fullness and power than another. Perhaps it is a sense of *pardoned sin* that you need. Jesus Christ is that pardon; His blood, His precious blood speaks pardon; one drop applied to your conscience will seal a sense of full forgiveness. "In whom we have redemption through his blood, even the forgiveness of sins." Perhaps it is a sense of *peace* with God you desire; the righteousness of Christ imputed to you will impart that peace. "Being justified by faith, we have peace with God through our Lord Jesus Christ." Perhaps it is to know that you are vitally *united* to Christ; faith in Christ will give you this union. Thus it all resolves itself into one grand truth—Jesus Christ, "whose flesh is meat indeed, and whose blood is drink indeed."

And if the spirit of God has given you a hungering and thirsting after Christ, then it is your privilege to receive, as the *free gift* of God's grace, the Lord Jesus Christ as the "living bread which came down from heaven." A most important truth is shadowed forth here, which we must prominently and distinctly place before you. You will observe that there was no direct response from Pharaoh to the cry of the Egyptians for bread. They appealed to him for bread, but he sent them to Joseph. "And Pharaoh said unto all the Egyptians, *Go to Joseph.*"

And why this? Because all the corn of Egypt was placed in the hands of Joseph, and Joseph was the man he delighted to exalt and to honor. He would teach them, too, that such was the order and administration of his government—all appeals to him must be through his prime minister, the governor and treasurer of the kingdom; and that what Joseph said and did had the royal authority and sanction. Words fail to set forth the importance and the preciousness of the gospel truth here shadowed forth.

The Lord Jesus is the "One Mediator between God and man." All the treasures of grace are placed in His hands; and He is the administrator of the everlasting covenant. "No man cometh unto the Father but by me." "I am the door." "Through him we both have access by one Spirit unto the Father." What can be more clear than this truth, that we can have no dealings in the way of salvation, and grace, and communion with the Father, *but through the Son?* It is in the righteousness of Christ we have acceptance with God. It is by the blood of Christ we draw near to God. It is in the name of Christ we offer our requests to the Father; and the bestowment of all the precious blessings, the daily bread, the continuous supply of every need, shall be in and through the Lord Jesus Christ, "that all men should honour the Son, even as they honour the Father."

This is a truth that may meet the tried, perplexed experience of some of our readers. How many there are who go to the Father for pardon, acceptance, and peace, and for all the blessings of daily life, without a recognition of the mediatorial character, relation, and fullness of the Lord Jesus Christ! Look once more at the shadow. These famished Egyptians passed by Joseph; they did not recognize the prime minister; they did not see that Joseph had all the granaries, all the corn of Egypt under his seal and in his hands. They went directly to Pharaoh, and met with no response.

This may just touch the spiritual state and position of your soul. You are wondering why for years you have been seeking, reading, and praying and doing, and yet have not advanced a single step in your spiritual course,—not a single beam of God's love has penetrated your soul—no sweet peace flows like a river in your heart,—no joy thrills your spirit; and you have no sense of reconciliation, adoption, and acceptance with the Beloved. And yet for weeks, and months, and years, you have been traveling to God, not recognizing that the Lord Jesus Christ is the true, the spiritual Joseph of the Church; and that it is in His hands all fullness of blessing is deposited.

"Go to Joseph." "Go to my Son," says the Father. "You petition for bread—you sue for pardon—you ask for reconciliation—you hunger and thirst for grace—go to my Son! I have laid help upon one that is mighty. I have exalted Him among His brethren, and will honor and magnify Him. He was humbled and slain, and now He is exalted and crowned. He died, and rose again, and lives to be the administrator of all the blessings of My covenant. Go to Him; and whatever you ask in His name, I will grant it."

Thus speaks the Father to you in this type. And thus our Lord confirms the truth—"Whatsoever ye shall ask in my name, that will I do, that the Father may be glorified in the Son: if ye shall ask anything in my name, I will do it." "Verily, verily, whatsoever ye shall ask the Father in my name, he will give it you. Hitherto ye have asked nothing in my name: ask and ye shall receive, that your joy may be full."

See why you have asked, and have not received,—you have not gone in the name of Jesus—you have not pleaded His merits—you have not honored His name—you have not gone to the Father with that one argument, that single plea that never fails—the ATONING BLOOD of Immanuel.

"You have asked, and have not received, because you have asked amiss."

We are thus instructed, not by the type only, but by the words of our Lord himself, that *prayer* is to be equally addressed to *the Son* as to the Father. No believer should have a moment's hesitation, or a single doubt on this subject. Admit His Deity, and you admit His claim to Divine worship. Acknowledge His Headship of the Church, and you admit His administration in the government of the Church. Allow Him to be the one Depositary of His people's grace, and you are forced to allow that petition for supplies of that grace must be preferred directly and personally to Him. Hesitate not, then, to address your confessions of sin, your pleadings for pardon, your petitions for grace, your breathings for sympathy, your praises and adoration to the Lord Jesus Christ, EVEN AS you address them to the Father.

And if it be your last, your latest, your expiring breath, let it be in the words of the dying Stephen, "LORD JESUS, receive my spirit!" Thus honoring Him, He will honor you. Then GO TO JESUS, and approach the Father through Jesus, and you shall have all your needs supplied, for there is corn in Egypt, bread enough and to spare, and you need not die. But oh, if you die, let it be in the very act of going to Jesus! Rouse to this work of shutting yourself up entirely to Christ. *Let not sins, nor backslidings, nor poverty, nor unbelief, keep you away from Jesus.* Say with the poet—

> "I'll go to Jesus, though my sin
>   Has like a mountain rose;
> I know His courts, I'll enter in,
>   Whatever may oppose.
>
> "I'll to the gracious King approach,
>   Whose scepter pardon gives,

Perhaps He will command my touch,
      And then the suppliant lives.

"Perhaps He will admit my plea,
      Perhaps will hear my prayer;
But if I perish, I will pray,
      And perish only there."

There is another gospel truth shadowed forth in this part of our type. In anticipation of the seven years' gnawing, grinding, crushing famine, Pharaoh had *laid up* in the granaries of Egypt an ample supply of bread for the people. Was there ever a more precious truth illustrated than this? *God, from eternity, has provided in the Son of His love, in the covenant of redemption, and in His eternal purposes, a full redemption, a free salvation for our poor famished, starving souls.* Do not think that Redemption was an afterthought of God; that Salvation was a subsequent idea of the Divine mind. Ah, no! Never was there a greater fallacy in theology than this.

God, from all eternity, knew that man would fall; foresaw the apostasy of our race, and provided for the event. In the counsels of eternity, God prepared and devised the great scheme of our salvation; laid up in the heavenly granary the bread that would meet the necessities of our famished nature, in original, unfailing, inexhaustible stores of pardoning, sanctifying, justifying, comforting grace—all treasured, provided in anticipation of the fall, the ruin, the famine of our poor sinful world. "Him, being delivered by the determinate counsel and foreknowledge of God, ye have taken, and with wicked hands have crucified and slain."

Beloved, the rivulet is sweet, the stream is sweeter, but the fountain from where both flow is sweeter than all. Let us follow the rivulet to the stream, the stream to the fountain. "I have loved thee with an *everlasting love:* therefore with lovingkindness have I drawn thee." What an additional element of sweetness will it give to that bread of life, how much more sparkling and refreshing will be the stream of the water of life, if you will blend it in your thoughts with God's everlasting love and purposes of mercy towards you! "Oh, how great is thy goodness which thou hast *laid up* for them that fear thee!" Thus, all the covenant blessings of redemption and grace are *anticipative*—anticipative of the circumstances, the needs, and the appeals of the Lord's people.

We may, therefore, believe that *no new exigency shall arise, no new affliction overtake us, no new event occur, which is not anticipated and provided for in the fullness of Christ, and in the supplies of the covenant of grace.* Leave, then, your future confidingly, calmly, hopefully. For all that future your heavenly Father has provided in and through Jesus. When the seven years' plenty have expired, and the seven years' famine commence, you shall find the Lord Jesus to be God's Treasurer and Almoner, "in whom it pleased the Father that all fulness should dwell," and your every need shall be amply and freely supplied. Let us, then, exultingly, gratefully exclaim, "Blessed be the God and Father of our Lord Jesus Christ, who hath blessed us with all spiritual blessings in heavenly places in Christ: according as he hath chosen us in him before the foundation of the world," (Eph. 1:3, 4.) Yes! before an atom of matter was formed, or a foundation-stone of this mighty fabric was laid, before a star shone in the heavens, or a ray of light trembled on the chaotic darkness, grace and glory were *laid up* for us in Christ Jesus.

Observe another gospel truth strikingly illustrated. Old as their supplies of corn were, they would, to the famished recipients, be as the blessings of a *new* harvest. Such are our gospel supplies. Ancient as the years of God, are the blessings of grace, yet to our daily life of faith they are as new blessings. Jesus is the "mediator of the *new* covenant." "This is my blood of the *new* testament." "If any man be in Christ, he is a *new* creature." "Who also hath made us able ministers of the *new* testament." God would thus teach us that we must come to Jesus for new, for *daily* supplies—daily grace for daily corruption—daily strength for daily service—daily sympathy for daily sorrow—daily support for daily trial— daily food for daily hunger.

"To whom *coming*." "Jesus Christ, the same yesterday, *to-day*, and for ever." *Go to Jesus, then, with each new circumstance and event and demand as it arises.* Jesus, our "Tree of Life," bears fruit every month, and every day of the month, and every hour of the day. He has taught you to pray, "Give us this day our *daily* bread," and He promises, "Open thy mouth wide and I will fill it." Let, then, the life you live in the flesh, encompassed by daily, hourly infirmities, trials, and sorrows, be *a daily drawing of new blessings from your Divine granary. Whatever your craving, you will find in Jesus a corresponding supply.* You have no sin His blood cannot cleanse—no grief His sympathy will not soothe—no infirmity His grace will not help—no perplexity His wisdom will not guide—no lack His sufficiency will not supply.

> "Grace taught my wandering feet
>   To tread the heavenly road;
> And *new supplies* each hour I meet,
>   While pressing on to God."

In all this we trace the will and purpose of God in the exaltation and honor to which He has advanced His Son Jesus Christ. The shadowing forth of this truth in the case of Joseph is most instructive. "And Pharaoh took off his ring from his hand, and put it upon Joseph's hand, and arrayed him in vestures of fine linen, and put a gold chain about his neck; and he made him to ride in the second chariot which he had; and they cried before him, Bow the knee." Behold the shadowing of our gospel Joseph! What do we read? "Wherefore God also hath highly exalted him, and given him a name which is above every name: that at the name of Jesus every knee should bow, of things in heaven, and things in earth, and things under the earth; and that every tongue should confess that Jesus Christ is Lord, to the glory of God the Father."

Reader, have you bowed the knee to Jesus? have you bowed the heart in adoration, faith, and love? Bow to Him you must, either in this world, or in the world to come—in time, or in eternity. To Christ all judgment is committed by the Father, "that all men should honour the Son, *even as* they honour the Father." "They will reverence my Son." Do *you* reverence Him? Are you exalting Him—crowning Him—serving Him? God will not hold him guiltless who dishonors His Son Jesus Christ—denying His Godhead, rejecting His atonement, refusing to love, serve, and glorify Him. Oh, bow your heart and bend your knee to Jesus! Place the diadem of Divine royalty upon His kingly brow, and worship Him in His priestly office, and He will make *you* a king and a priest unto God when He appears in glory!

"Go to Joseph." In their *gospel* significance, what words of fullness, solemnity, and hope are these! Interpreted in their spiritual import, they chime upon the ear more sweetly than an angel's harp, and more solemnly than the blast of the archangel's trumpet, "GO TO JESUS!" My reader, deem not these brief words of no interest to you. Words more momentous, more significant, more precious, were never uttered. It is a question of life or death. Go to Jesus you must, or you are lost! Your solemn future of happiness or of woe, of heaven or hell, is suspended upon your compliance or non-compliance with this invitation.

In some of its essential features your spiritual condition is portrayed by the case of the prodigal who took his journey into a far country, and when he had spent all, found himself in beggary and need amid a mighty famine; but encouraged by the recollection that there was bread enough in his father's house to spare, he arose and went to his father. It is for your life that we now urge you with all the earnestness and solemnity we can command, Go to Jesus. Nothing whatever must be allowed to intercept your coming; no reasoning must dissuade, no difficulty must daunt, no condition must discourage you. To Christ you *must* come, or perish! It is Christ—or Satan. Christ—or condemnation. Christ—or hell. The whole matter, more important to you than the interests of ten million empires, is narrowed to the finest point, the smallest compass—go to Jesus, or perish in the famine, with all the bitter pangs of the second and eternal death. Go, then, to Jesus—go at once, go as you are, go through a crowd of difficulties, opposition, and discouragements; go with your sins countless as the sands which belt the ocean, or the stars which bestud the firmament—sins of scarlet and of crimson hue; go with all the sad memories of the past crowding upon you—your caviling at Divine truth, your rebellion against God, your aggravated violations of His law, your ungodly deeds which you have ungodly committed, the hard speeches which you have spoken, even though you have plucked the crown from the Savior's head, trailing it in the dust, even—oh, crime of crimes!—even though you have scornfully trampled His atoning blood beneath your feet—even though you have made a covenant with hell, and with death are at an agreement; yet, in the face of all, in spite of all, notwithstanding all, with trumpet-tongue, the astounding, the marvelous, the gracious words peal forth upon your ear—GO TO JESUS!

Yes! to Jesus you may go! God is prepared to be reconciled to you in Christ, and He sends you to His Son for the merits, the worthiness, and the plea with which you may propitiate His justice, be restored to His favor, be adopted, accepted, and saved. And to make this momentous fact of your restoration doubly sure, you have both the efficacy of Christ's work—and the assurance of Christ's promise—annihilating, if you stand at His bar condemned, every excuse—"THE BLOOD OF JESUS CHRIST his Son CLEANSETH US FROM ALL SIN." "HIM THAT COMETH TO ME, I WILL IN NO WISE CAST OUT." Arise, then, and go. Be this your plea—"Blessed Savior! I come, I come to You as I am; I come vile, I come empty, I come as a bankrupt and a beggar, to receive as the gift of Your free grace the blessings of Your salvation."

> "Encouraged by Thy word of promise to the poor,
> Behold a beggar, Lord, waits at Thy mercies' door;
> No hand, no heart, O Lord, but Thine,
> Can help and pity needs like mine."

Believer in Jesus, regard not this act of going to Jesus as only primary and initiatory—once done, done forever. Oh, no! it is a continuous act all through the Christian's life. *The life of faith is a constant coming to Jesus for daily, hourly, and fresh supplies.* "To whom COMING,"—notice the tense—coming *now!* coming at this moment, and continuously coming. Let every circumstance and event, every trial, sorrow, and need, be an echo of the gracious life-inspiring words—"Go to Joseph!" Go to Jesus, confessing sin; go, unveiling grief; go, telling need; go, breathing love, desire, and hope. You are still in the land of famine and of need. But your heavenly Father would remind you that He has anticipated and provided for all your requirements, for all your history, for your daily demands, in Him whom He has made Head over all things to the Church, the fullness of Him that fills all in all.

Take the hard or the broken heart, take the cold or the glowing heart, take your barrenness or your fruitfulness, take the sunbeam of prosperity or the cloud-veil of adversity, take the joy, the sorrow, take *all* to Jesus; let Him participate in all, keep you in all, sympathize with all, for Jesus is your Brother, raised up to befriend, support, and preserve you in your time of need.

"What he saith to you, do." Implicit obedience to Christ's commands is as much enjoined by our heavenly Father, as it is the dictate of gratitude and the prompting of affection. "This is his commandment, That we should believe on the name of his Son Jesus Christ, and love one another, as he gave us commandment," (1 John 3:23.) Obedience to Christ is the evidence of discipleship and the test of love. "If ye love me, keep my commandments." And when our adorable Lord and Master, our King and Head in Zion, pledged to the apostles, and through them to all who should afterwards believe in Him, His presence to the end of time, He linked the precious promise with the obligation of obedience, "Teaching them to observe all things whatsoever I have commanded you: and, lo, I am with you alway, even unto the end of the world."

Let this, then, be your daily prayer—"Lord, what will You have me to do? I would bear Your yoke, and carry Your burden, and bind Your cross to my heart, and follow You, blessed Lamb of God, wherever You go." Whatever, then, Christ says to you, *do*. He bids you believe in Him; He commands you to obey Him; He invites you to come to Him; He asks you to confess His name before the world; to take up your cross and follow Him.

All this, and whatever more He bids you, you must do, as a loving, obedient disciple. There must be no debate, no demur. It's not for a soldier to question his commander's orders, nor for a child to debate his father's commands. "Ye are my friends, if you do whatsoever I command you." Let obedience to Christ in everything be the distinctive badge of your discipleship. His grace will sustain you, His counsel guide you, His presence will cheer you, His smile will reward you, and you shall know from heart-experience, that "in keeping his commands there is great reward."

"What He saith to you, *do.*" Saved by Jehovah's love from this wide-spread, this fearful famine—nourished by Jesus, the bread of life, God's unspeakable gift—and made to know both your hunger and its supply, by the Eternal Spirit—oh, to the Triune God be henceforth—your intellect, your wealth, your rank, your time, your life— wholly and forever CONSECRATED.

> "Father, Son, and Holy Spirit,
>   One in Three, and Three in One.
> As by the celestial host,
>   Let Thy will on earth be done;
> Praise by all to Thee be given,
>   Glorious Lord of earth and heaven!
>
> "Vilest of the sinful race,
>   Lo, I answer to Thy call;
> Meanest vessel of Thy grace,
>   Grace divinely free for all;
> Lo! I come to do Thy will,
>   All Thy counsel to fulfill.
>
> "If so poor a worm as I
>   May to Thy great glory live,
> All my actions sanctify,
>   All my words and thoughts receive;

Claim me for Thy service, claim
All I have, and all I am.

"Take my soul and body's powers;
Take my memory, mind, and will;
All my goods, and all my hours,
All I know, and all I feel;
All I think, or speak, or do;
Take my heart, but make it new!

"Now, my God, Thine own I am,
Now I give Thee back Thine own;
Freedom, friends, and health, and fame,
Consecrate to Thee alone
Thine I live, thrice happy I!
Happier still, if Thine I die!

"Father, Son, and Holy Ghost,
One in Three, and Three in One,
As by the celestial host,
Let Thy will on earth be done;
Praise be all to Thee be given,
Glorious Lord of earth and heaven!"

Joseph Recognizes His Brethren

CHRIST'S KNOWLEDGE OF HIS PEOPLE—THEIR IGNORANCE OF HIM

And Joseph knew his brethren, but they knew him not.
GENESIS 42:8

A MORE precious truth, or a sublimer idea our Lord Jesus Christ never uttered when on earth than in those words of His intercessory prayer addressed to the Father—"This is life eternal, that they might know thee, the only true God, and Jesus Christ, whom thou hast sent." It was our true Joseph beseeching His Father and our Father that this revelation of God and of Christ, in the knowledge of whom consisted their eternal happiness, might be fully disclosed to His brethren. Until this revelation is made, until this knowledge is attained, the range of thought and inquiry has been limited to objects which derive their sole interest and importance from a world passing away, and destined, before long, to be involved in the final conflagration of all things. What are a man's intellectual achievements worth, even though he "understood all mysteries and all knowledge," if yet he knows not spiritually, experimentally, and savingly, the only true God, and Jesus Christ whom he has sent? Such a one would deem the words of the apostle, himself no mean authority—extravagant and hyperbolical—"Yea, doubtless, and I count *all things but*

27

loss for the EXCELLENCY OF THE KNOWLEDGE OF CHRIST JESUS my Lord."

Added to which is his ardent aspiration—breathing from a mind already furnished as few were, with the precious spoils of this divine knowledge—"That I may know him"—know Him more in the power of His risen life-giving, life-sustaining, and life-securing life. It is to this train of thought we are led by the interesting and instructive period in Joseph's history that we have now reached. There are before us two opposites—*knowledge* and *ignorance*—knowledge on the part of Joseph, ignorance on the part of Joseph's brethren. "And Joseph knew his brethren, but they knew him not."

How full of Christ, and how replete with instruction to the saints of God is this incident! Oh, may the Holy Spirit be our teacher and revealer, opening to our understandings and applying to our hearts these scriptures of truth that so manifestly and decidedly testify of Jesus! The two points for consideration are, JOSEPH AS DISGUISED TO HIS BRETHREN, and THE RECOGNITION OF HIS BRETHREN BY JOSEPH, illustrating a vital, spiritual, and precious truth—CHRIST'S KNOWLEDGE OF HIS PEOPLE.

"They knew him not." There was, doubtless, much to account for this ignorance on their part. Joseph was now exalted to the government of Egypt. Twenty-two years had passed since they last saw him, then a young lad, a beardless youth, a slave sold to the Egyptians. He was now full-grown, had arrived at maturity, and was arrayed in courtly, costly apparel, speaking to them in the language and with the air of an Egyptian prince. All this tended to throw a profound veil over the person of Joseph, and to disguise from them the fact that they were, unconsciously to themselves, in the immediate presence of their long dead but now living brother.

The spiritual reader, in whose mind thoughts of Jesus are pre-eminent, will in a moment recognize the Lord here. The disciples, the Lord's brethren, knew not their Lord immediately after His resurrection. So changed was He in those three days—His countenance so altered,—His whole appearance so transformed, invested as with a resurrection glory so great—when He appeared in their presence and spoke to them, they failed to recognize Him—they knew not that it was Jesus. Mary at the sepulcher, the two disciples journeying to Emmaus, the gathered Church in the upper room, were all alike unconscious that their once crucified but now risen Lord was in converse with them.

Oh, what must be His changed appearance now! How glorious! Wearing still the same body He wore on earth—perchance still associated with the imagery of the sacrificial death He endured—the print of the nails, the gash of the spear, "looking like a lamb that had been slain;" yet so transformed, so glorified, so glorious, that, but for His own manifestation and unveiling, none who knew Him in the days of His humiliation and sorrow, would know Him again.

But oh, bright and joyous prospect!—we shall know Him—we shall see Him as He is—and we shall be like Him, for He "shall change our vile body" (the body of our humiliation) "that it may be fashioned like unto his glorious body." Dear Lord, we thank You for what we see and know of You now; and are looking for that blessed hope, Your glorious appearing, when the window will be uplifted, and the veil be withdrawn, and You will stand before us as our true Joseph, raised from the deepest humiliation to the most exalted and resplendent glory, honor, majesty, and power.

But the point of analogy which now arrests our attention is more solemn and instructive—the *spiritual* ignorance of the Lord Jesus Christ which marks, for the most part, the brethren of the Lord. This is exhibited, in the first place, in the natural, unregenerate state of the Lord's hidden people. What knowledge have we naturally and in our unenlightened state of Jesus? It is true, He may be our Brother in an everlasting covenant, our Savior to be revealed and made known to us in the sovereignty and effectual calling of His grace; but, while we are in that natural and unregenerate state, we are totally and profoundly ignorant of the Lord Jesus.

The condition of the Jews is an example of this: "He came unto his own, and his own received him not." He was their long-promised, long-looked-for Messiah, their Redeemer, their King; but when He came, wearing a human disguise, a poor man, a man of grief, they knew Him not, and, knowing Him not, they scornfully, utterly rejected Him. The apostle John alludes to the same state when He says, "The world knoweth us not, because it knew Him not." This is the condition of every unconverted, unrenewed reader of this book—ignorance of Jesus Christ, and, in consequence of this ignorance, the rejection of the Son of God, which I hesitate not to say constitutes the sin of sins, the crime of crimes! Our Lord says, "THIS IS THE CONDEMNATION, that light is come into the world, and men love darkness rather than light, because their deeds are evil." He is the Light, and Him they reject!

Another truth is illustrated here. Observe the disguise that Joseph wore. He revealed himself, or stood before his brethren in the character, not of their brother, but as the governor of Egypt, in his legal, executive character as the prime minister of the land. And why is it, beloved, that we who are spiritually enlightened, who are taught by the Holy Spirit, and who may have had some favored discoveries of Christ to our souls, how is it that we do not know *more* of Christ? Is it not because we deal with Christ too much in the spirit of legality? We do not sufficiently see Christ to be our Brother, our own Brother, our living Brother—bone of our bone, and flesh of our flesh.

Is there not too much of a Jewish faith in our professed Christian faith? Do we not too much deal with Christ as a Law-giver, rather than as a Law-fulfiller? Is there not too much in our going to Christ of a bondage spirit? Do we not often come to Jesus for bread, for the spiritual blessing for which we are longing, too little as our own Brother, our next of kin, our Goel, our Joseph, and too much as if He were the governor, the prime minister of Egypt?

Oh that the Lord may vouchsafe to us more of a *gospel* faith! May He give us to see that Jesus Christ is the "end of the law" for righteousness to everyone who believes; and that it is our privilege to bear our needs, our sorrows, our trials to Jesus as our Brother, and not as clothed with a character and sustaining a relation that fills the mind with awe, inspires a bondage spirit, and arrests that free and full communion that ought ever to mark the approach of a sin-pardoned, accepted believer into the presence of Jesus.

Take another point of analogy—the speech of Joseph to his brethren. "He spake roughly unto them." "Joseph saw his brethren, and he knew them, but made himself strange unto them." My reader, you can testify how often this has been your spiritual experience. What a page is here, corresponding with our Christian and spiritual exercise of soul! Is not the voice of Jesus oftentimes rough, as it were, in the ears of His brethren? Does He not often make Himself strange to us in His conduct and dealings? And when He uplifts the rod and smites—when He draws the dark cloud over life's sunny landscape—when, by His providence, He seems to muffle the loving, tender tones of His voice, and speaks roughly to us, filling us with alarm, and dread, and apprehension—oh, does He not then wear a disguise which seems to veil from us the clear and tender relation in which

He stands to us as His brethren? And yet beneath this roughness of speech and strangeness of manner, there dwells and beats in the bosom of Christ a Brother's tender, sympathizing, loving heart.

But not only does He speak roughly, and make Himself strange to them, He sends them to prison; He puts them in ward three days. "Ye shall be kept in prison, that your words may be proved, whether there be any truth in you. And he put them all together into ward three days," (Gen. 42:16, 17.) But what had they to fear? It was Joseph's prison, he was their jailor, their keeper, and they were in good custody. How often has the Lord Jesus Christ, in the spiritual exercises of our soul, dealt thus with us. He has brought us into a strait place, He has sent us into a solitary place; He has permitted us to recede into a legal, bondage frame of spirit; and our prayer has been that of David—"Bring my soul *out of prison*, that I may praise thy name."

Oh, beloved, thank God if you are Christ's prisoner! Better, far better, to be the prisoner of Jesus than of Satan; better to be sent into Christ's ward than into the devil's. What though at times your Joseph, your Jesus, your Brother, to try your faith, to test your sincerity, to deepen His work in your heart, to make you better acquainted with the nature of the bondage spirit, puts you into a narrow place, a strait place—oh, it is but ultimately to bring you into greater largeness of soul, to prepare you to walk more in the holy liberty of adoption—it is but to sweeten, to intensify His own love, and to intensify in your heart a longing, panting, and thirsting after the free Spirit of an adopted child.

And, let me add, in that prison-house into which your Lord and Savior permits you to enter, how many a lesson have you learned, how many a precious truth have you been brought into the experience of, how many a sweet spring of comfort has been unsealed to your spirit, which, humanly speaking, you would otherwise never have known. Then, be not cast down and discouraged if your Joseph, to prove you and teach you, sends you for a while into His prison. Many a man of God has had to thank Him for the prison-house, for the sickroom, for a suffering, sleepless bed. "The Lord hath *set apart* him that is godly for himself;" and God the Lord often sets him apart from his daily calling in life, from his family, from the Church, puts him in ward that he may turn over the page of conscience, clear his evidences, examine his own heart, look more closely into the heart of Christ; and if he can but realize, "it is my Joseph who has put me here, and this is the prison-house of Him that loves me," he will bow with submission to the Savior's will, and say, "Thy will, not mine be done."

There is another very instructive point. I refer to the trying of Joseph's brethren. "Ye are spies; to see the nakedness of the land ye are come." Among your greatest blessings you have to thank Christ for, are those that try the reality of your religion, test the genuineness of your faith, and prove the sincerity of your love. The process may be humbling and painful in the extreme; to be taken for a false man, when you profess to be true; for a spy, when you deem yourself a brother; to have your religion called in question, your love doubted, your faith put to the severest test, flung like wheat into the sieve, or cast like gold into the crucible—this is a trying, humiliating process!

Nevertheless, in the catalogue of your spiritual blessings, you may place this high up in the list as one of the choicest and costliest. Thank God for that which tests the reality of your religion, which separates the wheat from the chaff, the gold from the foil, which brings your faith into exercise, proves the strength of your confidence in God, and the extent of your knowledge of Christ; which brings out your Christian principles in bold relief, emerging from the trying process with a purer faith, a deeper love, and a brighter hope. Then you will not quarrel with God, nor chide your Elder Brother for having dealt with you as a spy, and not a brother beloved of God.

But there is another striking and solemn view of the subject upon which we would lay great stress. Joseph spoke through the medium of an interpreter. Thus we read:— "And they knew not that Joseph understood them; *for he spake unto them by an interpreter.*" And who is the interpreter of Christ and of His words but the Divine and Eternal Spirit? His is the office, as taught us by Christ himself, to make known and reveal Him. Thus Christ testifies:—"But the Comforter, which is the Holy Ghost, whom the Father will send in my name, he shall teach you all things, and bring all things to your remembrance, whatsoever I have said into you." Again:—"He shall testify of me." "He shall glorify me; for he shall receive of mine, and shall shew it unto you."

Behold our true Interpreter! We know nothing spiritually, understandingly, of Divine truth, and of Him whom that truth reveals, and who is Himself "the truth," but as the Holy Spirit interprets it to us. The words of Christ are enigmas, the language of Christ is a foreign tongue, the revelations and mysteries of Christ unintelligible and inexplicable, and Christ himself unknown, unseen, until the Holy Spirit becomes our Teacher. The Interpreter of the Bible is He who wrote the Bible—Himself the Author of the Bible.

Men, professed theologians, who are bringing to the elucidation, interpretation, and study of revelation, the light of reason, the aids of philosophy, the results of learning, the discoveries of science, the means and appliances of human thought, utterly and avowedly abjuring the necessity and the illumination of the Holy Spirit as the sole Interpreter of the Scriptures of truth, will not only have to take up the lamentation of old—"We grope for the wall like the blind, and we grope as if we had no eyes: we stumble at noonday as in the night,"—but will be found to have done contempt to the Spirit of truth, and, abandoned to their willful and judicial darkness, will be left to believe a lie!

But, beloved, you have not so learned Christ, if so be that you have been taught the truth as it is in Jesus. To you the Holy Spirit has made known the Savior. He has uplifted the veil from your heart, has purged the film from the eye of your understanding, and has revealed the Son of God in you. He it is who has given you to see all merit, all worthiness, all righteousness, all salvation in Jesus; and, removing the covering of this Divine Ark—the Scriptures of truth—has discovered to you JESUS in all His glory, fullness, loveliness, and love.

Yes, the Spirit is Christ's interpreter. All that is obscure in His teaching, profound in His doctrine, discrepant in His revelations, unintelligible in His words, mysterious, strange, and painful in His dealings, the Eternal Spirit stands, as between Christ and the lowly disciple, prepared to unfold, explain, and reconcile all. Oh, seek more earnestly and prayerfully than ever the teaching of the Holy Spirit in the study and understanding of the Scriptures, especially those parts that more particularly testify of Christ; and *ask the Spirit* to make Christ more clearly and fully known to your soul. Beseech Him to unfold to you the finished work—the complete salvation of Christ; to apply the atoning blood to your conscience, and to testify, by His inward witness, to your personal interest in His love, obedience, and death.

Blessed and Eternal Spirit! Divine Interpreter of Christ! Revealer of Jesus—lead me into all truth concerning Him. Reveal His glory, unveil His beauty, disclose His love, interpret His language, and unfold and apply His truths to my soul, until I stand in His glorified presence, and know Him even as I am known!

Not only must the interpretation of the gospel be divine, but equally so must be the interpretation of the Divine dealings with us. God alone can elucidate and explain the mysteries of His providential dispensations. If we attempt to unveil and interpret them, guided by no other light than that which emanates from ourselves, we shall inevitably be involved in a labyrinth of perplexity and doubt. But waiting patiently on the Lord, trusting also in Him, He will bring it to pass, and interpret the dark symbols of a Providence whose wheel within wheel must ever baffle and confound the most sagacious and far-seeing mind of man.

Are the ways of God with you a great deep? Is He enshrouding your path with mystery? Does He in His transactions make Himself strange? Are your expectations blighted, your plans crossed, your purposes baffled, and, on these broken waters, do the fragments of wrecked and disappointed hopes float around you? Be still! and know that He is God! Before long He will break the silence, and all shall be explained, and this shall be your joyous cry,— "He hath done all things *well!*"

> "Blind unbelief is sure to err,
>   And scan His work in vain;
>   God is His own interpreter,
>   And He will make it plain."

We are now conducted to the second part of the subject—*Joseph's knowledge of his brethren:* "And Joseph knew his brethren." Of this fact there could be no doubt: we need not, therefore, occupy any time in proving it. He had outgrown their recollection, but they had not outgrown his. We are not informed by what indices Joseph recognized them. Perhaps it was—and I think this is the most probable solution of the mystery—by a direct Divine communication to his mind. He was but a stripling when he last saw them. They had advanced in life, perhaps were bald and gray-headed. Yet Joseph knew them; God doubtless gave him a direct revelation that these were his brethren, for we read—"And Pharaoh said unto his servants, Can we find such a man as this is, a man *in whom the Spirit of God is?*" It was by the illumination of the Spirit that Joseph interpreted the visions of the king, and, doubtless, by the same Spirit he knew his brethren.

We pass from Joseph and his brethren to our true Joseph and His spiritual brethren, unfolding one of the most blessed, precious, and sanctifying truths that can possibly be opened up and applied to you by the blessed Interpreter, the Spirit of Christ—*Christ's knowledge of His people.* Let this one truth be engraved on your heart—Christ's full, personal, minute knowledge of you, and you have found the secret of all happiness in adversity, joy in sorrow, succor and support when heart and flesh fail you. Jesus knows His brethren.

Let me first remind you that Christ's knowledge of His brethren is an *eternal knowledge.* It is not a knowledge arrived at in time, attained since they had a being. The knowledge of Christ is an eternal knowledge of His Church. He knew them when they were chosen in Him before the foundation of the world. He knew them when the Father gave them to Him to be His peculiar treasure. He knew them when they were entrusted to His hands to be redeemed, ransomed, and saved. He knew them when He wrote their names in His book of life. He knew them in the everlasting counsels of eternity, when He loved them with an everlasting love.

What a precious, sanctifying truth is this! Oh, do not rest in the streams, sweet as they are, but follow them up to the source where they flow. It is the everlasting love of God to His Church, the everlasting knowledge that Christ has of His brethren, which gives sweetness, reality, and substance to all the covenant blessings that flow into the soul of a child of God.

A few remarks further—Christ knows His brethren in their unregeneracy, worldliness, and sin. Were not this the case, how could He ever find them? Where would He go to look for His hidden jewels? How could He direct His message of salvation to their souls if He did not know them in the great mass of fallen creatures?—if He did not know them in the rags and ruin and famine of our nature? But the Lord Jesus Christ knows His brethren, walking "according to the course of this world, the children of wrath even as others."

He knows them in their rebellion, in their fall, in their sinfulness, and in their self-righteousness. He knows where they are, what they are, and who they are. Oh! what a solemn truth is this! How it throws memory back on the past, and explains many a mystery in our unregenerate history hitherto inexplicable. You can think of periods when your life seemed to hang by a hair—of circumstances that brought you to the very confines of eternity. Ah, why were you preserved? What was it that guarded you, rescued you, brought you back?

It was Jesus's knowledge of you in your darkness, unregeneracy, and rebellion! It was Jesus having His eye on you, His hand over you, the yearning of His heart towards you! It was He who kept your feet from falling, your soul from destruction, your life from the grave. It was He who followed you along all your dark, winding way, never losing sight of you for a moment, nor withdrawing His hand until the appointed, the blissful moment arrived, when He called you by His grace. "Preserved in Christ Jesus, and called."

"That was a time of wondrous love,
   When Christ, my Lord, was passing by;
He felt His tender pity move,
   And brought His great salvation nigh.

"Guilty and self-condemned I stood,
   Nor thought His mercy was so near,
When He my stubborn heart subdued,
   And planted all His graces there.

"When on the verge of endless pain,
   He gently whispered, 'I am thine;'
I lost my fears, and dropped my chain,
   And felt a transport all divine."

We go further, and remind you of Christ's knowledge of His brethren in deep spiritual necessity, famine, and need. Oh, this is a blessed view of Christ's recognition of us— His acquaintance with our true spiritual condition. Jesus knows that we have not a righteousness with which we can present ourselves before God—that we have nothing good in our flesh; that we have been brought to the end of our own strength, merit, and righteousness. "Who remembered us in our low estate: for his mercy endureth for ever." "I am poor and needy; yet the Lord thinketh upon me."

And what a special knowledge Jesus has of us when, by the Holy Spirit, and under the deep conviction and consciousness of this necessity, poverty, and famine, we are led to arise and go to Him, traveling in our emptiness to His fullness, and in our necessity to His supply, and in our famine to Him, the Bread of Life. Ah, do not think that the Lord Jesus Christ is not aware of your soul's necessity, whatever it may be. If the Eternal Spirit is breaking up the fallow ground of your heart, and showing you its plague and emptiness—if He is creating in you a spiritual hungering and thirsting after righteousness, showing you more and more that your soul can live only by the bread that comes down from heaven, it is a sweet, blessed thought that Jesus knows those deep gracious exercises of soul.

Oh, you have not a desire after Christ, faint though it is, your heart goes not out after Christ, longs for Christ, and rests in Christ, but Christ knows it, and rejoices in it with exceedingly great joy. And is it not a delightful thought that Christ is cognizant of the work of His own Spirit in the soul? You may not at times be able to discern that work yourself; so concealed is it by infirmity, unbelief, and the mists that exhale from inbred sin and corruption; nevertheless, here is a truth worth untold gold—Jesus knows His own work, recognizes His own image, and calls us His brethren. The saints may not know it, your dearest friend may not know it, you may not know it yourself, enough that Jesus knows it; He sees the flickering spark which nothing can extinguish, traces the lineaments of His own image which nothing shall efface, and interprets as none other can, the language of our groans, tears, and desires.

It is also a blessed thought that Jesus knows His brethren *individually*. Christ does not, as we too frequently ourselves do, lose sight of our individuality. We too imperfectly deal with Jesus personally. We too little bring our individual sorrows, needs, and circumstances to Christ. And yet what a comforting truth is this, and not comforting only, but deeply sanctifying—Christ knows me personally, has my name on His heart, has my position in His mind, has my circumstances in His eye, is acquainted with my individual state in society, with my trials, temptations, sorrows, and wants. Such is His individual and discriminating knowledge, He knows me as if I were the only brother He owns and acknowledges on earth. Sweet truth is this! If you retire to your chamber to brood in solitude and silence over your lonely griefs, perhaps, with the sad thought, "no one knows me, no one sympathizes with me, no one is acquainted with my case, I am like a sparrow alone on the housetop, I pray, and sigh, and groan in lonely places, and no man cares for my soul," oh, beloved, there is One who knows you, knows your name, your position, your griefs, your temptations, your loneliness, who says, "I know their sorrows"—it is Jesus, your Joseph, your brother.

"The foundation of God standeth fast, having this seal, the Lord knoweth them that are his." Well may we with surprise inquire with Nathanael, "Whence knowest thou *me?*" Are you acquainted with such a poor, sinful worm as I? Do you, Lord, care for *me*—think of *me*—love *me?* Such knowledge is too wonderful for me—it is like Yourself, Divine.

Let me remark, too, that our highest source of comfort lies, not in our knowledge of Christ, but in Christ's knowledge of us. There stood Joseph's brethren; they were as safe, as tenderly, kindly cared for, had awakened as profound an interest in the heart of Joseph, as at the moment when his disguise fell, and he stood before them revealed and manifested as their brother. Let this comfort you, my reader; if there are times when Christ conceals Himself from you, when God is a hidden God; if there are periods when, as with Mary at the sepulcher, a veil so conceals Him, that you do not know Him to be your risen Lord; if, like the disciples, you are tossed upon the dark waters, and Christ comes walking on the sea, and you mistake Him for a ghost, and cry out for fear; nevertheless, here is your comfort, your safety, and your hope—Jesus knows you, is acquainted with you, has His unslumbering eye upon you, and you can be in no circumstance of sorrow, of peril, of darkness, and of need, in which Christ shall not know and recognize you as His brother, and most dearly beloved.

You, then, who are walking in darkness, who are tossed upon the stormy waves of adversity, who do not see Christ in the mist, oh, take this comfort to your heart—"I may not see Jesus in this storm, He may wear a disguise, speak roughly to me by His providence, make Himself strange to me by His conduct, nevertheless, my faith grasps this precious truth—"I know my sheep," and it is enough. "Enough, Lord, that You know me."

This is a peculiarly consolatory truth in view of a trial to which the saints of God are often much and painfully exposed—the ignorance of them, their principles, actions, and motives on the part of their fellow-believers. In consequence of this we are often exposed to much misjudgment and unkind censure. Our Lord drank of this very cup. His brethren did not know Him, and even His disciples misunderstood Him. Let this comfort you in the misjudgings and misinterpretations, the reproofs, and rebukes of men, especially those of your fellow disciples. "Lord, it is enough that You have said, I know my sheep, and that *You* know me. You know the principles that govern me, the motives that influence me, the end that I seek in this act, and I can calmly, safely leave the inspection of my heart to Your eye, and the issue of this step to Your judgment and decision." Thus you will rise superior to the human opinion of an honest, upright, conscientious cause, and will be enabled to say with the magnanimous apostle, "With me it is a very small thing that I should be judged of you, or of man's judgment; yea, I judge not mine own self." Blessed Lord, YOU know me, and it suffices!

We venture upon yet another truth. These brethren of Joseph were standing as petitioners in his presence without the least conviction of their relationship. There was reverence to his authority, faith in his ability, and repose in his willingness; but not one feeling of confidence or of comfort inspired by the assurance that he was their brother. This fact illustrates a remarkable feature of the believer's experience. We often go to Jesus, live upon His sufficiency, and exercise faith in His kindly feelings towards us, without the comfort and joy of a full assurance that He is ours.

Nevertheless, He *is* ours, and we have still a measure of faith that binds us to Him, and that faith, though it be like the unseen anchor dropped into the ocean, keeps the soul firm and stable, and nothing shall separate it from Christ. Then, though you may not have the full assurance of faith, of hope, and of love, yet "cast not away therefore your confidence, which hath great recompence of reward;" but in your darkness, depression, and loneliness, keep a firm grasp on this truth—"I am empty, Jesus is full; in my poverty and ignorance I throw myself on Him by faith; and although I have but a dim perception of Him as my Brother, still, though He put me in ward, yes, though He slay me, yet will I love and trust in Him."

We would not repress your ardor after *full assurance* of your interest in Christ; yet, for the sake of the feeble in grace, we would remark that it is not *essential* to your salvation, nor is it your warrant to go to Jesus. You may still be Christ's, and in simple faith be living upon His fullness, yet lack the clearer, fuller, and more assured manifestation of Himself to your soul—the sealing of the Spirit. But, since this degree of knowledge is attainable, and its attainment will contribute materially to your spiritual enjoyment and personal holiness, we would earnestly plead with you to seek it.

Assurance may not be essential to your salvation, but it is essential to your happy, holy walk; and the feeblest child of God may arrive at the confidence expressed in these words of the great apostle—"I know whom I have believed, and am persuaded that he is able to keep that which I have committed unto him against that day." And what *is* assurance? It is nothing more nor less than—*faith* in the Lord Jesus Christ. And the fullness of assurance is in the same ratio with the fullness of our faith in the Son of God. In the smallest degree of faith there is the germ of assurance, and assurance develops and deepens, strengthens and brightens, as faith becomes rooted and grounded in Christ.

The poor man in the Gospel who could only say with tears, "Lord, I believe, help thou mine unbelief," had as really the germ of assurance in his heart as Paul, who could say, so unequivocally, "I KNOW whom I have believed." Poor soul! have you but touched the hem—but seen the cross distant and dim—but ventured, tremblingly, hesitatingly upon Jesus? Can you say, "Lord, I believe in the midst of my much unbelief; I believe that you are *able* to save me, though I have such misgivings as to your *willingness*"?

Dear heart, cheer up! you shall never be lost! Jesus has spoken it, and it is enough. He says, "Him that cometh unto me,"—no qualifications, no limitations, as to the amount of guilt, or the multitude of sins, or the degree of faith—simply, "him that cometh;"—take Christ at His word; come to Him as you are, and He will in no wise discourage or reject you.

Meditate much upon Christ.—You will find this habit an effectual antidote to those vain, carnal, earthly thoughts, which, alas, obtrude themselves so frequently and so powerfully upon the believing mind. Let the mind be preoccupied and solely with Jesus, and the world and the creature and sin will find no play. Oh, it is a sweet theme of meditation—Jesus! You are in mental converse with One who has access to the innermost recess of your soul, the most sacred cloister of your heart; who is in communion with the most delicate shade of thought, with the finest tone of feeling, and who knows you, can understand you, and feel for you as no other being in the universe can.

Do not deem this mental meditation unattainable, this spiritual concentration of the soul on Christ in meditation so high that you cannot attain unto it. What others have experienced you may experience. Cultivate this devout meditation upon Christ. Meditate upon His person, study His work, muse upon His love. Endeavor to blend Him with your thoughts, to entwine Him with your affections, to associate Him with your daily life of service and of suffering. Such an effort to think of Christ will soon bring down to your soul the dear Object of your thoughts, for He regards them who only *think* upon His name; and while you are musing upon His person, the fire of His love will burn within your heart, and your tongue will give utterance to such precious sentiments and feelings as are contained in this experience of an eminent divine, recorded more than a century ago—"The thoughts of Christ have become exceedingly frequent with me; I meditate on His glorious Person, as the eternal and the incarnate Son of God: and I behold the infinite God as coming to me, and meeting with me in this blessed meditation. I fly to Him on multitudes of occasions every day, and am impatient if many minutes have passed without some recourse to Him. Every now and then I rebuke myself for having been so long without any thoughts of my Savior; how can I bear to keep at such a distance from Him? I then look up to Him, and say—Oh, my Savior, draw near unto me! Oh, come to dwell in my soul, and help me to cherish some thoughts wherein I shall enjoy You; and upon this I set myself to think of what He has done, is doing, and what He will do, for me: I find the subject inexhaustible; and after I have been thus employed in the day, I fall asleep at night in the midst of some meditation on the glory of my Savior; so I fall asleep in

Jesus, and when I awake in the night, I do on my bed seek
Him whom my soul loves. On awaking, the desires of my
soul still carry me to Him who was last in my thoughts
when I fell asleep." (Rev. Dr. Cotton Mather.)

Let the thought of Christ's knowledge of us be an ever-
present, ever-abiding remembrance. When darkness or
sorrow veils Him from our view, still let us cling to the
truth that He knows us; and when sin would tempt, and
the world seduce, and the creature ensnare, and some false
attraction would disturb the central fixedness of our heart
on Christ, oh, let the solemn truth that Jesus knows us
then instantly break the spell, dissolve the enchantment,
and win back the soul to its allegiance and love.

The Sacks Filled with Corn

A FULL CHRIST FOR EMPTY SINNERS

Then Joseph commanded to fill their sacks with corn, and to restore every man's money into his sack, and to give them provision for the way: and thus did he unto them. GENESIS 42:25

HOW close to the fountain of their supply did these famishing brethren of Joseph now stand; yet how unconscious that he was their brother! Ignorant of this fact, they were awe-struck by his commanding presence, and were filled with fear and trembling by the authority and tone with which he spoke to them. It is thus with us. How often do we appear in the presence of God as these brethren in the presence of Joseph! He is our Father, and Jesus is our Brother, and all the fullness of Deity, and all the treasures of the covenant of grace are His. Yet, this fact of Divine relationship, so much concealed by the veil of unbelief, fettered by a legal spirit, and misinterpreting the providences of our God, we too frequently present ourselves in His presence—in communion, in supplication, in service—with the trembling of a servant, and wearing the manacles of a slave.

And yet, what is the true spirit and posture of a child of God, of a brother of Christ? It is this, "Ye have not received the spirit of bondage again to fear; but ye have received the Spirit of adoption, whereby we cry, Abba, Father. The Spirit itself beareth witness with our spirit, that we are the children of God." Oh, if, in the case of these brethren, the veil had been but uplifted, and the astounding fact had burst upon them in all its startling truthfulness, "I am Joseph, your brother," what a revolution had taken place in their feelings—their confidence restored, their fears quelled, their hopes inspired, and overwhelmed with emotion, they would have fallen at His feet, bathing them with tears of contrition, gratitude, and love.

In all this, do we trace nothing analogous to some of the holiest and sweetest experiences of our soul? In the prosecution of our subject, we have arrived at a most spiritually instructive part of the narrative—the ample supply meted out by Joseph in response to the pressing needs and appeal of his brethren. The points which will illustrate the great gospel truths, we pray the Eternal Spirit to unfold and apply, are simply these:—

THE SUPPLY—THE RESTORED MONEY—THE PROVISION FOR THE JOURNEY.

Let us turn our attention, in the first place, to *the supply,*—"Then Joseph commanded to fill their sacks with corn." It was for corn they had gone down into Egypt, impelled by the grievous and sore famine that raged throughout their land, and corn they found and obtained. Now, to a spiritual mind viewing this part of the narrative in its gospel light, how full, instructive, and precious it is. Keep in view the fact, that Christ is our Brother, that as our Brother He is at the head, yes, that He is *the Head*, of all spiritual blessings, and you will be provided with a key to the gospel interpretation of this part of the story, so striking and instructive in its teaching.

Now, the first remark under this head of supply is this,— *It was sheer necessity, urgent, pressing need,* that brought these brethren into the presence of Joseph. Does any other motive, or principle, or errand bring us to Christ? Will a sinner in his unrenewed state ever go to the Savior not under the pressure of necessity? Will a soul ever betake itself to Christ without the conviction of its deep, spiritual need of Christ?—Never! With all the sweet, powerful attraction of the Lord Jesus Christ—His love, loveliness, and grace—so completely depraved and dead is our nature, it is utterly insensible to the power of this great magnet, and will never repair to Christ until the Holy Spirit, awakening a conviction of sin, creates in it the pressure of need.

Here learn what is the first stage of real conversion, my reader—it is the spiritual, enlightened conviction, sense and sight of our lost and perishing condition as sinners. None value a crucified, atoning Christ but the sick, the poor, the empty, the helpless; those who know the plague of their own hearts, feel their condemnation by the law, and are driven out of every refuge, and from every hope but that which meets them in these wondrous words,—"This is a faithful saying, and worthy of all acceptation, that Christ Jesus came into the world *to save sinners.*"

Have *you* thus been brought under sin's conviction by the Spirit? And will not this illustrate a humbling page of your own advanced history, saint of the most High? So weak is your faith, so languid your love, so worldly your spirit, at so great a distance, ofttimes, do you find yourself from Jesus, that but for pressure, but for a feeling of necessity, but for a conviction of some need, alas, with all the attraction of Christ, His beauty, His love, His graciousness, how seldom would you betake yourself to Jesus! Sorrow brings you to Him, perplexity brings you to Him, exhausted resources bring you to Him. Your heavenly Father, in the infinite wisdom and righteousness of His dealings, lays His hand upon you, and, under the heavy pressure of that hand, you arise and come to Jesus, and then learn the lesson of the rod in the necessity, the conviction of want, the pressure of trial and sorrow which has won back your truant heart into the blessed presence of your Lord.

Secondly, what was it they brought to Joseph? They brought vessels—*empty* vessels. How many of these empty sacks, or of what size, is of but little moment, nor would it have been a matter of any moment to Joseph if they had brought all the sacks in Canaan since his resources and his benevolence would have filled them. Enough for our present illustration that they brought *empty* sacks.

What is the state, the moral, spiritual state of the soul that is spiritually brought to Christ, and that savingly receives Christ? Ah, we little know the process that soul has to pass through, the discipline it undergoes before it is fit to come to Christ, or before Christ is fit for that soul. One word, profoundly significant, expresses that condition—EMPTINESS! And this annihilates all those fancied and fanciful ideas that thousands entertain of some self-sufficiency, some previous moral fitness in their souls before they come to Jesus; that, before they avail themselves of His salvation, they must place themselves in a kind of salvable state, that is, that they must partially save themselves before they come to the Savior to be saved!

But one word—oh, that the Spirit of God may write it on our hearts!—expresses the condition in which Christ expects a sinner to come to Him—EMPTINESS! And whether the soul is conscious of this emptiness or not, it is there! Spiritual blindness to the fearful fact does not invalidate its existence. The soul of man in its natural condition is empty of all holiness, of all righteousness, of all goodness, of all strength, of all love. It is a vast moral void, into which were you to empty the universe of created good, would remain a void still. As well might you attempt to extinguish the fires of Vesuvius by casting into its crater a drop of water, as to extinguish the burning cravings of the human soul with any good but GOD. God only can satisfy the soul of man; and happiness is a stranger to the human heart until it finds its way back to Him. "The Lord is my portion, saith my soul; therefore will I hope in Him."

But although we assert that there is this vast spiritual emptiness in the soul, deem it not paradoxical when we remind you that there is yet much of what that soul must be *emptied* before it is prepared to receive out of Christ's fullness. The soul of man is full to overflowing with self-righteousness, with rebellion against God, with the love of sin, and the reigning power of all iniquity. It is brimmed and overflowing with all the elements of destruction, which, if left to work their own results, will infallibly plunge the soul into the chambers of eternal darkness and despair. The idol self must fall, your own righteousness must be renounced, there must be the deep spiritual conviction of the plague of your own heart; you must feel that you are under the condemnation of the law, and that you have not one claim to God's mercy, nor one plea springing from yourself whereby He should accept and save you.

Here let me pause and ask you, Have you thus been emptied? Or are you still filled to engorgement with self, and with the world, with sin, and with your own conceit, there being no room in your heart for the Savior? Dear reader, the *lowly* stable where the Incarnate God made His advent to our world images the spiritual state of that heart into which He enters, and with Him His "kingdom of righteousness, and peace, and joy in the Holy Ghost."

It is only a heart deeply, spiritually conscious of its poverty, lowliness, and uncleanness, and emptied and humbled thereby in the dust, that opens its doors to receive and welcome Him who came "not to call the righteous, but *sinners* to repentance," to "die for the *ungodly*," to "preach good tidings unto the meek, to bind up the brokenhearted, to proclaim liberty to the captives, to give the oil of joy for mourning, the garment of praise for the spirit of heaviness." Oh, if your heart is lowly, empty and penitent, Jesus will make His gracious advent into it, and dwell there forever!

With regard to the process of emptying, if any work ever proved itself Divine it is this. Not all the eloquence, the philosophy, the learning, the moral persuasion, of man or angel can produce it. The soul can attach itself to what is vile, can absorb into itself what is unholy, and can yield to what is contrary to God's truth, but it has not the moral power of an infant's strength to expel one solitary evil, to free itself from one dominant sin.

My reader, it is the power of God alone that empties a man, that makes him clearly to see the imperfection of his own righteousness, his ignorance of truth, of God, and of Christ. It is the work of the Holy and Eternal Spirit to show to the poor sinner that all his righteousness is as filthy rags, that he has no spiritual strength, and not one pulse of love to God throbbing in his bosom. Oh, it is a power as great, as mighty, and as Divine as that which spoke this universe into being—which said, "Let there be light, and there was light,"—which alone can empty your soul of all its darkness, its rebellion, its ignorance, its love, homage of self, and bring you to the cross of Christ, to the feet of Jesus as a poor, empty beggar.

The means by which God the blessed Spirit accomplishes this great work are various. To begin with the minor ones: it is often by trial, adversity, and sorrow, that God opens a man's eyes to see the emptiness of himself and of all created things. Travel through the Church of God, and ask, What was it that first led you to Jesus? What first awoke spiritual, solemn, serious, and devout reflection in your mind? What first embittered and beclouded to you the sweet, sparkling streams and rivulets of created good?

The answer of thousands would be—God blighted my lovely flower, felled my stately cedar, laid low my heart's choicest treasure, blew on the accumulated earnings of many years, laid me on a sick and suffering bed. And thus was I brought to Jesus. Sorrow impelled me, the storms drove me, adversity led me to Him as the hiding-place from the wind, and the covert from the tempest. I sought the creature's sufficiency, the world's vanity, my own emptiness. He drew me with His love to seek and find all I needed in Himself. And now I can bless and praise Him for blighting all, for blasting all, for ruining all, since it was but to make my soul His kingdom, my heart His home, my body His temple, and Himself more precious than countless worlds— my all and in all.

> "In days when health and joy were mine,
> And cloudless seemed my morning's shine,
> I thought each bliss would still remain,
> Nor knew how precious Christ was then.
> But soon was dimmed my early light,
> And sickness came with withering blight;
> I turn'd to past delights in vain,
> But only Christ seemed precious then.
> When sorrow sent her searching dart,
> To probe and prove my erring heart,
> Fainting beneath the bitter pain,
> I *felt* that Christ was precious then.
> And when before my startled eyes,
> Sins past, and scarcely mourned, arise;
> In vain my tears would cleanse the stain,
> My Savior Thou art precious then.
> And oh, when trembling near the tomb,

My spirit dreads the approaching gloom,
Then let the Cross my soul sustain,
And bid me think Thou'rt precious then."

But the grand, the chief instrument of spiritual emptying, is *the truth of God.* The Holy Spirit, bringing home the truth with light and power to the sinner's heart, shows him the emptiness and sinfulness and darkness that are there. There is nothing so illuminating, so quickening, as the truth of God. "The entrance of thy words giveth light; it giveth understanding unto the simple." "The law of the Lord is perfect, converting the soul: the testimony of the Lord is sure, making wise the simple: the statutes of the Lord are right, rejoicing the heart: the commandment of the Lord is pure, enlightening the eyes." (Ps. 19:7, 8.)

There is no light, no candle like that of the Lord's word, no truth like that of God's truth, when the Holy Spirit holds it up as a mirror, showing to a man his self-righteousness, ignorance, depravity, and worldliness. There is a Divine power going forth with God's word which all the opposition of the heart within, all the darkness that shades the mind, all the usurping power of evil dwelling in the soul cannot possibly resist. It is indeed and in truth "the sword of the Spirit, *which is the word of God.*" "Being born again, not of corruptible seed, but of incorruptible, *by the word of God.*" (1 Pet. 1:23.)

Now this instrument of spiritual quickening, sanctification, and comfort God will honor. He has magnified His word above His name, and will have us magnify it too. He is jealous of the purity, honor, and glory of His revealed word. Heaven and earth shall pass away, but the word of God lives and abides forever. Reader, has God's word come to your soul with a life-giving, soul-emptying power? and is it sweeter to you than honey, and more precious than much fine gold?

Let us now turn our attention to the *replenishing* of these empty sacks, "Then Joseph commanded to fill their sacks with corn." Observe from whom the supply of corn came—it was from Joseph. A more vital, important, and precious gospel-truth could not be illustrated than this. Let us dwell upon it—*the* FULLNESS *of our Lord Jesus Christ.*

We select, as the groundwork of our statement, the remarkable words of the apostle, "It pleased the Father that in him should ALL FULLNESS dwell." (Col. 1:19.) More precious, or more pregnant words are not to be found in the Bible than these. Of whom does the apostle speak as the Depositary of this fullness? "In Him,"—the Son of God, our Lord and Savior, it pleased the Father that all fullness should dwell. This fullness is not deposited in angels or in men, but in Him who, in the preceding passage, is spoken of as "the image of God," "the firstborn of every creature," in Him, "by whom were all things created that are in heaven, and that are in earth, visible and invisible," as "before all things, and by whom all things consist," as "the head of the body, the church," as "the beginning, the first-born from the dead; that in all things he might have the preeminence."

In Him, this Divine, this wonderful Being, ALL FULLNESS dwells. In whom could all the fullness of the Godhead—all the mediatorial fullness of the Church dwell, but in the Son of God! But take the "fullness" particularly spoken of in this passage, the *mediatorial* fullness of Christ; and in whom, other than a being essentially God, could all fullness of merit, all fullness of righteousness, all fullness of grace, all fullness of pardon, all fullness of sanctification, all fullness of wisdom, all fullness of love, all fullness of sympathy, all fullness of compassion, in a word, all fullness of all supply, possibly dwell?

But all this fullness dwells in Christ! And who can comprehend this fullness? What plumb-line can fathom, or what scale can measure the height, the depth, the length, the breadth, of this fullness of salvation for sinners—the inexhaustible stores; the vast supplies, the incalculable abundance from which countless myriads have drawn, and are drawing still, and yet the sacred treasure, the precious fullness, remains unexhausted by a drop, unsunk by a hair's-breadth? Infinity alone can give us its dimensions and sound its depths.

In Christ, essentially, there is all "fulness of the Godhead bodily;" and in Christ communicatively there is all the fullness which *it pleased the Father* should dwell in Him. The one He possesses in virtue of His absolute Deity—He being essentially one with the Father; the other He possesses in virtue of His covenant relation to the Church—He being her Mediator, Head, and Redeemer. It is in the light of the latter we are more especially to interpret the fullness which it pleased the Father should dwell in Christ. It is, distinctly and emphatically, a MEDIATORIAL FULLNESS.

The same thing is spoken of by the evangelist John, "Of his fulness have we all received, and grace for grace." Behold, then, our true Joseph! It was the good pleasure, the sovereign will, the gracious purpose of the Father, that all the treasures of His love, all the riches of His grace, all the fullness of the covenant should be placed in the hands of Christ, to be dispensed by Him according to the collective and individual necessities of His Church.

And in what does this fullness consist? A fullness of dignity to atone, a fullness of life to quicken, a fullness of righteousness to justify, a fullness of virtue to pardon, a fullness of grace to sanctify, a fullness of power to preserve, a fullness of compassion and sympathy to comfort, and a fullness of salvation to save poor sinners to the uttermost;

in a word, ALL fullness; a fullness commensurate with need of every kind, with trial of every form, with sorrow of every depth, with sin of every name, with guilt of every hue, yes, with every conceivable and possible necessity in which the children of God may be placed; fullness of grace here, and fullness of glory hereafter; a fullness which the Church on earth will live upon, and boast of until time be no more; a fullness which will be the delight and glory of the Church in heaven to behold, until eternity shall end. In whom could all this fullness be enthroned?—In a mere *creature?*—Preposterous thought!

Now, as from Joseph these empty vessels of his brethren were replenished, so from Christ, and from Christ alone, our spiritual supplies are to come. The Church of God has but one Spiritual Head, the sinner but one divine Savior. God has not distributed the treasures of His grace, or delegated spiritual authority and power in its communication to others, but has deposited all grace, and all power, and all glory solely and only in His Son.

No Church, no minister, no ecclesiastical body has one particle of this grace in its power to bestow. The sole possession and power of spiritual interpretation of God's Word is delegated to no Church under heaven. The authority and the power to absolve from sin, and to communicate the grace of pardon to the soul belongs to no priesthood on the face of the earth. The fullness of merit, and of grace, and of power necessary to the salvation of one sinner, is exclusively in the Lord Jesus Christ.

His Church has no legislative, no administrative power whatever to rule, and govern, and supply—all, all is invested in her one Divine, spiritual, glorious Head—the Lord Jesus Christ. And don't we find all we need in Him? What is the demand? Is it the pardon of sin? "In whom we have redemption through his blood, even the forgiveness of sin."

Is it righteousness to justify? "We are made the righteousness of God in him." Is it spiritual life? "I have come that ye might have life, and that ye might have it more abundantly." Is it grace to subdue the power of sin? "My grace is sufficient for thee." Is it compassion and sympathy in times of trouble, in seasons of sorrow? "We have not an high priest which cannot be touched with the feeling of our infirmities." Oh, what is the need that shall not find in our full Christ its own commensurate supply?

And what will our true Joseph give us? With what will He replenish the exhausted vessel? It was corn, real food, with which Joseph filled the empty sacks of his brethren. Our Lord Jesus gives His brethren "the *true* bread from heaven." There is no mockery, no delusion in His gifts. We shall receive nothing at His hands but what will enrich, strengthen, and advance our soul's well-being. It may come in a disguised form—a rebuke, a reproof, a warning, a lesson difficult to learn, a cross heavy to bear; it may empty us from vessel to vessel, may fill us with shame and self-abhorrence, may lay us low in the dust, nevertheless, it is the true bread He gives us, and just in that form which our soul's necessities required.

"He fed them with manna in the wilderness that He might *humble them*." The truth of God is humbling, the grace of Christ is self-abasing; and the soul that is the most emptied of self, self-dependence, self-seeking, self-will, who walks the nearest and the most softly with God, gathers the most abundantly of this divine, this heavenly, this precious manna. Oh, there is nothing so promotive of our soul's abasement, so humbling to self, as living by faith, poverty, and nothingness, upon the fullness and sufficiency of a crucified and present Christ.

The gospel is humbling, faith is humbling, grace is humbling—the place, the circumstances in which we are found, are humbling; and He feeds us with this manna in the world's waste howling wilderness *that He might humble us.*

Oh, blessed discipline this! "Thou shalt remember all the way which the Lord thy God led thee these forty years in the wilderness, to *humble* thee." "And he *humbled* thee, and suffered thee to hunger, and fed thee with manna, which thou knewest not, neither did thy fathers know; that he might make thee know that man doth not live by bread only, but by every word that proceedeth out of the mouth of the Lord doth man live." (Deut. 8:2, 3.)

As Christ is taken into our hearts by faith, He becomes a part of our moral nature, an integrated element of our spiritual being. Consequently we grow Christ-like, or rather, Christ grows in us. We become more holy, more meek, more gentle, more humble; in a word, the image of our Lord is more developed in us, and we grow less man-like and more God-like; and the quietness of our spirit, and the courtesy of our demeanor, and the lowliness of our minds, and the gentle, winning sweetness of our whole carriage and speech are but the image and reflection of Christ.

In view, then, of this statement of Christ's fullness let me exhort you to bring your needs, your sins, your trials, your case, whatever its character, to Christ. He will not send you back to a creature-power, or to human compassion for that which will replenish and solace you, but will unlock the hidden treasures, the full fount of His own resources, sympathy, and compassion, and pour it like a tide into your soul, and your heart shall abound with joy. Come when, or where, or how you may, He will cast into your emptiness, nothing but His own infinite and unwasting fullness— nothing but Himself! And then, with Mary, you shall exclaim—"My soul doth magnify the Lord, and my spirit hath rejoiced in God my Saviour. He hath filled the hungry with good things; and the rich he hath sent empty away."

Ah! none are sent away from Christ, except the rich, the full, the self-sufficient. But the empty, the poor, the hungry, the penniless are filled out of His fullness of grace and dismissed, rejoicing in Christ Jesus, having no confidence in the flesh, and magnifying His great name.

But to proceed to the second point, THE RESTORED MONEY—"Then Joseph commanded to fill their sacks with corn, and to restore every man's money into his sack." You will observe, my reader, in the first place that they *brought with them* this money. They had no conception that corn could be obtained without it, and took care, doubtless, to supply themselves with the current coin of the realm; and with this came down into Egypt, and presented themselves in the presence of Joseph.

What a deep-rooted principle of our nature does this illustrate—the principle that would *purchase* the salvation of the soul, that brings the *price* of human merit in its hand, and with this rushes into the presence of the Savior! Self-righteousness is as natural, as innate a principle of our fallen, sinful nature, as any principle within us! No, more so, it is the strongest and most powerful. The very first idea of a conscience-roused, a soul-awakened sinner, is to bring a price in his hand to Christ—something that will merit the Savior's regard—that will commend the case to Christ's notice—something that will be a kind of return for, or an acknowledgment of, the boon thus asked—something that will be a barter between Christ and the sinner—some previous fitness, previous self-preparation; in a word, money in the empty sack.

Oh, how few of us, when first we came to Christ, came entirely without money! But this principle must be up-torn, root and branch. This part of our subject may just meet the spiritual condition of some of my readers. Why are you not *rejoicing* in Christ Jesus? Why have you not *found Him* whom you have been so long seeking? Why are you not happy in a sense of pardoned sin? Why are you not knowing your adoption into the family of God? You have been *seeking* Jesus for years, why have you not *found* Him? Because, perhaps, unconscious to yourselves, you have been waiting to find some money, some feeling or condition with which you can come to Christ with a degree of dignity and self-respect; not to receive the boon He has to confer as a sinner, as a beggar,—not to receive the good He has to bestow as a poor mendicant, or as a starving man receiving bread—but as a purchaser, and not as a receiver, as a claimant, and not a recipient, as a thing merited and not a gratuity bestowed.

But all this, as I have said, must be torn up root and branch before Christ will pour His fullness into your soul. What says the Scriptures?—"Ho, every one that thirsteth, come ye to the waters, *and he that hath no money:* come ye, buy and eat; yea, come, buy wine and milk *without money and without price*." (Isa. 55:1.) "Being justified FREELY by his grace, through the redemption that is in Christ Jesus." (Rom. 3:24.) "For by grace are ye saved through faith; and that not of yourselves: it is the gift of God: not of works, lest any man should boast." (Eph. 2:8, 9.) "It is of faith that it might be of grace." "Whosoever will, let him take the water of life FREELY." (Rev. 22:17.) "And when they had *nothing to pay,* he frankly forgave them both." (Luke 7:42.)

Thus it is written as with diamond, that salvation is of *free grace;* that we are justified and pardoned without any works of righteousness, or human merit of our own; that none are rejected by Christ who come empty and poor. He only is spurned who brings his money with his sack; his coin in his hand with which to purchase that which is unpurchasable; his price with which to purchase that which is above all price—the bread of life—the fullness of Christ's salvation.

Take another spiritual truth here illustrated. Joseph *returned the money*, commanding it to be replaced in the sacks' mouths. It is the glory of God that He is not only a prayer-answering, but also a *prayer-exceeding* God. We never go to Christ with the most enlarged desires, supplicating the greatest blessings, but He gives us more than we ask. You have gone with limited requests, circumscribed petitions, and stinted desires, but so full is Christ, so large is His heart, He has given you far beyond all that you asked or thought. Blessed, precious encouragement this to go to Jesus with our utter emptiness, to arise and give ourselves to importunate prayer. What encouragement is this to draw near to God and ask what we will; to make known to Him our needs, great and pressing as they are.

So full, so gracious, and so loving is our spiritual Joseph, He will never give us less, but always infinitely *more* than we ask at His hands. Well may we—and who should louder swell the note?—unite in the glowing doxology, "Now unto him that is *able to do exceeding abundantly above all that we ask or think*, according to the power that worketh in us, unto him be glory in the church by Christ Jesus throughout all ages, world without end. Amen."

Joseph gave his brethren, too, *provision for the way*. How like a brother this! Not only did he fill their sacks with corn and replace their money, but he also gave them an extra provision for their personal necessities, until they arrived at home. How thoughtful and how kind was this of Joseph! These brethren had injured him. Yet he forgives all, forgets all, and returns them a blessing for their wrong. Now that they are in distress and need, the ocean of his love rolls over all the past, and hides and obliterates it forever. What a type of Jesus! Though we have sinned against Him, crucified Him, wronged Him a thousand times over, yet He loves us still. Hear Him in His dying agonies praying for His murderers, "Father, *forgive* them, for they know not what they do." Sinner! will not your rebellion, your unbelief, your impenitence give way before this matchless love? Bow the knee, bend the heart, and crown Him with your faith, your love, your life!

But take another truth here shadowed forth. Where were these brethren traveling? what was the end of their journey? They were journeying *homeward*, home to their father's house. If, believer in Jesus, we are the children of God, we, too, are journeying toward home—home to our Father's house. Through this world of famine, of sin, of suffering, and sorrow, we are journeying to the family home! Sweet thought, could we but realize it!

O believer, cherish amid all the weariness and roughness, the toil and battle, the privation and disappointment, the suffering and sorrow of this life, the sweet, the holy, the soothing reflection, "it is my way home; it is my path to my Father's house. I am going home to be with God and with Christ forever! This sickness, languor, and decay—is but opening wider the door through which the light and glory of heaven beams in upon my soul, and by which I shall, before long, pass to my ineffable and eternal rest above!"

Study your pilgrimage in this light, and it will chase many a shadow from your brow, pour sunshine into many a dark nook of your heart, and smooth many a rough stage of your journey. Every step, be it in darkness or light, grief or joy, is bringing you nearer, and still nearer, to the bright, blissful, happy home Christ has gone to prepare for you!

Then notice, there is provision for this journey. Do you think that your blessed Lord has left you to take this journey at your own cost? relying upon your own resources? Do you think that He will not meet all its necessities, sustain all its trials, anticipating every incident and circumstance of that journey? O beloved, we little know Christ if we do not receive this truth in all its fullness. When you lift your head from your pillow in the morning, let this be the first thought to occupy your mind—"for all this day's history, my covenant Head, my Joseph, my Savior has provided. Then, I will bring to Him the needs that press, the perplexities that embarrass, the anxieties that chafe, the disappointments that grieve, the temptations that assail, the sins that wound me. I will bring my fears, my infirmities, my griefs, yes, every circumstance as it occurs to Jesus, and I will draw from His fullness of grace, sympathy, and strength, by prayer and faith, provision for this day's travel home to my Father's house."

Keep this truth constantly in view—a full Christ for an empty sinner. With no other will He have dealings; the rich He will send away empty, the poor He will send away full. The only sinner whom He rejects is he who comes with a price. His salvation is for the *lost*—His blood is for the *guilty*—His grace is for the *poor*. Come now—come as you are—come though you have been a thousand times before; yours shall be all the blessing—His all the praise.

> "A fullness resides in Jesus our Head,
>   And ever abides to answer our need;
>   The Father's good pleasure has laid up in store,
>   A plentiful treasure to give to the poor.

> "Whate'er be our wants, we need not to fear,
>   Our numerous complaints His mercy will hear;
>   His fullness shall yield us abundant supplies,
>   His power shall shield us when dangers arise.

"Whatever distress awaits us below,
Such plentiful grace will Jesus bestow
As still shall support us, and silence our fear,
For nothing can hurt us while Jesus is near.

"When troubles attend, or danger, or strife,
His love will defend and guard us through life;
And when we are fainting, and ready to die
Whatever is lacking His hand will supply."

Jacob's Lament

A GOOD MAN'S MISINTERPRETATION OF
A DARK PROVIDENCE

And Jacob their father said unto them, Me have ye bereaved of
my children: Joseph is not, and Simeon is not, and ye will take
Benjamin away: all these things are against me. GENESIS 42:36

THE deep, long shadows of life's evening were now gathering
and darkening around the close of Jacob's course—but
deeper, darker still were the shadows of God's providence.
His sun, whose race had been so long and so prosperous,
was now setting—but setting, oh, how gloomily! It would
seem as if the residuum of life's cup of sorrow were reserved
for life's close. And thus it pleases our heavenly Father
ofttimes that a believer's deepest affliction, his heaviest woes,
shall come upon him at the moment that he is about to bid
farewell to them forever: as if his Father would make heaven
all the sweeter by imparting an added bitterness to earth,—
all the brighter by accumulating around its last stage the
darkest dispensations,—all the more a perfect rest, by letting
loose the wildest storms as the vessel enters the port. Thus
was it with the patriarch.

And as he contemplated the cloud, he could think of
nothing but a speedy grave to which his gray hairs would
descend with sorrow. And yet, how different the reality of
the whole scene to the aspect which it wore to his dim and

darkened vision! In those clouds of woe he could see no silver light. Those mystic symbols of God's providence he could not decipher; the handwriting upon the wall he could not interpret. The only conclusion to which he could come was—*all these things are against me!*

In nothing is a child of God wider from the mark, more truly at sea, drifting away among the breakers of doubt and uncertainty, than when, unaided by the Spirit, he attempts to interpret the strange, trying, inexplicable procedure of God. Thus it was with Jacob. We propose, in the further prosecution of this subject, reviewing some of those DARK PROVIDENCES now accumulating around the patriarch— his MISINTERPRETATION of their import—and the TRUE SOLUTION of the whole.

Affliction seldom comes alone. A single, solitary trial is but half the recipe designed by our heavenly Physician to effect the cure. God seldom works by units in the unfolding and perfecting of His gracious purposes of love and mercy towards us. There is a combination, a plurality of trials, all uniting, aiding, and assisting each other in working out the great, the grand, the holy result. David's experience is the experience of all God's people—"He sent from above, he took me; he drew me out of *many waters.*" Thus was it with good old Jacob: many waves were surging around him—but his covenant God drew him out of all.

Let us look at these dark providences in their order. His first sorrow was that of *bereavement.* The shadow of death was upon his home. "Joseph is not." To him Joseph was virtually *dead.* The supposed circumstances of his end were of so painful a character as to greatly aggravate the affliction of his loss; and long and sorely had the patriarch mourned his rude and early death, doubtless treasuring, as a sad and only relic of his slaughtered child, the bloodstained coat of many colors that he wore, woven by his mother's hand. This, the saddest of all sorrows, still lingered in the good old man's heart, shading its brightest and latest joys.

How few of us are exempt from this sorrow! Who has not accompanied far into the shaded valley, loved ones of the heart? It pleases God sometimes to visit us with this calamity under circumstances peculiarly and unspeakably aggravating and distressing. We are born to die. The treasured ones around us have within them the seeds, and upon them the sentence, of death. The brilliant eye, the rosy cheek, the vermilion lip, the tall, graceful form shooting up, as in a night, like a cedar, are often to a skillful and discerning glance but as flowers blooming for the tomb.

Our home-circles, with all the powerful barriers that affection and influence can cast around them—guarded as by angel-sentinels of love—are not proof against the entrance of the "king of terrors." Youth cannot resist him— beauty cannot awe him—wealth cannot bribe him— eloquence cannot persuade him—learning cannot confound him—skill cannot baffle him—tears cannot move him— religion cannot evade his icy touch. To all this, his uplifted dart is inexorable. He takes the prince from the throne, the ruler from the state, the orator from the senate, the judge from the bench, the minister from the pulpit, the head from the family, the light from the home, the babe from its mother's arms. None, *none* are spared.

What mean those echoes of the muffled bell still lingering on the ear? What mean these broken circles— this vacant chair—those unread books—those portraits on the wall—this treasured locket—this unworn apparel? Oh, how sad, how touching their mute, expressive eloquence! They remind us of the departed—they tell of the spirit- land where they have fled, where they will return not again until time is no more.

And often does our heavenly Father see fit to take the dearest and the fairest first. Precious thought! if He plucks the ripe and leaves the green—transplants the tree of righteousness to a sunnier sky—and leaves the barren tree for time and culture, perchance for fruit.

But what is this sad visitation of bereavement but one of the appointed dispensations of our heavenly Father, sent in unerring wisdom, righteousness, and love? It is in the covenant of grace, and must therefore be included in the schedule of the believer's charter of blessings. "All things are yours—*death*"—be it our own, or be it that of one nestling in our bosom, sheltered beneath our wing—it yet is a covenant mercy. Christ has changed both its character and its name; and death to the believer is now a covenant *privilege* and a peaceful *sleep*. Is our Joseph no more?—God Himself has done it—has done it righteously. Sleeps he in Jesus?—Then he sleeps sweetly, and shall do well—for "them also which sleep in Jesus will God bring with him."

Yes! they are not lost, nor lost to us, who die in Christ. With Him they are now, with Him they will come again, and with Him will ever be. Even at this present we seem to be nearer to them, and in converse holier and closer, sweeter and dearer, as faith deals closely with the invisible, than when they were on earth.

> "God calls our loved ones, but we lose not wholly
>   What He has given.
> They live on earth in thought and deed as truly
>   As in heaven."

We owe them much! They have taught us how to die; and by their death we are learning how to live. They have lessened and loosened our ties to earth, and have increased and strengthened our ties to heaven. And now that they are gone, heaven is nearer and dearer, and is to our conception more than ever a reality and a place.

Oh yes! we are their debtors! We are well repaid for our anxious, weary watchings, tears and parting. They have, by sanctifying grace, made room in our hearts for Jesus, have brought God more fully into our souls, have made earth less sweet, death less bitter, Christ more precious, and heaven more winning.

Another dark cloud resting on the home of the patriarch was—*separation*. "Simeon is not." Simeon was still alive, but far removed from the eyes of his father. He had been detained in Egypt by Joseph as a hostage, as a pledge and covenant of the return to him again of his brethren. This was an added drop of bitterness to the full cup of the aged saint. Another link was broken, another tie severed of domestic happiness, a new sorrow blending with the many now shading the parental heart. Are *we* entirely exempt from this peculiar form of trial—*separation* from those we love, whose presence and companionship seemed necessary to our happiness, yes, essential to our very being?

Ah no! Who, in this life of vicissitude, this world of change, has not felt it? It is part of the moral discipline— the discipline of the affections—the fitness for heaven— through which our God sees fit we should pass. He loans us the blessing of human companionship a while—the loving heart, the kindred mind, the responding spirit, the sympathizing nature—to cheer, and soothe, and help us on our way: then removes it. The noblest specimens of our nature have been sensible of this sorrow.

Listen to the elder Edwards—a man whose colossal intellect might be thought to have absorbed every drop of sensibility, and yet he possessed a nature as exquisitely tender as a woman's—"My heart is heavy at the remembrance of all the miles that lie between us. Oh, I can scarcely believe that you are so distant from me. We are parted, and every parting is a form of death, as every reunion is a type of heaven." He seems to have caught the poet's idea,

> "To die and part
> Is less evil; but to part and live,
> There—there's the torment."

Listen to the words of the Psalmist—"Lover and friend hast thou put far from me, and my acquaintance into darkness." Yes! the tie that bound us, as we thought, too closely and too fondly ever to be broken, to a loved minister, a faithful friend, a fond relative, our Father dissolves, but to instruct us not to set our hearts inordinately upon any place or being on earth, and to remind us that if He separates us from friends—from the society, the counsel, and the soothing of those who had lessened life's sorrow and had increased its joy by affection and sympathy—it is but that He himself should enter and enshrine Him in the vacant recess, and be all in all.

The Lord Jesus sometimes holds our blessings as hostages. They are not entirely and forever removed from us, but are reserved to Himself for a while, as pledges of our unswerving confidence, filial obedience, and supreme love—that we will perform the vows and fulfill the promises we made when His hand was upon us. If this be the sorrow you are called to experience, dear reader, be still and know that He is God; yes, that He is your own God, and that whatever may be the painful, distant, and prolonged separation from the creature, there shall be no separation from Himself—His love, care, and sympathy.

And God would have us remember, too, that all present separation, whether by the distance of place, or the bereavement of death, from the holy objects of our affections, is but temporary and for a *little* while; that, in heaven, in our Father's house, we shall find them all again, and with them spend eternity. Blessed separation from the human, that brings our soul into this high experience of the Psalmist in his fellowship with the divine, "Whom have I in heaven but thee? and there is none on earth that I desire beside thee."

Another dark providence around this aged man of God was—*the sorrow of surrender.* "And ye will take Benjamin away." This was a peculiarly keen and poignant grief to the heart of Jacob. Benjamin, the child of his old age, his fondling, the youngest, the sunbeam, doubtless, of his house, was to leave him; he was to part with this the last, the dearest, and most precious treasure. My reader, our heavenly Father often asks of us a similar surrender, to prove the strength of our obedience, the sincerity of our affection, the reality of our faith—to test whether or not He were the supreme object of our homage, adoration, and love.

To surrender the youngest, the loveliest, and the dearest is often asked by God. The Lord sees fit to enter the domestic circle, and separate from it its light and its charm. And whether the removal is by death, or by the changing scenes of life, to surrender our Benjamin is often a trial hard to bear. Be it so. Our blessings are not ours; they are His. He has a right to extinguish this sunshine of our home—to remove this charm and sweetener of life, this treasure that seemed to shed around the winter gray of old age the light and warmth of the spring tide of youth!

Let us not, then, sorrow and repine; God never asks us to yield anything that seems necessary to our happiness and essential to our being, but, as we would remind you again, He asks His own. Your Benjamin is His; and if He enters your domestic enclosure and breaks the stem of some beautiful flower, it was His plant, and He had a right at any moment, and under any circumstances, to remove it to another and a distant place on earth, or to transfer it to the richer garden and the brighter skies of heaven.

But, superadded to these, there was one more cloud that gathered around Jacob's house. The *famine* was raging in the land. A man of wealth and of large possessions, he was still, with his beloved ones, dying of hunger. "The famine raged sore in the land." Yes, beloved, God may see fit, in His dealings with His people, to add to the sorrow of bereavement, to the grief of separation, and to the pain of surrender, impoverished circumstances, narrowed income, exhausted supplies.

God ofttimes deals with His people as if His heart were callous, His mind displeased, as if He were cold and indifferent to their temporal comforts and necessities. Be it so. He may see fit to reduce you in life, to blow upon garnered resources, to send a biting famine, as it were, to your home. It is but a page in your history corresponding with the experience of the most eminent of His people. The Lord would thus teach us that this life is not our portion, worldly wealth is not our treasure, created good is not our God.

Thus some of the saints are called to endure this reverse of fortune, this trial of poverty in extreme old age. The affluence of youth, the wealth of riper years has melted away, and poverty and hoary hairs have come together. But this has its blessings. God intends by this to confirm His love and faithfulness to His people. "Even to your old age I am he; and even to hoar hairs will I carry you." When has God ever failed His people? When has He ever forsaken His saints in the decline of life? Straitened circumstances may come—sickness may come—dependence may come—the wintry blast may blow—the snowflakes fall thick and fast—but GOD will come too, and His love and providence will turn winter into spring, and spring into summer, and summer into the ripe, golden fruit of autumn; "for he hath said, I will never leave thee, nor forsake thee."

Now, all these dark clouds, thus draping around the aged patriarch, were well calculated to fill his soul with distrust and trembling, to lead to an adverse interpretation of the infinite wisdom and righteousness and goodness of his covenant God. Let us then turn our attention to this.

"All these things are against me." What affecting, yet what significant words are these! And recollect that they are the words of a man of God; one with whom God had had very close transactions, with whom He had, as it were, talked face to face. Yet behold him, after all the long and deep experience of the divine dealings, a mere child, reduced to the lowest condition in his religion, his faith staggering, his feet sliding and almost gone, his past experience abandoning him, succumbing to trying circumstances, misspelling mystic symbols, writing hard and bitter things both against God and himself. It was a good man misinterpreting a dark providence. He was reading his spiritual Hebrew from left to right, rather than—as Hebrew properly is read—from right to left. To properly understand God's dispensations, they must often thus be read *backward*, and not forward. They must be studied in their results— must be viewed in the light of their ends—in the purposes which they are designed to accomplish. Faith must look rather at the *end*, than at the beginning, of a dark providence.

Beloved, we are but little acquainted with our own selves if we do not find much in our Christian and personal history that corresponds with this. Therefore, forgetting for the moment the case of the patriarch, let me state when it is, and how it is, that the child of God, tried and afflicted by the dispensations of his heavenly Father, is led to misread, misspell, and misinterpret these dispensations, and come to the conclusion, the wrong and erroneous conclusion, that because he cannot penetrate the darkness, unravel the mystery, and solve the problem, therefore God and His dispensations are against him.

In the first place, when spiritual exercises, when the dark dispensations of God's providence are viewed simply and only *with the eye of sense*, it will invariably lead us to a misconception, a misunderstanding, and a misinterpretation of His dealings with us. It is utterly impossible for you thus to look at a dark cloud, a paralyzing event, a crushing calamity, an unfortunate circumstance in your history, and not feel that it is a foe coming to despoil you of happiness; that it is a frown of your God; that it is an electric cloud surcharged with some element of destruction.

But, beloved, this is not the eye with which we are to look at God's dealings. The moment *faith* made its home in our hearts, that moment God gave us a new eye, a divine organ of vision; we professed to have ceased to deal with God and His dispensations as men of the world, as men of sense who looked at things only through the spectacles of carnal reason; we then professed to become believers in Christ, to commence the life of faith, to walk by faith, to fight by faith, and by faith ever to look at and deal with the visible, as with the invisible; by faith spelling the dark letters, and interpreting the mystic symbols of God's providences, and by faith resting in the firm conviction and assurance, that though clouds and darkness were round about *Him*, righteousness, faithfulness, and love, are about *us*, pointing, ordaining, and guiding every step of our feet homeward.

Looked at with the eye of sense and the eye of faith, the aspect of God's providences will be essentially dissimilar. If seen with the eye of sense, they will appear dark and overwhelming, and you shall come to the conclusion that all is against you, conspiring to destroy your happiness and well-being. But looked at with the eye of faith—faith's far-seeing vision—the picture changes, and those very events, circumstances, and incidents in your history that looked so somber and threatening, are all disguised blessings, veiled mercies, elements under the control and government of God, all combining for your greatest good and His highest glory.

Cease, then, to view your dark shadows, your trying dispensations, your overwhelming afflictions with the eye of sense, and look at them more simply, directly, and constantly with the eye of faith. "I would have fainted, unless I had *believed* to see the goodness of the Lord in the land of the living."

Again; when God is judged by His *dealings* rather than by His *sayings*, by what He *does* rather than by what He *is*, the child of God will invariably be involved in doubt and perplexity, and come to the conclusion that God's dealings with him, clothed with the drapery of woe, and uttering the voice of the stranger, are making against him. My beloved ones, God will not be judged by His saints according to His dealings; He will be judged by them according to His words. If you judge God's character, His love, His purposes, and the intents of His heart towards you, by His conduct, rather than by what He is in Himself, marvel not that you come to this conclusion, "all these things are against me."

But let us thank God that we have this high principle of interpretation of what He does—namely, His revealed and written Word—His promises sustaining, tempering, interpreting His providences. The Lord's government of His saints is like a dissolving panorama. Scene after scene, picture after picture, each one differing from the other, passes before the eye. Some are tinted brightly, others are shaded darkly; some portray battles lost, others battles won. Yes! what is life but a daily succession of dissolving views? But what is

God, He whose pencil tints and whose hand moves the picture? He is immutable, unchangeable, and eternal. He may change the lesson, vary the discipline, diversify His dealings, but He will never change in His love, falter in His faithfulness, or falsify His word. Life shall change—others shall change—most of all, we shall ourselves change; but our covenant God and Father never changes.

And it is by what He has written, and what He is, that He will have us judge of Him, and not by what He does. Doing this, you will not come to the incorrect and depressing conclusion, that all these changing, dissolving scenes of life, which form a perfect whole, are working against you, but you will be still and calm in the conviction that the power that controls and moves it all is the hand of a wise, loving, and gracious Father. It is here, beloved, our invested interests are so safe. In all life's chequered, variable history, we have to deal with a Father!

Is our bark amid the breakers? Our Father is at the helm. Does the sword's point press our heart?—a Father's hand holds it. Is the cup brimmed and bitter?—a Father's love has mingled it. Has the bright and hopeful picture of yesterday dissolved into the somber and despairing one of today?—a Father is behind the scene, ordering and controlling all things after the counsel of His own will. Thus, be your daily life what it may, it is just what He makes it. If our nest be pierced with a thorn, He has planted it; if it be soft with down, he has lined it. God makes people, and places, and scenes exactly what they are to us, and with this assurance we may calmly receive all at His hands as sent in love.

One more reason accounting for this strange misinterpretation of God's providences on the part of His people. When we forget that, in reality, nothing can possibly be *against* the child of God, we shall be plunged in a sea of doubt and perplexity. When you lose sight of the fact that nothing can really touch the interests, imperil the well-being, or affect the everlasting safety of a child of God, you are as a cork tossed upon the ocean. What a grand truth is this to keep hold of! "It is *well* with the righteous." "The *blessing* of the Lord is upon his people." "There is no enchantment against Jacob, neither is there any divination against Israel."

Man may curse; but God blesses. Let God's dispensation be ever so dark, painful, and afflicting, it is utterly impossible that anything can be against the best interests of a believer in Christ. If there is one being in the universe that is tenderly loved, daily cared for, prayerfully guarded, vigilantly watched over, and that, moment by moment—whose personal interests are bound up in the heart of God, and on whose everlasting safety He has pledged the honor of His name—it is the child of God, the believer in Christ, he for whom the Savior spilt His precious blood, and whom the Holy Spirit has made His temple.

"If God be *for* us, who can be *against* us?" Every being, and everything that is great, holy, and powerful, is on the side of the Triune Jehovah—angels—the spirits of just men made perfect—all the holy on earth—the Church above and the Church below—are all in league and in sympathy with God's elect. Why, then, should we yield to despondency and fear, or believe that anything can really be against us? Oh, it is only when unbelief and sense survey the scene that we extract from God's way with us material for misgiving, despondency, and despair. Environed by His perfections, yes, encircled by God Himself, it is, it must be *well* with the saints forever, and nothing shall prevail against them.

Having thus portrayed a few of the dark providences which ofttimes shade the Christian's path, tracing the misconstruction of these Divine dispensations to some of their causes, we now proceed to vindicate the character and glory of God in His conduct of His saints. What, in fact, was the true interpretation of all those trials now accumulating around the last days of the patriarch? The very reverse of that to which in unbelief and ignorance he arrived! All those things were working for him and in his favor.

Each event was a link in a chain of blessing, each cloud embosomed a mercy, each symbol was the token of love. The error into which the good man fell was that into which we are constantly, in like circumstances, gliding—the error of a rash and hasty interpretation of Divine providence. We seek to unravel what is explicable only to God—to sound what He only can fathom, and to anticipate, rather than quietly, patiently wait the unraveling of His thoughts, purposes, and end. We distrust God, and suppose it possible that He could have one hard thought, one unkind feeling towards His people. Impatient of mystery and delay, unsubmissive to the law of restraint, so divinely imposed, we wish to break the hedge with which our God has shut us in, to burst through the web of circumstances which infinite wisdom and love has drawn around us. In doing so, thwarted, lacerated, and wounded, we find ourselves involved in difficulties and exposed to perils from which a love that knows no chill, a patience that knows no weariness, a wisdom that nothing can baffle and a power with which nothing can cope, alone can rescue us. Oh, the patience and goodness of our God! Had we not Him to deal with, no creature in the universe could bear with our rebellion and folly for an hour!

Before we take a wider scope of this subject, let us trace the illustration afforded by the case of Jacob. Where was Joseph whom he supposed was not? He was alive, and exalted to great power, distinction, and wealth. His supposed death was a dark sorrow, yet that sorrow was but preparing the way for a bright sunset of Jacob's life. Out of that death life was to spring—out of that cloud light was to flow—the event that appeared to curtail so much domestic joy and hope was just the one that would prove the salvation of his house. It was not against him, it was for him!

And where was Simeon? He, too, was one of the links in this unbroken chain of mysterious providences. Detained in Egypt as a hostage, he was, in fact, but a pledge and security of the glad tidings and the good things that were about to chime upon the ear, and unveil to the eye of the perplexed and sorrowing patriarch. Beloved, the very blessings that the Lord takes from us are but pledges and foreshadows of yet greater and costlier ones! God seems to say, "Surrender this mercy, and I will replace it with a better. Yield in obedience this one blessing, and I will return it sevenfold. Lend me your Simeon, and I will return him again to you, and Joseph with him."

Thus it is that God buries our treasures but to raise them again to life, clad in deathless bloom, more precious, beauteous, and fragrant than ever. "Except a corn of wheat fall into the ground and die, it abideth alone: but if it die, it bringeth forth much fruit." Tremble not, then, when God veils your creature-treasures from your sight—it is but to fasten your eye more exclusively upon Himself; and when the trembling needle oscillates back to its center, when the wayward, foolish, idolatrous heart, smitten, sad, and lonesome, yet disciplined and sanctified, returns again to its "first love," God ofttimes reinspires its earthborn joy, and restores its creature-blessing.

And what of the famine? Sore and grievous as it was, even it was a link in this golden chain of wondrous providences. It was trying to the heart of Jacob—a large landholder, the possessor of great estates, yet famishing for bread—to behold his family and dependents reduced to such a calamity. Don't we learn something from this? While God can keep alive the soul of His saints in famine, He can cause the worldly to starve in the midst of plenty. The words of inspiration testify, "In the fulness of his sufficiency he shall be in straits," (Job 20:22.)

Many a man has great power, large possessions, beautiful domains, and every blessing that earth can supply, and yet his soul famishes for good, his heart pines for joy, his mind searches in vain for peace—he is poor in his wealth, and starves amid his plenty. Nothing but the love of God can satisfy the soul of man—none but God Himself can make him truly happy. My reader, acquaint yourself with Him, and be at peace; cease chasing the bubble, catching at the straw, eating ashes and feeding upon the wind of worldly creature-good. You will never be satisfied. Oh, listen to the voice of Jesus! "Wherefore do ye spend money for that which is not bread? and your labour for that which satisfieth not? hearken diligently unto me, and eat ye that which is good, and let your soul delight itself in fatness."

But what of the scarceness in Jacob's house? It was evolving God's thoughts of peace and purposes of love. The very famine was sowing the seeds of harvest—the crushing need was creating a full supply. It was providing wealth, honor, and food for Jacob's family. But for the famine—we speak after the manner of men—would Jacob ever have heard that Joseph was yet alive? Would life's close have been amid such golden sheaves of plenty? Would its autumnal sunset have been so serene and glowing? Thus, then, each of these painful events transpiring in the closing history of the aged patriarch was working out God's hidden love in the experience of His beloved child.

A few words of exhortation in conclusion. Thank God for the *hedge*. He planted it—He encircled you with it, and for your highest well-being, present and future. Satan never uttered a truer word than that which he spoke to God about Job, "Hast thou not made *an hedge* about him, and about his house, and about all that he hath on every side?" When God thus hedges a man, the gates of hell shall never prevail against him; nor can Satan touch him without God's permission. But there are often providential hedges in one's path, which, at the first blush, seem to wear an aspect militating against us. But be still. When God plants a hedge around us, we have as much reason to thank Him as when He breaks it down—as much when He closes, as when He opens, our path. That thorn-bush is but interposed between you and some impending, unseen, unsuspected evil from which God would shield you.

Oh, little do we suspect how much one evil is sent to prevent another and a greater! When our purposes are frustrated, our plans reversed, our hopes disappointed; or, when some sudden, distressing calamity overtakes us, then we begin to exclaim, "This is *against* me." Oh, could we see, as our Father does, the end from the beginning, could we unravel that mysterious web, decipher the meaning of that unlooked-for trial, unfold the blessing veiled and shaded in that somber cloud—in a word, could we see from what calamity we were saved, from what temptation we were shielded, from what sin we had been kept, from what fatal injury to our happiness and usefulness we have been preserved, we should bless God for the hedge, nor think the discipline too severe, or the mode too painful by which hopes, now crushed, would spring again into brighter bloom, in sweeter and undying fragrance. "Light is *sown* for the righteous; and gladness for the upright in heart."

Be cautious, then, of coming to rash hasty conclusions as to God's dealings. "I said *in my haste*," says David. It is the dictate of true wisdom and of sound faith, to wait patiently until God explains His own providences. He will do this in His good time.

> "God is His own interpreter,
> And He will make it plain."

Tried, afflicted child of God! be not hasty in your conclusion that God does not love you, that Christ cares not for you, and that all those untoward, painful, and inexplicable events in your history are confederate against your well-being, and are evidences against your conversion, your adoption, your saving interest in Christ.

Satan will strive hard to lead your reasoning to such a conclusion. Was not Jacob loved of God? Yes, God affirms it—"*Jacob* have *I loved*." And does He not call Himself—"the God of Jacob?" And yet, who was ever more sharply tried by God than he? Upon whose path to heaven did larger, darker shadows gather? Tried by undutiful children—tried by mournful bereavement—tried by painful separation—tried by crushing poverty—and yet, the beloved of God! "Whom the Lord *loveth* he chasteneth, and scourgeth every son whom he receiveth. If ye endure chastening, God dealeth with you as with sons; for what son is he whom the father chasteneth not?" "As many as I love, I rebuke and chasten."

Accept, then, these afflictive dealings of your heavenly Father as evidences of your belonging to the seed-royal of Christ, as seals of your adoption, as parts of the discipline by which the Lord is promoting your sanctification and preparing you for glory. Read in this hallowed, soothing light of God's love, you will not conclude that all these things are against you, but rather will exclaim—"He has done all things *well*."

We learn from this subject that God sometimes removes a blessing but to return it to us again. He never intends to curtail our real happiness. He loves His people too well for that. We know but imperfectly the GREATNESS of God's love to us. It is infinite—how should we fully know it? And yet this should be our constant prayer, especially when His dealings are trying to faith, "Lord, show me *how* You love me. Lead my heart into Your love. Let me, with all my cares and sorrows, infirmities and sins, sink into the soundless depths of this vast sea."

He asked of Abraham the surrender of Isaac, He took from Jacob first Joseph, and then Simeon, and lastly Benjamin, but He kindly restored them all again, all the sweeter, all the dearer, all the more hallowed and precious from their temporary removal. Relinquish, then, without a murmur or a misgiving what the Lord asks, dear though it be as the heart's tenderest fiber.

From the grave in which God entombs it, it shall, at His bidding, leap again into life, more beauteous, more sacred, and more precious than ever. And the discipline of the heart, the deepening of God's work in your soul, the weanedness, the prayerfulness, the lowliness, the endearing of Christ that the removal of the blessing has induced, will be an infinite compensation for its painful and temporary withdrawment. Joseph was but a mere stripling, poor and despised, when God removed him from Jacob; he was full-grown, the governor of all Egypt, wealthy and honored, when God gave him back!

> "Saints, at your heavenly Father's word,
> Give up your comforts to the Lord;
> He shall return what you resign,
> Or grant you blessings more divine."

And what is the conclusion of the whole? It shall be in the words of God, and not of man, "ALL THINGS WORK TOGETHER FOR GOOD TO THOSE WHO LOVE GOD, TO

THEM THAT ARE THE CALLED ACCORDING TO HIS PURPOSE." Blessed Lord! be Your dispensations bright or cloudy, mysterious or plain, on this Divine truth I can live, upon it I can die, and it shall be my study and praise through eternity!

> Courage, brother!—yes, take courage,
>   In life's battle dare to fight;
> Though the strife may seem unequal,
>   "Trust in God, and do the right."
>
> Stand up boldly—never falter;
>   Stand up, though you stand alone;
> God will nerve your arm for warfare,
>   He will make His strength your own.
>
> Is your heart well-nigh to fainting?
>   Seems the future hopeless, drear?
> Is there none to ease your burden—
>   None to whisper words of cheer?
>
> Courage, you are not forgotten:
>   Learn dark doubts aside to fling;
> God would teach your heart the lesson,
>   Sweetest joys from sorrows spring.
>
> Fierce may be the outward conflict,
>   Fiercer still the strife within;
> But how sweet the resting, brother,
>   When we stand "complete in Him!"
>
> Weary heart, then, take fresh courage,
>   Sins, and fears, and self despite;
> Look above!—with faith unshaken,
>   "TRUST IN GOD, AND DO THE RIGHT!"

Joseph Making Himself Known to His Brethren

CHRIST REVEALING HIMSELF TO HIS PEOPLE

Then Joseph could not refrain himself before all them that stood
by him; and he cried, Cause every man to go out from me.
And there stood no man with him, while Joseph made himself
known unto his brethren. And he wept aloud: and the
Egyptians and the house of Pharaoh heard. GENESIS 45:1-2

WE have now reached the *conclusion* of this interesting and
persuasive story. The veil is uplifted, the disguise is removed,
and JOSEPH stands before his brethren manifested and made
known. The whole scene is inimitably beautiful and richly
instructive, such as neither the pen of the poet, the pencil
of the painter, nor the tongue of the orator can adequately
depict. Talk of human fiction! Scripture history is infinitely
more fascinating and marvelous; added to which is the
irresistible power and charm of revealed and confirmed
truth. Reserving for the next chapter of our work the *relation*
in which Joseph manifested himself, in the present we have
to do only with the *manifestation*. This one particular is
sufficiently suggestive of most precious truth, touching
Christ and His brethren, to engage our study. Upon JESUS,
the central object of our story, we must keep the eye
undividedly and intently fixed; for, wonderful and
exciting as the story itself is, its charm and its teaching

were as nothing if we see not JESUS in it. The most suggestive points for our meditation are—THE PRIVACY— THE MANIFESTATION—THE EMOTION.

"Then Joseph could not refrain himself before all them that stood by him; and he cried, Cause every man to go out from me. *And there stood no man with him, while Joseph made himself known unto his brethren.*" The occasion was eventful and solemn; there were entwined with it memories too sacred, feelings and emotions too tender, for any other to share with themselves. He resolved, therefore, that it should be veiled with the profoundest secrecy. There was, too, remarkable delicacy of feeling on the part of Joseph in this arrangement. He considered his brethren—the thoughts and feelings that would overwhelm them at the astounding discovery that he was their very brother whom they had injured. The memory of their sin and wrong rushing back upon their minds with overpowering force, might so fill them with shame and confusion of face as to expose them to the rude stare and reproach of the Egyptians. From this humiliation, the kind and considerate brother would sincerely screen them.

Added to this, Joseph was now about to divest himself of his official dignity, and to exchange the distant, stern address of the governor of Egypt for the unreserved, familiar, and affectionate communion of the brother, and no eye shall gaze upon the spectacle except their own. "And there stood no man with him, while Joseph made himself known unto his brethren."

It was an occasion and a joy with which a stranger should not intermeddle, and with which another could not sympathize. We pass to its spiritual and gospel teaching. Do you see in this, my reader, a remarkable page of your own spiritual history? Are not your thoughts at once thrown back upon some of the most sacred and solemn periods of your experience, when, separated and alone, not a human eye seeing, not a human ear hearing, there has been a gracious manifestation to you of God in Christ, the most personal, touching, and overwhelming?

The Church of God is *hidden* and *invisible*. Her divine life, her spiritual conflicts, her joys and sorrows, are, for the most part, concealed from the rude gaze of an ungodly world; and that which transpires between the child of God and his Father in heaven, between Jesus and His brethren, is cognizant only to Him whose most confiding, solemn, and gracious interviews are reserved for hours and places of the profoundest privacy. Let us turn our attention to two or three periods of our spiritual history illustrating this.

There is, in the first place, God's separation of His people from all others *in election*. God's people are a "remnant according to the election of grace." His Church is truly and emphatically an elected body. They are a people taken out of the world according to His eternal purpose and everlasting covenant, designated and set apart as His special and peculiar people. This truth flashes from the page of God's Word as with electric light. Thus we read, "God at the first did visit the Gentiles to take out of them a people for his name." "He hath chosen us in him before the foundation of the world." "Knowing, brethren beloved, your election of God." "All that the Father giveth to me shall come to me." "Ye are a chosen generation, a royal priesthood, an holy nation, a peculiar people." What need we of further testimony?

Here is the first and most ancient separation of God's people, invisible and unknown; no angel, no creature present when that choice was made, when that covenant was entered into, when that Church was chosen. It was a secret eternally, solemnly veiled in the infinite depths of Jehovah's mind. He alone was cognizant of it who dwelt in the bosom of the Father. "Secret things belong unto the Lord our God." How worthy of Him this eternal act of sovereign grace and love, "who worketh all things after the counsel of his own will," and "who giveth not account of any of his matters!"

In nothing does He appear more like Himself—more completely and gloriously the eternal, independent, holy, sovereign Lord God. Receive in faith this truth, because it is revealed—adore it, because it is divine—love it, because it entwines the holiness and comfort of the saints with the glory and praise of God.

Then, there is the separation of God's people *in their spiritual and effectual calling by the Holy Spirit.* Real conversion is a *secret and separating* work. It separates a man from himself, from the covenant of works, from the world, and often from his family. It touches and dissolves the ties which in unregeneracy so closely and so fondly bound him to earth's sinful associations. Where divine and sovereign grace thus enters the heart, oh what a division, what a separation transpires, in the experience of that individual, from all the antecedents that at one period of his history formed the charm, the sweetness, the very sun of human existence!

Who can describe the awful privacy of that transaction, when the worshiped idol 'self,' the cherished righteousness, the adored object of creature-affection was laid at Jesus' feet, and Jesus and the soul were left alone in the discovery of a relation, and in the manifestation of a love such as heaven must have looked down to see! My dear reader, has your professed religion thus separated you? Has the great divorce taken place? Have you been separated from the self-righteous world? from the gay world? from the ungodly world? from the intellectual world? disenthralled from that form of worldly fascination and power by whose spell you were held a willing captive? If so, then the snare is broken and you are escaped. Divine and sovereign grace has exerted upon you its mightiest power, and conferred upon you its richest boon!

This is true conversion—a separation from self-righteousness—from the dominion of sin—from the captivity of Satan—and all other that is false. O solemn stillness, O holy privacy of that moment when this great change takes place—this grand secret is disclosed—this wondrous discovery is made! Truly does our true Joseph cause every man, every object, and every feeling to retire from the scene, when, by the Spirit's quickening and His converting grace, He draws the soul in love to Himself, and reveals the secret of the covenant. It is an occasion too holy, too sacred and solemn, for any other to be present save Christ and the Soul.

The *providential*, not less than the gracious, dealings of God often bring us into this experience of isolation. When the Lord intends to reveal His ways, and to make us better acquainted with Himself and with our own selves in these ways, there is that in His dealings which seems to sequester us from all but Himself. He removes us from the crowd—from the busy hum of men—from the whirl and excitement of daily life; and, bidding all retire, there is no creature present while He talks with us.

Ah! there is a silence in that bereavement, a solitude in that sickness, a secret in that adversity, a mystery in that event, known only to Christ and the soul. There is heart-searching, and conscience-probing, and sin-revealing, and divine discoveries, veiled from every intelligence but the believer and God. And when the hand of our Father is thus laid upon us, the stricken deer seeks not more instinctively the lonely glen to nurse its wound in solitude, than does our heart prompt us to retreat from our fellows and seek the cloister of a sacred privacy, to think and feel and act alone with God.

And what an unfolding is there here of the tender, delicate consideration of Jesus! With His solemn rebukes, His deep heart-searchings, His gracious discoveries, no one shall be cognizant except Himself. Our secret sins, which He places in the light of His own countenance, He kindly veils from everyone else. What deep instruction may we receive from this! How considerate we should be of the case, how careful of the feelings, and how jealous of the reputation of the Lord's brethren and ours! Our Joseph will never needlessly and unfeelingly expose us to the rude gaze, the changed affection, the lessened esteem and confidence of others; but, veiling our infirmities, failures, and sins from the world and the saints, will deal with them in the solemn privacy of our own souls. So let us deal with our brethren!

But it is in the act of *private communion* with God that the believer and Christ are the most truly and solemnly alone. Then, if ever, every being and object retires, and Jesus draws near and holds the soul in the spell of a fellowship and joy with which the stranger intermeddles not. Such was the communion of the patriarch at Peniel. He was alone. The curtain of night draped the scene from every eye; all sound was hushed into silence but the voice of prayer. Jacob and the Angel of the Covenant were the sole actors in that scene. It was then that Christ made Himself known, conferred a spiritual knighthood upon the holy auditor, and retiring, left him a conqueror and blest.

Beloved, our greatest strength in prayer is, when we wrestle *alone* with the Strong One. Our thoughts, and feelings, and sympathies, are shared by others when with others we draw near to God. But do you, O son of Jacob, aspire to his dignity and blessing? Then cause everyone to go out when you would hold your most sacred season with

Christ. O blessed hour, when Christ and the heart meet in holy, confiding, loving fellowship! There dwells not in that bosom a sin, in its depths of sensibility a sorrow, in its clinging affections a rival, in its intense yearnings a desire, in its fervent breathings a petition, in its bright sunshine a cloud, which may not at that moment find pardon, sympathy, and repose in converse with Jesus.

Oh, cultivate these seasons of privacy, these moments of separation for communion with God! Christ Himself needed and sought them. How frequently did He leave the busy world, and the thronging multitude, and the presence of His disciples, to meditate in pensive loneliness on the seashore, or to pour forth His midnight supplications amid the mountain's solitude! If He, the Strong One, the Sinless One, felt the need of retirement for thought, and prayer, and self-communion, how much deeper our need, whose nature is so fallen, whose heart is so sinful, whose path is so thickly paved with temptations to evil, and so deeply shaded with the storm-clouds of sorrow!

Oh, see that your hours of conversation with Jesus are not rudely invaded! Go at morning's dawn, at midday's turmoil, at evening's shade, yes, in the still hour of night, when sad thoughts encircle, and tears bedew your pillow, and, dismissing the world and the creature, draw near to the Mighty One, the Compassionate One, the All-seeing One, and tell the Savior all! Oh, cultivate sacred retirement! It is as essential to the nourishment of your piety, the increase of your spirituality, the comfort of your soul as the morning's sunbeam and the evening's dew is to earth's fertility.

The richest fruit and flower of truth grow beneath the cross, the purest springs of grace flow in the hidden, shaded walk with God. There you can confess sin, and unveil grief, and breathe needs, and make known trials, seek and obtain renewed supplies of pardon and strength, peace and comfort, as nowhere else. And realize how beautifully and wisely God has harmonized the time and place of separation from all others, with the special season of communion with Himself.

> "The calm retreat, the silent shade,
>   With prayer and praise agree,
> And seem by Thy sweet bounty made
>   For those who follow Thee.
>
> "Then, if Thy Spirit touch the soul,
>   And grace her mean abode,
> Oh, with what peace, and joy, and love,
>   She communes with her God!
>
> "There, like the nightingale, she pours
>   Her solitary lays;
> Nor asks a witness to her song,
>   Nor sighs for human praise."

Joseph, having commanded every man to retire, then makes himself known. This conducts us to the MANIFESTATION of Joseph to his brethren. "Joseph *made himself known* unto his brethren." What must have been the varied thoughts, the conflicting emotions of Joseph's brethren, and of Joseph himself, when they found themselves face to face alone! In the minds of the conscious brethren what solemn awe, what memories of sin, what forebodings of evil, what strange reflections and fears now crowd! In Joseph's heart, what concealed emotion, what smothered feelings, what loving, tender thoughts and purposes were revolving! Is there nothing corresponding with this in the divine and gracious manifestations of Christ to the believing soul?

How impressive the thoughts and feelings of the believer when he finds himself alone in the Divine presence! What sad memories of sinful departure, of wilful backsliding, of unfaithfulness and unkindness to Christ, crowd the mind! What trembling, and fears, and self-abasement fill the heart! The remembrance at that moment of wrong, and injury, and unkindness to a Being so good, to a Savior so gracious, to a Friend so loving, to a Father so tender and faithful, overwhelm the soul with awe, humiliation, and dread.

But oh, what a contrast does the Lord Himself present! In the heart of Jesus, what love, what compassion, what yearning tenderness, and in the mind of God, what thoughts and purposes of peace dwell, panting, as it were, for the expression and the outflow!

But let our thoughts for a moment dwell more exclusively upon this single element of experimental religion—the Divine manifestation to the believing soul. It is the very essence of a holy, happy religion. A Christianity without it is but the name, the profession, the resemblance. A man of God is a living soul; a believer in Christ is in vital union with his Head; he is a temple of the Holy Spirit. All this involves close dealing and communion with the Divine. With such an individual, thus quickened with divine and spiritual life, there must of necessity be much transaction with God, with the spiritual and invisible.

Water does not ascend more naturally to its level, than does the grace of God, welled within a gracious soul, rise in communion and aspiration and praise to Him from whom it came. It is no hallucination, nothing visionary and ideal, that a child of God may so walk with God, a believer in Christ so commune with Christ, as to realize on earth a conversation with the divine, and the invisible, and the spiritual, but one remove from the pure and perfected fellowship of heaven itself. The man of God is as conscious of having God's ear open to him, God's countenance beaming upon him, God's heart responding to him, as a loving child is who stands in the parental presence, and wakes from a father's lips words of response and love. I cannot illustrate a feature of real vital religion of greater moment than this.

And I am all the more earnest in enforcing it, seeing there are so many religionists who are satisfied with their round of religious duties, unaccompanied and unsanctified with a moment's consciousness of the Lord's manifestation to their souls. Ask them if they know from personal experience the significance of these gracious words of Christ, "We will come and *manifest* ourselves to you," and how unmeaning and blank their look!

Let me remark that the first and most memorable discovery of Christ to the soul is in its earliest stage of grace. What pen can portray, or tongue describe, the experience of that moment when Jesus first stands revealed to the believing soul; when words of pardon are first spoken, and a sense of acceptance is first realized, and the love of God is first felt! If the reader can recall that hour when Jesus stood before him, the veil uplifted, the disguise removed, all manifested and revealed in surpassing loveliness and love, your Savior, your Lord and Sovereign, then, methinks, he can recall a period in his existence upon which memory will feast with delight, lasting as the duration of eternity. Oh, heaven alone can supply a joy comparable with the joy of that hour!

Does this page meet the eye of a Christ-seeking, Christ-longing soul? My beloved reader, the Lord Jesus waits to be gracious to you. He is prepared to throw off the disguise, to rend in twain the veil, to lay aside the appearance that may have filled your mind with awe and your heart with fear, and to reveal Himself as bearing your sin, as exhausting your curse, as delivering you from condemnation, and as reconciling you to God by His blood. Oh, He is ready to burst through the dark clouds with which your sin and guilt and unbelief have invested Him, and to stand before your trembling spirit in His true relation, full of grace, overflowing with love, uttering assurances of a forgiveness that will leave not the shadow of a sin uneffaced, of a righteousness that places you in a present acceptance, and insures you a future glory.

Only believe! give full credence to the assurances of His gospel. That gospel tells you that He came into the world to save *sinners;* that He came to call not the righteous but *sinners* to repentance; that He died for the *ungodly;* that He casts out none who come to God by Him; that He saves to the uttermost; that pardon and justification, adoption and salvation, are the *free* gifts of His grace. Only believe these simple yet wondrous statements, and the result will be a true and settled joy unspeakable and full of glory.

Oh, what a blessed realization of Jesus to your soul will there be the moment doubt yields to confidence, fear gives place to love, despair merges into hope, and guilt and condemnation are supplanted by pardon, peace, and assurance forever! All these precious streams will flow like gentle wavelets into your soul the moment you embrace in childlike faith the Savior.

Then there is the Divine manifestation to the believing soul, after a season of spiritual gloom, depression, and despondency. It pleases God to discipline and instruct the believer by darkness as by light. Indeed, the one is as essential to the progress of our Christianity as the other. Astronomical science achieves its most glorious discoveries when earth's beauties, clad in evening's shadows, fade upon the view. Infinitely greater and more glorious are the spiritual discoveries of God, of Christ, of truth, and his own heart, made by the child of light when walking in darkness. He learns in the shade what he did not in the sunshine.

The storm has tested the strength of his bark; the lee shore has proved the firmness of his anchor; the darkness of a starless night has increased his confidence in the correctness of his compass. In this season of spiritual gloom, of severe soul-exercise, what lessons the believer learns of God's love, power, and faithfulness; how confirmed is his faith in the truth of God's Word; what experimental discoveries he makes of the love, the fullness, the sympathy of Jesus; and how more thoroughly schooled he becomes in, perhaps, the most difficult, as the most humiliating, of all knowledge—the knowledge of himself! "Such honor have all the saints."

O beloved, there is no event or circumstance of your life, however simple or inexplicable, profound in its gloom or dazzling in its brightness, pleasing or painful, by which God does not intend to instruct and bless you. He taught David as much in the cave of Adullam as He ever did upon the throne of Israel. He taught Joseph as a prisoner in his dungeon what he never learned as the governor of all Egypt. Deem not, then, days and nights of spiritual adversity, trial, and storm, through which you course your way, blank and unfruitful periods in your history. Oh, no! Christ is in all, and by all He is but deepening His work of grace in your heart, promoting the divine life in your soul, and training you for heaven.

But these seasons of spiritual depression and gloom in the believer's experience are but temporary. There follows the season of Divine manifestation, when Christ, the Sun, breaks through the dark clouds, and all is light and joy again. "He restoreth my soul." "The Lord will command his lovingkindness in the daytime, and in the night his song shall be with me." Our Joseph removes the momentary obscuration, the cloud-veil that He wore, and stands before us our Joseph still. Oh, can you not testify to such blessed seasons in your experience, when the Lord has, after a night of weeping, caused the morning of joy to dawn; when, after a long and dreary road, you have emerged into a large and wealthy place, bathed with the sunshine of His love?

These are blessed manifestations of Jesus. And but for the hidings, the withdrawings, the suspensions of His sensible presence and love, how little should we know of the sustaining power of faith in darkness, and of the enhanced sweetness and pleasantness of the light when the darkness is past! All this is to endear Jesus to our soul,—to make us better acquainted with our true Joseph. We learn as much what He is by His disguises as by His manifestations, by His hidings as by His revealings. In both He is our immutable Christ.

If it is now a time of darkness with your soul, hope in God, for you shall yet praise Him. Jesus will not always speak to you in a reserved and rough tone, to test your faith and prove your love and make the manifestation all the sweeter. Wait but the Lord's time, and though for a little moment He has hidden His face from you, yet with great mercies He will appear again.

> "Encompassed with clouds of distress,
>   Just ready all hope to resign,
>   I pant for the light of Thy face,
>   And fear it will never be mine.
>
> "Disheartened with waiting so long,
>   I sink at Thy feet with my load;
>   All plaintive I pour out my song,
>   And stretch forth my hands unto God.
>
> "Shine, Lord! and my terror shall cease;
>   The blood of atonement apply;
>   And lead me to Jesus for peace—
>   The Rock that is higher than I.

"Almighty to rescue Thou art;
  Thy grace is my shield and my tower;
  Come, succor and gladden my heart—
  Let this be the day of Thy power."

Nor must we fail to quote *afflictive seasons* in the believer's history, as occasions of special manifestation of Jesus to the soul. Affliction is a separating process. The Lord, by these dispensations of trial and sorrow, draws us aside into solitary places, and there converses with us. And when dark adversity or sore affliction has thus withdrawn us from man, or, perhaps, has impelled man from us, and we are left alone, we are surprised to find how near we are to Christ, or, rather, how near Christ has brought Himself to us.

It is only in the sorrows and trials of human life that *real* friendship is fully tested. A friend who loves us, clings to us, acknowledges and aids us at *all* times, is a friend indeed. *That* Friend of friends is—JESUS. We have but to be in trial, in sorrow, in need, to realize that Christ is standing at our door asking admittance to our grief. The storm has borne Him on its wing, the clouds have provided Him a chariot, death has brought Him in its wake. Where a suffering, sorrowing, needy servant of God is, there is Jesus.

The season of *sickness* is a touching illustration of the special manifestation of Christ to His people. I cite this instance, as it is more or less the experience of many of God's people; and sooner or later will be the experience of all. A sickroom is often the audience-chamber of Christ— the King's private room where He meets His saints alone. Thus sequestered from all—the world excluded, the creature shut out, business suspended—lo! Christ has entered; and, oh, what solemn transactions, what gracious communion, what Divine manifestations, what interchanged affections, then transpire between Christ and the soul. The sickroom was necessary for the separation, the separation was needed for the manifestation, and the manifestation for the health and comfort of the soul.

And thus a dispensation which the man of God thought a calamity so adverse and a cloud so threatening, has but developed God's purpose of mercy, wisdom, and love, in the closer communion into which it has brought the heart with Christ. So that the season of sickness and suffering— a sleepless pillow and a couch of weakness—has been irradiated and soothed with gleams of heaven, with the presence of Jesus and the smiles of God.

Exiled from the privileges of the public worship of God, severed from those means of grace and useful employments in which your soul has been accustomed to delight, deem not yourself, sick one! the inhabitant of a dry land, or as an exile whom no one loves, for whom no one cares. Oh, no! Your sick and suffering couch God may place near by the vestibule of heaven, yes, within the very precincts of the coming glory—such may be the divine manifestations to your soul. Angels sent from above minister to you, happy spirits encircle you, the odors of paradise float around you, the breezes of heaven fan you, the eye of God watches over you, and the manifested presence of Jesus strengthens you to bear the exile with cheerfulness, the languor with patience, and the suffering with a heart that meekly exclaims, "As my Father wills."

Thus, beloved, adversity, whatever its form—be it the loss of property, the decay of health, the bereavement of friends—has been the door through which Christ has entered, bent on a loving, gracious revelation of Himself to your soul. He has constructed the furnace, kindled the fire, controls the heat only to melt and then to mold, to purge and then to purify and refine your soul, that you may have less of sin and more of holiness, less of the creature and more of Christ, less of self and more of God, less of earth and more of Heaven.

> "Pain's furnace-heat within me quivers,
>   God's breath upon the flame does blow:
> And all my heart in anguish shivers
>   And trembles at the fiery glow.
> And yet I whisper: *As God will!*
>   And in His hottest fire hold still.
>
> "He comes, and lays my heart, all heated,
>   On the hard anvil, minded so,
> Into His own fair shape to beat it
>   With His great hammer, blow on blow:
> And yet I whisper: *As God will!*
>   And at His heaviest blows hold still.
>
> "He takes my softened heart and beats it;
>   The sparks fly off at every blow;
> He turns it o'er and o'er and heats it,
>   And lets it cool, and makes it glow.
> And yet I whisper: *As God will!*
>   And in His mighty hand hold still.
>
> "Why should I murmur? for the sorrow
>   Thus only longer-lived would be;
> Its end may come, and will tomorrow,
>   When God has done His work in me,
> So I say trusting: *As God will!*
>   And, trusting to the end, hold still.
>
> "He kindles, for my profit purely,
>   Affliction's glowing, fiery brand;
> And all His heaviest blows are surely
>   Inflicted by a Master hand.
> So I say praising: *As God will!*
>   And hope in Him, and suffer still." —*Julius Sturm*

Nor must we overlook the gracious manifestations of Christ's restoring grace and changeless love after seasons of spiritual and penitential backsliding. Such was the look of Jesus to the fallen Peter. Such the language of God to His repentant Ephraim: "I have surely heard Ephraim bemoaning himself...Therefore my bowels are troubled for him; I will surely have mercy upon him, saith the Lord."

Oh, what a mercy that the Lord curbs our waywardness, checks our wanderings, restores and heals our backslidings; and when in contrition we lie at His feet bemoaning our departures, confessing our sins, covered with shame and confusion at our base, unkind, ungrateful requital of love so deep, mercy so great, grace so free, how blessed then the manifestations of His restoring mercy, His healing grace, His unchanged and forgiving affection! We marvel not that the gentle word, the expressive look of Christ, breaks the heart with contrition, and dissolves it into love.

But the most gracious, manifest, and sustaining revealings of Christ to His brethren are reserved for the lone, shaded valley of death. What can meet that solemn period but faith in Christ? Who can so tread it with us as that its loneliness shall create no depression, its gloom no obscurity, its appearance no terror, its dart no sting, its remote consequences no fear—but Jesus?

When death confronts a believer, he confronts Christ in that believer, and meets his Spoiler and his Foe. And so near is Jesus, so absorbingly conscious is the departing soul of His presence, it sees not death, but Him only who is the Conqueror of death, the Resurrection and the Life, and so it fears no evil, and passes over to the other side, its song of victory, in dying cadence, fading in the distance.

Fear not, then, the coming hour! You shall not be deserted nor desolate; separated from others, you will be all the more engaged with Christ. That solemn crisis will find

Him at your side; and although sad recollections of chilled affections, of unfaithful services, of an uneven walk, it may be, a wound inflicted upon the bosom that now pillows your languid head may crowd upon the memory, yet, oblivious of it all, and forgiving it all, Christ is there to give you dying, God-glorifying grace for the hour and article of death.

Dismissing the revelation of Joseph to his brethren, we next approach the SENSIBILITY he displayed on the occasion: "And he wept aloud." The long pent-up feelings of his heart now found vent in that intense audible mode peculiar to oriental grief. Emotions he had struggled to conceal now threw off their guise, and he wept. These were marvelous tears of Joseph! Who gave him that sensibility? who kindled these feelings? who unsealed these tears?—He of whom it is written, "Jesus wept."

Ah, beloved, if such was the sensibility of Joseph—a man of like infirmities, selfishness, and sin, with ourselves—what must be the sensibility, what the sympathy, and what the tears of Christ? The love, the tenderness, the sympathy, those tears thus expressed in the presence of his brethren, were welled there by his glorious, gracious Antitype—they were but distillings from the nature and spirit of Christ. It is a beautiful shadowing forth this of the hidden love and sympathy of the Savior—hidden and unknown until our circumstances elicit and reveal it.

Did the heart of Joseph overflow? Did the sight, the need, and the affliction of his brethren unseal the fountain of sensibility? Do you think that when you stand in the presence of Christ He will feel and exhibit less kindness, sympathy, and love? Oh, no! His nature is so identical with your own, there is not a shade of sorrow, nor a form of temptation, nor a peculiarity of need to which the sensibility and sympathy of His heart is not toned.

A weeping Joseph! it is a touching spectacle, and I envy not the feelings of the individual who can read the story without emotion. A weeping Savior! it is a sublime study, and I envy the pencil that can livingly portray, and the loftiness and delicacy of that perception that can vividly realize its image, its tenderness, and its grandeur. Yet more deeply do I covet the feelings of that saint who, with a heart of leaden grief, with mental beclouding and depression, its stricken and bleeding affections wandering through the vacant and desolate cloisters of the soul whose beloved occupants death has removed, can believingly, calmly, silently sink into the depths of this boundless sea of Christ's human sensibility, and realize the all-sufficiency of His sustaining grace, and the exquisite soothing of His sympathizing love. "Jesus wept"—words we can never weary of repeating, and which will continue to fall sweet as heaven's music on the ear until He wipes the last tear away.

But if of human sorrow there is one with which the sensibility of our true Joseph is the most closely and tenderly entwined, it is the sorrow which the inroads of *death* produce—the grief which the departure into eternity of loved ones leaves in its long, lingering shadow, and anguish in the heart. This is a loss which we feel only One can meet; it were irreparable but for Christ. We may part with health, but by skill, kindness, and care, win back again the boon. We may part with wealth, but by patient and self-denying industry retrieve our loss. We may part with endeared and sacred places, but by new friendships, scenes, and associations, experience a sweet and soothing mitigation of the sorrow.

But no skill of science, no efforts of kindness, no voice of love can redeem from the grave, or win back from eternity, the beloved spirits that have left us. They have gone beyond our recall. The treasure of our heart—the light of our home—the companion of our pilgrimage—the charm and sweetness of life has departed, leaving a grief Christ only can soothe, a shadow He only can illumine, a vacancy He only can fill. There is but one Being in the wide, wide world, but one in the boundless universe, who can occupy that lone and desolate niche.

Our dearest Lord was disciplined by this very sorrow of parting, that He might be able to succor and soothe this grief of ours. Oh, sweet sorrow, which none but Christ can soothe! Oh, sacred loss, which none but Christ can supply! It is often necessary that the tenderest fiber of our affections should be severed, the most sacred cloister of our hearts should be emptied, the fondest idol of our souls displaced, that we might learn the reality and power of Christ's sympathy in parting.

Who can supply a parent's care, fill a child's place, be more than husband, brother, friend, minister, but Jesus? Then let the swelling billow of your bereavement but cast you more completely upon Him—the Rock that is higher than you. If this be the fruit, a rich and golden harvest will your faith have sickled from this sowing of tears. Weep on! and weep not only at the feet, but on the very bosom of Christ, that your sorrow may all the more partake His sympathy. Wish not to recall the absent one—that were selfish sorrow—rather seek greater nearness to the Lord, a deeper sanctification of the heart, a more full, unreserved surrender to God. Let Christ be more precious to you now than ever; and all the future of your path be cheered by His presence, and all the future of your pilgrimage be consecrated to His glory.

"Oh! weep, sad heart!
The loved, the lovely, from this earth have flown;

The beautiful have left you all alone.
Autumn its dead leaves o'er their graves has strewn.

"Oh! weep, sad heart!—
The Savior wept for you, and bore the smart
Of your deep grief in His own bleeding heart.
You may not sit alone, and mourn apart.

"Then weep a while;
You'll miss the cheerful voices in their mirth,
That brightened many a lonely path on earth.
Ah! gentle ones, you have a heavenly birth.

"Weep not for *these:*
They've passed from this tempestuous land of ours
Into a clime of endless love and flowers,—
Crowned with immortal bliss in heavenly bowers.

"Then dry your tears!
Sheltered so kindly in the Savior's breast—
You would not call your loved ones from that breast.
Oh! with the angels leave them, pure and blest:
Weep not, sad heart."

In conclusion, allow me to exhort you to cultivate seasons of holy privacy. Beware of losing yourself in a crowd of religious purposes, and in the turmoil of religious doings. You may be "religious overmuch!" Allowing things and engagements professedly religious, and for a religious purpose, to become too encroaching and absorbing, you may leave no time for *private* prayer, for *closet* transactions, for *personal* heart converse with God. Many an individual has lost his Christian evidences, his spiritual joy, his assured hope, in the pious activities, the religious excitement, the mere outworkings and paraphernalia of Christianity.

But receive this truth in the love that offers it—Your soul cannot advance in the Divine life, you cannot be a lively, joyful, happy Christian, you cannot learn to look at death with calmness and at eternity with confidence, unless you cultivate those seasons which find you closeted with Christ. These seasons form the most powerful aids to religious progress. It is then we understand more of the mind and insinuate more deeply into the heart of our Lord.

We read that when Jesus took His disciples apart from all others into a desert place, He then explained to them the parables which, amid the din and excitement of the populace, they could but imperfectly understand. Ah, beloved, Christ our Teacher explains and expounds many an obscure saying in His Word, many an abstruse parable in His providence, and many a profound problem in our history, upon a couch of suffering, upon a sleepless pillow, in the house of adversity, in the season of bereavement, and even on a bed of death. The shadows reveal marvels and beauties of a landscape that the dazzling rays of the sun *darken* with their excessive brightness.

The sequestered walks of life, shaded and retired, impart an air of reality and solemnity to life, which the sunshine of prosperity, bathing the scene in bright effulgence, veils from view. Oh, what rapid scholars we become in the school of adversity! How we dive into the mind, and nestle in the heart of Jesus then! What a new revelation does the ancient Book of God become to us! How much of our own mysterious being is unveiled, and of our past inexplicable history is explained, when the heart, isolated from the world, withdrawn from the creature, at rest from itself, is in repose with God. And as we emerge from the sacred cloister that has been to us a Bethel and a Peniel, we exclaim, "Blessed is the man whom thou *chasteneth*, O Lord, and *teachest* him out of thy law. O Lord, by these things men live, and in all these things is the life of my spirit."

Be watchful, then, lest the attractions of the world, the anxieties of life, even the exacting and absorbing influence of religious external engagements invade the sanctity, and encroach upon the solitude of your hidden walk with God. Be jealous of every object and of every being that would give Christ one pulse less of your heart, one thought less of your mind, one moment less of your life. In all things give Him the pre-eminence. Bind the first and last sheaf of the harvest upon His altar—lay the first-fruits, and the gleanings of the vintage at His feet—give Him the earliest and the latest—and entwine Him with your first and last thoughts of love.

He who has declared, "I am the First and the Last," demands and deserves the first and the last of the life purchased by His blood: youth in its bloom, age in its golden fruit; yes, life in each stage of its onward and endless being.

> "My God, I would not coldly offer Thee
> The withered hue of feeling's flower,
> The fragment of a passing hour,—
> Gifts which have nothing cost to me.
> But, looking down into my heart,
> Whatever treasure it has hidden deep,
> Whatever talent it would strive to keep,
> With these, to You, O God, I part.
> I should not dare to bring affections blighted
> By the rude blasts of worldliness and pride,
> Nor lay a worn-out heart the earth had slighted
> Upon the altar of the Crucified.
> But in Life's dewy hours, when hope is on the wing,
> My love, myself, my all, to Thee I bring."

Joseph Making Himself Known to His Brethren as Their Brother, and Comforting Them

CHRIST OUR BROTHER

And Joseph said unto his brethren, I am Joseph; doth my father yet live? And his brethren could not answer him; for they were troubled at his presence. And Joseph said unto his brethren, Come near to me, I pray you. And they came near. And he said, I am Joseph your brother, whom ye sold into Egypt. Now therefore be not grieved, nor angry with yourselves, that ye sold me hither: for God did send me before you to preserve life. GENESIS 45:3-5

A MORE full and perfect discovery of Joseph yet awaited his brethren—a discovery of the *name* and *relation* that he bore to the men now awestruck and discomforted by his presence. It was not enough that he should reveal himself as no stranger. He would do more than this. He would give an emphasis to his name, and an unmistakable affirmation of his relation: "I am JOSEPH—your BROTHER." No announcement less distinct, emphatic, and thrilling than this would have disarmed their fears, inspired their confidence, and revived their love. In one moment they were placed in an attitude of the most perfect repose.

Beloved, partial views of Christ but partially meet the spiritual requirements of the believer. The moral feelings, as the spiritual necessities, of the soul are many, varied, and complicated. There is but one Being possessing the skill, the delicacy, the resources, or the power to meet them. The inventor of a curious and complicated mechanism alone can understand its working, feed and control its movements. No one knows, no one understands, and no one can keep in motion the wondrous mechanism of the believing soul but Him who created it. We must have then a full Christ, and must know Him fully—know Him in His Divinity and humanity—know Him in His atoning sacrifice—know Him in His finished work—know Him in the infinite sufficiency of His grace—and know Him in all the relations He sustains to us in the covenant of redemption, if would we stand in the Divine presence with the filial confidence, the perfect peace, the assured hope, inspired by a spiritual and experimental knowledge of God, and Jesus Christ whom He has sent.

The subject of the present chapter presents the Lord Jesus in two delightful aspects—the NAME He bears, and the RELATION He sustains to His people. These are suggested by the words—"I am JOSEPH, your BROTHER." The reader will observe that Joseph drops his Egyptian and assumes his Hebrew name. He does not say, "I am Zaphnath-paaneah," the name by which he was distinguished in Egypt; but, "I am *Joseph*," the name by which he was known in Canaan. Beloved, what is the name by which our spiritual Joseph the most delights to reveal Himself to, and to be recognized by, His brethren? Is it not JESUS? His birth and His mission were both announced by the celestial visitant in mysterious relation to this expressive and precious name, "Thou shalt call his name JESUS, for he shall save his people from their sins."

Here allow me to pause and remark that you will often obtain a clue to a more perfect understanding of the Scriptures of truth by studying the significance of the *proper names* of Scripture. The names conferred by Divine authority are always intended either to commemorate a historical event, to illustrate a Scripture fact, or to express a revealed truth. Two instances from the Old and the New Testaments are in point. The Angel of the Covenant, after the long night of wrestling and before the day began to dawn, thus spoke to the holy wrestler: "What is thy name? And he said, Jacob. And he said, Thy name shall be called no more Jacob, but Israel [that is, *A prince of God*]: for as a prince hast thou power with God and with men, and hast prevailed." How significant and sacred this new name of the patriarch!

Turning to the New Testament, we read that, after Peter had made his noble confession of the Godhead of Jesus, "Thou art the Christ, the Son of the living God. And Jesus answered and said unto him,…Thou art Peter, [*a stone*,] and upon this rock [His own Divine person] I will build my church." The significance of the apostle's name illustrated the nature of His confession, and the confession embodied the Foundation of Christ's Church. Now, if this be the case with regard to His disciples, how much more true and impressive as it regards the Lord himself! Thus, "Thou shalt call his name Jesus,"—the Hebrew signification of which is, THE SAVIOR, JESUS, and then it is added, as an explanation of the title, "for he shall save his people from their sins." It will at once appear that the *name* of JESUS was intended by the Holy Spirit to be profoundly and impressively significant. The whole of salvation, the entire gospel, is contained in this one Name.

An individual may know intellectually but little of the Bible—he may be unable to decipher its symbols, scarcely able to read its syllables. He may but imperfectly have studied systematic theology, or not have studied it at all; he may be unlearned in the geography, the chronology, the geology, the philosophy, and the poetry of the Bible, and yet, if the Holy Spirit has revealed to his soul the Name of Jesus, and he has been enabled to study the deep significance, to feel the marvelous power, and to taste the unutterable sweetness of that "Name which is above every name," he has penetrated into the essence of revealed truth, he has found the marrow of the gospel, he understands the way of salvation better, and knows more of God, and of Christ, and of the Bible, and of spiritual peace and Christian hope, than many a man who has studied the Bible intellectually, theoretically, and speculatively, but has never broken that box of precious ointment—the *name* of JESUS.

The Bible reader will recall to mind that notable instance in the conversion of Saul of Tarsus of our Lord's manifestation of His name: to the question of the amazed persecutor, "Who art thou, Lord?" the answer was—"I am Jesus." What must have been the electric power with which that word fell upon the ear of Saul! Dwell for a moment, my reader, upon the precious significance of this Name. What a body of divinity, what a mine of truth does it contain! It designates the office and work of Christ as the Savior of His brethren. Joseph was a temporal savior. He was the instrument, in the hands of God, of rescuing his father's house from the terrible calamity of death by starvation. The office of our spiritual Joseph, though in a higher sense, is the same. This is signified by His title: "He shall be called JESUS, *because he shall* SAVE *his people from their sins.*"

This is just the office and the mission that our condition demanded, and in the execution of which He becomes so endeared to those who are saved. We are lost, self-destroyed, destitute, originally and practically, of every particle of holiness and righteousness, without strength, utterly impotent to save ourselves. Under the sentence of eternal death, shut up to the condemnation of the law, the carnal mind at enmity, and the will armed in rebellion against God, the heart hating holiness and loving sin, inclined and powerful to all that is evil, disinclined and impotent to all that is good, with a hopeless deathbed, and an eternal hell confronting us, truly we needed a Savior!

And just such a Savior is Jesus. How precious, then, the declaration, "He shall SAVE his people from their sins!" This was the high mission on which He was sent from the court of heaven—a mission of benevolence worthy of Him who is essential and infinite Love. For this He made His advent to our world, lived a life of poverty and toil, and endured a death of humiliation and suffering, all to save us poor lost sinners. What wondrous words are these we have already quoted, and which are worthy of endless reiteration: "He shall save his people *from their sins*." This is just what we needed—to be saved from our sins, from their guilt, their power, their condemnation. This Jesus does.

It may be instructive to the mind and establishing to the faith of the reader to trace the mode by which Jesus accomplishes this marvelous and blessed work. The views of salvation, as held by many, are sadly crude and obscure, and in many cases scripturally and essentially wrong. Seeing it is a matter of vital and momentous interest, the most important and solemn study that can engage human thought, and that a fundamental error here is fatal to the eternal safety of the soul, let us approach its study with all seriousness of mind, and expound it with simplicity and godly sincerity.

How, then, does Jesus save us from our sins? He saves us, first, *meritoriously* by His obedience. The obedience of

Christ to the precepts of the law repaired, honored, and magnified it; and that sinless, perfect obedience to its every precept is, and becomes when *imputed* to those who believe, our righteousness or justification before God. And thus the glorious title well befits Him—"This is *the name* whereby he shall be called, THE LORD OUR RIGHTEOUSNESS." "As by one man's disobedience many were made sinners, so by the obedience of one shall many be made righteous." Thus Christ's merits become, by imputation, our merits. By a perfect obedience to the law, He merited our justification; and having no merits of our own, His merit is made over to us, and God justifies, or acquits, or counts us worthy in and through the infinite and imputed merits of Jesus. This, in a few words, explains the doctrine of our justification.

Hold fast, my reader, the doctrine of imputed righteousness received by faith. Truly the Church stands or falls, and the sinner is saved or lost by it. If saved, how truly blessed and secure is the state into which our justification places us! The believing soul is clothed with Christ's righteousness—yes, is made "the righteousness of God in him;" consequently, there rests not on the justified soul, as such, the shadow of condemnation, or spot or wrinkle of sin or unrighteousness. Believe this to be the state into which your justification by faith places you, and sweet will be the peace, deep the joy, and bright the hope you will experience. More than this: it will inspire and intensify your longings and endeavors *after holiness*. You will desire and aim after deeper sanctification, and your highest, noblest ambition will be to please God in all things, to walk worthy of your high calling, daily to wear Christ's yoke, to bear His burden, "having your fruit unto holiness, and the end everlasting life."

Jesus also saves us from our sins *virtually* by His atoning sacrifice and death. As the *obedience* of Christ honored the

Divine law, so equally did the *death* of Christ satisfy Divine justice. The one is our righteousness, the other is our pardon. The vicarious sacrifice of the Messiah was the full belief of the Old Testament saints; hence the Levitical sacrifices, all shadowing forth the Great Sacrifice to be offered by the "Seed of the woman who was to bruise the serpent's head." Hence, too, the concurrent prophetic testimony of Scripture. Isaiah prophesied of Jesus as "wounded for our transgressions, as bruised for our iniquities." Daniel foretold of Jesus as "cut off, but not for himself." And this agrees with the uniform testimony of apostles—"He was made sin for us, who knew no sin, that we might be made the righteousness of God in him;" "He was delivered for our offences, and was raised again for our justification." "Christ died for us."

What a broad foundation has Jesus thus laid for the salvation of sinners in His atonement! By it all the Divine attributes are harmonized, and the moral government of God is glorified, and thus it becomes Him who is infinitely righteous as He is essentially love, to people and adorn heaven with the vilest sinners, redeemed from earth. On this basis, the sacrifice of Jesus, God and the sinner stand side by side—God pardoning, the sinner pardoned; and this the divine act of His most free and sovereign grace.

And when we remember *from what* Jesus saves us, oh, how glorious and gracious does this salvation appear! It is from our sins—saved from which, we are saved from the parent, and the greatest, of all evil. By bearing sin—its load, its curse, its penalty, He saves from sin. His obedience saves us from the condemnation of sin, His blood saves us from the guilt of sin, His grace saves us from the power of sin, His intercession saves us from the temptations and assaults of sin. This is just the salvation we needed, and anything less than this would have left us still shut up to a just and endless condemnation.

We do not pray—it would neither be wise nor holy in us so to do—to be saved from discipline, from the hallowed results of sanctified trial, from the winnowing process of temptation, from the daily cross that, in pain and weariness, we bear after Jesus. But we do ask Jesus to save us from the dominion, the power, and the guilt of sin. Oh, when we ask this, we ask for that which is not only in accordance with His will to grant, but which was the great end of His death to accomplish, and of His intercession to secure.

And if the Lord seals this on your conscience by the application of the blood, you may calmly and safely leave all the rest in His hands. He will save you from as much adversity as will be for your good, and will not allow a stroke to settle upon you, or an element to mingle with life's cup of sweet, more bitter than is essential to your well-being. But from all your sins—sins past, present, and to come— His most precious blood will cleanse you, His finished salvation will save you.

Do not allow the fact of indwelling sin, or the conviction of its daily outbreak to veil this truth from your eye, or to rob you of its precious comfort. The full, free, and entire forgiveness of our sins does not insure the utter extermination of sin, although it does constrain us, by the most persuasive, holy, and powerful of all motives, to seek its mortification and death. Still, its existence and struggle will remain until the Christian warrior shall fight his last battle and achieve his last victory, and exchange his sword for a palm, and his cross for a crown.

Jesus also saves us from our sins *vitally* by His Spirit. The office of the Spirit, as a Quickener of spiritual life, is an essential and precious provision in the economy of redemption. Apart from an arrangement that should secure the spiritual renewal and renovation of the soul, and give a vital and virtual application of the work of Christ to the heart, we do not hesitate to say that the Atonement of Calvary, with all its costliness and glory, would have availed us nothing! Added to our guilt, which needed pardon, and to our condemnation, which demanded justification, both of which the blood and righteousness of Christ supply, we possess a soul so entirely inoperative and dead to all spiritual life and holiness, so insensible to all that is heavenly, so impotent to all that is good, so totally "dead in trespasses and sins," as to demand a Divine power to renew its nature, regenerate its faculties, and quicken it with a new and spiritual life.

Oh, how utterly fallen, low totally depraved, how entirely void of spiritual holiness, strength, and love are we! Talk of our nature being in a *salvable* state—preposterous idea! "When we were without strength, in due time Christ died for the ungodly." "There dwelleth in our flesh no good thing." "There is none righteous, no, not one." If there is any, the least, moral power, or inclination, or light innate in the soul, by which we can assist the work of our recovery, then Christ becomes a *Helper* only, and not a *Savior*, and the Holy Spirit is simply a secondary and subordinate Agent, aiding a mind already spiritually enlightened, a will already rightly disposed, a heart already pulsating with love, and yearning with desire toward God! See to what a 'reduction to absurdity' the theory of innate moral ability in the natural and unrenewed man conducts the reasoner.

But the case is fully met by the office and work of the Holy Spirit. Oh, it is a wonderful and glorious provision this of our salvation! "It is the SPIRIT that quickeneth; the flesh profiteth nothing." It is the Spirit who enlightens: "The things of God knoweth no man, but the Spirit of God." It is the Spirit who convinces of sin, "He shall convince the world of sin." It is the Spirit who reveals Jesus: "He [the Spirit of truth] shall glorify me: for he shall receive of mine, and shall shew it unto you." It is the Spirit who sanctifies: "Being sanctified by the Holy Ghost." It is the Spirit who authenticates our new nature, and witnesses our adoption: "The Spirit itself beareth witness with our spirit, that we are the children of God." It is the Spirit who comforts us: "I will pray the Father, and he shall give you another Comforter, that he may abide with you for ever; even the Spirit of truth." Thus might we traverse the entire circle of the Holy Spirit's operations, describing an indispensable part of our salvation, and exhibiting the divinity and personality, the love and power of the Holy Spirit in our recovery equally with the Father and the Son.

Jesus saves us from our sins *fully* by His power. Never was *power* exerted in a way so glorious as this—power to *save*. God has power to destroy, and will fearfully exhibit that power in the great day of His wrath, in the everlasting punishment of the ungodly. But Christ came into the world, not to destroy men's lives, but to save them. His power, the power of Deity, is exerted in salvation. No power short of this could possibly save us from our sins. The power of sin over the soul could only be met and vanquished by the superior power of Christ over sin. He alone had strength to bear sin by imputation, to efface sin by His blood, to pardon sin by His grace, and to convince of sin by His Spirit. "Wherefore he is *able* to save them to the uttermost that come unto God by him."

What a warrant and encouragement is this for you to come penitentially to Christ with all your sins—the greatest, most aggravated, and innumerable—sins original, sins actual—sins against light, knowledge, and conviction—sins willful, sins ignorant—sins before, and sins after conversion. Jesus is able to save you from them all! "Yes," you reply, "I doubt not His *ability*, seeing He who created all things must be divine and illimitable in power. But is He as *willing* to save me as He is able?" Question it not! Listen to the confirmation of this precious fact: "Lord, if thou wilt, thou canst make me clean. Jesus saith unto him, I WILL, be thou clean." Here is a proof that Christ's *willingness* to save is as equal and as prompt as His *power* to save. Yes! His will is in harmony with His power, and goes every step with it in the salvation of a poor sinner from his sins.

"He is *willing*, He is *able!*
Doubt no more."

Jesus saves us from our sins *freely by His grace*. Were this not so, were our salvation uttered with conditions and contingencies, were the efficient cause our willingness, or our faith, or our worthiness—were there anything in us required to supply the turning-point, then salvation would never be given, and heaven would never be our home. But, bankrupt of all worthiness, having nothing to pay, cast wholly upon the mercy of God in Christ, to save or to condemn us as He willed, lo! Jesus undertakes to save us from our sins by an act of His most free grace, cancels our great debt, supplying our merit, imparting His worthiness, and, without money or price, fee or reward, receiving, and accepting, and saving us just as we are. "Being justified *freely by his grace*, through the redemption that is in Christ Jesus." "And when they had *nothing to pay*, he frankly forgave them both."

Hesitate not, then, to approach the Savior. What though you are bankrupt and beggared of all goodness, what though you have not a holy thought, or a spiritual impulse, or a gracious desire, or a solitary good action with which to conciliate Divine justice, or claim Divine mercy. Yet, seeing God asks no merit, requires no worthiness other than what

Jesus supplies, seeing that He is well-pleased in Him, and is prepared to pardon, and justify, and adopt, and accept you in and through Christ, demur not to believe, hesitate not to come, and be fully and freely saved from all your sins. "By grace are ye saved."

Beloved, His name is JESUS; and this blessed name is the pledge that He will save you. Are you burdened, crushed beneath the weight of your transgressions? Are you debating, questioning, doubting, whether Jesus will save such a sinner as you? Oh, take hold of *His name* in simple faith, and you shall be saved! He saves meritoriously, He saves vitally, He saves powerfully, He saves willingly, He saves gratuitously, He saves to the uttermost, and will reject none that come to Him. His arm is as strong as His heart is loving. And if you will approach Him as a poor, burdened, worthless sinner, and cast yourself at His feet; oh, not so brightly beamed the eye of Joseph upon his brethren whom he was about to redeem from famine, not so tenderly did his affections yearn over them as, trembling and astonished, they stood in his presence, than will the Lord Jesus delight in and rejoice over you while He reveals to your soul His precious name—"I am JESUS, your Savior, your Redeemer, your Lord."

"Precious Jesus! Your name is to my soul as ointment poured forth; therefore do I love You. In adversity, it is my sheltering tower of strength into which I run, and am safe. In moments of conscious guilt, I fly to it, and it removes my fears, and gives me peace. In the hour of temptation, I breathe it, and the foe retires, and I leave the fight victorious. I breathe it in prayer, and my petition prevails. In sorrow, when my heart is overwhelmed within me, it distills inexpressible soothing, and I am comforted. The power of Your name is mighty. It illumines my darkest, and cheers my loneliest hours. It subdues my rebellious will, silences my murmuring heart, and wins all my soul to love. It strengthens me in service, animates me in duty, stimulates me to obedience, and raises my affections to God and to heaven. In life, in death, in eternity, I will wear Your name on my heart, chant it in my song, and prolong its endless praise!"

The deathless, magic power of Jesus' name, when all other names on earth have lost their charm, or have faded from memory, has often been illustrated. The touching instance of the pious Bishop Berridge may be familiar to the reader. When on his deathbed, he did not know any of his friends or relatives. A minister, with whom he had been well acquainted, visited him, and when conducted into his room, he said, "Bishop Berridge, do you know me?" "Who are you," said the Bishop. Being told who the minister was, he said that he did not know him. Another friend came, who had been equally well known, and questioned him in a similar manner—"Do you know me, Bishop Berridge?" "Who are you?" said he. Being told it was one of his intimate friends, he said he did not know him. His wife then came to his bedside, and asked him if he knew her. "Who are you?" said he. Being told she was his wife, he said he did not know her. "Well," said one of them, "Bishop Berridge, do you know the Lord Jesus Christ?" "Jesus Christ!" said he, reviving as if the name had produced on him the influence of a charm; "oh yes! I have known Him these forty years. Precious Savior, he is my only hope!"

> "There is a name I love to hear,
>   I love to speak its worth;
>   It sounds like music in my ear,
>   The sweetest name on earth.

> "It tells me of a Savior's love,
>   Who died to set me free;

It tells me of His precious blood,
    The sinner's perfect plea.

"It tells me of a Father's smile
    Beaming upon His child;
It cheers me through this 'little while,'
    Through desert, waste, and wild.

"It tells of One whose loving heart
    Can feel my deepest woe;
Who in my sorrow bears a part
    That none can bear below.

"It bids my trembling soul rejoice;
    It dries each rising tear;
It tells me, in a still small voice,
    To trust and never fear.

"Jesus! the name I love so well,
    The name I love to hear!
No saint on earth its worth can tell,
    No heart conceive how dear!

"This name shall shed its fragrance still
    Along this thorny road,
Shall sweetly smooth the rugged hill
    That leads me up to God.

"And there, with all the blood-bought throng,
    From sin and sorrow free,
I'll sing the new eternal song;
    Of Jesus' love to me."

From the name of Jesus, let us pass to consider the *relation* that He sustains to us as our BROTHER. "I am Joseph your brother." With what astounding, yet subduing power must this announcement have fallen upon their ears! "What! is this great man, this mighty man, *Joseph?* Is this governor of all Egypt our *brother? Can* it be?" Incredulity must have been the first feeling of their mind, this ripening into confidence, and confidence deepening into love.

Beloved reader, not less surprising nor less true and touching is the announcement of the gospel, that the Son of God, the Lord of heaven and earth, sustains to His Church the close and tender relation of a BROTHER. In His address to His disciples when on earth, He recognized this fraternal bond—"Go, tell *my brethren;*" "Behold *my brethren!*" "*My brethren* are these which hear the word of God and do it." "Inasmuch as ye have done it to the least of these *my brethren.*" Such is the relation Jesus would have us recognize. It is a more close, sympathizing, and holy relation than earth's dearest and tenderest. Look at His dignity as such.

He is the Elder Brother of His Church, "The *first-born* among many brethren." The law of primogeniture (birthright) was especially instituted by God in the time of the Jewish Church, and its wisdom and equity in all future ages has ever been acknowledged. Modern jurisprudence has never been able to improve upon it; and our own English law has, with certain modifications adapted to the age of the world and the changed face of society, engrafted it upon its code as one of the profoundest and healthiest enactments. Not only did this law of primogeniture entitle the elder brother to a double portion of the paternal estate and a large degree of power, it also invested him with the office of domestic priest of the family.

It was, doubtless, the remembrance of all this that added such keenness to the remorse, and such pungency to the sorrow of Esau, when he awoke to a conviction of his sin, infatuation, and loss, in bartering on terms so easy, and for a motive so frivolous, the sacred and precious inheritance of the birthright. "Afterward, when he would have inherited the blessing, he was rejected: for he found no place of repentance, though he sought it carefully with tears." As our Elder Brother, Jesus possesses, in a higher, holier sense, all the privileges and power of the "*first-born* among many brethren." The paternal inheritance is His—illimitable power is His—the priestly office is His—the Divine and heavenly birthright is His, in all its fullness of grace, and in all its perfection of glory—and in this His brethren share. He retains all the privileges and power of the heavenly birthright, that He may lavish its blessings upon them.

Still closer has He brought Himself to us as our Brother by the assumption of our veritable nature. We could not claim as our brother an angel, or the inhabitant of any other world, if such there be. He who asks our relationship, bespeaks our confidence, and inspires our love, must be linked with our humanity, must wear our nature, must be bone of our bone, and flesh of our flesh. Such was Jesus. It was this fact which flashed upon the minds of the brethren of Joseph with such bewildering power: they were conscious they were in the presence of a brother who felt as they felt, wept as they wept, loved as they loved, and the first touch of nature made them feel they were kin. "Forasmuch as the children are partakers of flesh and blood, he also himself likewise took part of the same; wherefore in all things it behoved him *to be made like unto his brethren.*"

How near to us does this cardinal truth of our holy religion bring the Son of God! How human is His love, His compassion, and sympathy! Is there a brother on earth to whom we can repair with the same assurance of a quick and a full response to the appeal of humanity, as to Jesus? That brother has infirmities and burdens, sorrows, anxieties, and needs of his own, so weighty, keen, and absorbing, that though there throbs within his bosom a brother's kindly heart, it is too much to ask him to make our necessities and our griefs all his own. But not so Jesus! We resort to Him in difficulty, we fly to Him in temptation, we repair to Him in sorrow, we betake ourselves to Him in need, and, lo! we find Him as accessible, as prompt, and as interested in our personal case, as though there poured into His ear no other appeal, or were laid on His heart no other grief, and upon His shoulder no other burden than our own!

"MY BROTHER!"—how sweet the relation! how thrilling the recognition! The moment faith realizes it, the heart, stunned with surprise, or wild with grief, or sorrowing with despair, is in perfect repose. Beloved, think that all the dignity, the power, the honor, the wealth of the Elder Brother of the Father's one family is centered in JESUS; and that the influence of this extends, in all its enriching, ennobling, soothing power, to the youngest, the lowliest, the least of the Father's house—perchance to *you!*

The dignity conferred upon us by this fraternal relation of Jesus, and the nearness into which it brings our nature, laden and shaded with need and sadness, to God, is a marvelous and tender illustration of its preciousness. Is Jesus our Brother? Then God is our Father; for He is the Son of the Father, eternally and well-beloved. No angel in heaven is clad with such dignity, is invested with such glory, moves in an orbit so near the center as Christ's brethren now glorified, and as will be our privilege when our true Joseph sends for us to be with Him.

Amid the world's ignorance and unkindness, the scorn with which it derides our saintship, the malignity with which it plots our downfall, the fetters with which it would enslave, the dungeons in which it would immure, or the fires with which it would consume us, let this truth sustain and cheer us: the most glorious, and powerful, and loving Being in the universe stands to us in the relation of our—BROTHER! What have we, then, to fear?

"Jesus, who passed the angels by,
Assumed our flesh to bleed and die;
And still He makes it His abode,—
As man, He fills the throne of God.

"Our nearest Friend and BROTHER now
Is He to whom the angels bow;
They join with us to praise His name,
But we the nearest interest claim.

"Though now ascended up on high,
He bends on earth a BROTHER'S eye;
Partaker of the human name,
He knows the frailty of our frame."

A striking and touching feature in this stage of the narrative arrests our attention, which will be found to illustrate a precious part of the believer's experience. Awed by the presence of Joseph, their minds oppressed with doubt and trembling, his brethren stood *at a distance* from his person. Their position betrayed fear and distrust, "for they were troubled [marg., *terrified*] at his presence." Joseph, perceiving their position and their feelings, instantly and tenderly spoke to them in language winning and assuring: "And Joseph said unto his brethren, *Come near to me*, I pray you. And they came near."

Beloved, it is the will of Jesus that His brethren, His saints, His beloved people, disarmed of all legal bondage and servile fear, should be very close to Him, sitting at His feet, sheltered at His side, leaning on His bosom. He will allow no distance of place, no circumstance of trial, or of temptation, or of backsliding, to separate between Him and the brethren. The relationship is too close, the redemption is too great, the salvation is too precious to allow any degree of distrust, servility, or congealed affection on their part towards Him.

"We who were sometime afar off, are *brought nigh* by the blood of Christ." United to Him by the Spirit, engrafted upon Him by a reciprocated nature—on His part by the assumption of the human, on ours by the impartation of the Divine—what opposites could be more closely united, what extremes could more perfectly meet, what being could be more closely and indissolubly one than Christ and His brethren? Imagine, then, how keenly sensitive must He be to any show of distrust, shyness, or distance on the part of His brethren towards Him! He is jealous of our love, our confidence, and our companionship. And seeing that at an expenditure so costly, by a sacrifice so great, and by love so transcendent, He has bridged the gulf, annihilated the distance, and broken down every barrier between Himself and His Church, He would work in them that faith, and enkindle in them that affection, that which shall draw them into the greatest nearness to Himself.

The language of Jesus to you is, "Come near to me, my disciple. Why this distance, these fears? Come near to me, shelter beneath my side, nestle in my heart, take hold of my strength, commune with me. I am Jesus your Brother." Oh, let *nearness to Jesus* be the distinctive feature of your religion! He is always near to you—invisible, indeed, His person, and noiseless His tread—yet still, oh how near! "Thou art *near*, O Lord." And He would have you perfected in that love which reassures the timid mind, composes to rest the fluttering heart, disenthralls the bondage spirit, and establishes the soul in the firm, unwavering conviction that the interests of His brethren are identical with His own— that the ephod is still upon His shoulder, and the breastplate is still upon his heart, the symbol and the pledge that His *strength* and *sympathy* are ours.

Seeing, then, that His blood is your plea, His invitation your warrant, and His love your attraction, *draw near* to

Him by prayer in perplexity, and He will guide you; in assault, and He will shield you; in adversity, and He will shelter you; in necessity, and he will supply you; in conscious departure, and He will heal your backslidings, and restore to you the joy of His salvation. Oh, nothing dishonors Jesus more than our distrust of faith! Nothing wounds Him more than our fickleness of love. He cannot, He will not, allow distance to interpose between Him and His brethren—wronged Him though they may have done to the utmost. They are too precious to Him to allow the slightest degree of confidence and love to be lost between them. He will not only—as we shall see in the process of this work—have them near to Him in heaven, but they shall cultivate the most loving intimacy, the most perfect confidence, the closest fellowship with Him on earth.

And, if need be—if His beauty will not attract them, if His glory will not charm them, if His love will not win them, if the prospect of being with Him forever will not allure them, He commissions the loving correction, the gentle chastisement, to effect what milder and more persuasive means failed to accomplish—their greater *nearness* to Himself. Be jealous, watchful, and prayerful, then, lest the world in its fascination, the creature in its fondness, life's battle in its fierceness, means of grace neglected, affection allowed to congeal; should, separately or combined, create a distance between Christ and your soul.

Let every incident and circumstance in the daily walk of your life—be it exalting or depressing, a test of principle, a trial of faith, an appeal of love—but bring you nearer to the Lord; that, less like Peter, who "followed Jesus *afar off,*" and more like Caleb, who "followed the Lord *fully,*" you may tread the dusty, lonely paths of your earthly pilgrimage:

your heart sequestered from earth, your spirit in close converse with Jesus in heaven.

But there was deep emotion on this occasion of Joseph's revelation of himself to his brethren, which he skillfully and tenderly met. They were evidently troubled and discomforted in their minds by the sad memories that the presence of Joseph awoke. Joseph's quick eye saw their mental conflict; he seemed to read every thought of their mind, and to touch every pulse of their heart. He threw himself, as it were, within their very bosoms. And if ever there were an illustration of the truth that "a brother is born for adversity," it was this. Mark how he sought to comfort them: "I am Joseph your brother, whom ye sold into Egypt. Now therefore *be not grieved*, nor angry with yourselves, that ye sold me hither: for God did send me before you to preserve life. For these two years hath the famine been in the land: and yet there are five years, in the which there shall neither be earing nor harvest. And God sent me before you to preserve you a posterity in the earth, and to save your lives by a great deliverance."

How delicately, tenderly, and effectually did Joseph now comfort his brethren! He sought first to disarm them of the weapons of self-accusation with which their hearts were so deeply wounded. "Be not grieved, nor angry with yourselves." Our blessed Lord alone can disarm us of our self-accusations. But for the words of comfort that He speaks, the faith that enables us to look from within ourselves and from all our willful acts of sin, and the evils which our own doings have brought upon us, we should not only be grieved, and angry with ourselves, but, overwhelmed with self-abhorrence and abasement in the remembrance of our vileness, we should never more lift up our head.

Oh, there is no reproach so bitter, no accusation so
keen, as that which our own conscience and heart inflict—
none so true, or that lays us more deeply in the dust before
God! Remorse for his sin, and despair of its forgiveness,
would have led the Philippian jailor to self-destruction but
for the words of Paul. Are you filled with remorse, self-
reproach, and anger, at the remembrance of all the sin and
neglect, rebellion and wrong Jesus has received at your
hands? Hear Him say to you—"Be not grieved, nor angry
with yourself; I can forgive all, cancel all, forget all. I do
not condemn you; go, and sin no more."

Blessed are those who, in the spirit of self-abasement,
abhor and condemn themselves; they shall never be
abhorred and condemned by God. Christ will not trample
upon a poor sinner who tramples upon himself, and will
never accuse one who at His feet is filled with self-accusation.
The Lord will never take part with His people against
themselves. Oppressed with self-reproach, abhorring
themselves in dust and in ashes, He will draw near to them
with words of kindness, soothing, and love: "Be not grieved,
nor angry with yourself; I have pardoned all, and will no
more remember your sins." Oh, it is utterly impossible for
Christ to speak harshly, unsympathizingly, or condemnatory
to a humble, penitent, contrite soul, standing in His
presence filled with trembling and self-condemnation.

But what is the great panacea of a wounded conscience,
terrible and true in its self-impeachment, keen and galling
in its self-reproach? The BLOOD of Jesus! Nothing short of
the blood of sprinkling can reach the *conscience*. This alone
cleanses, heals, comforts, pacifies. The sin-distressed, sin-
accusing conscience, brought into *believing* contact with
atoning blood, is in one moment at rest from sin, at rest
from itself, at rest in Christ. The apostle's argument is, "How
much more shall the BLOOD of Christ, who, through the

Eternal Spirit, offered himself without spot unto God, purge your CONSCIENCE."

And then, based upon this truth, he thus exhorts, "Let us draw near with a true heart in full assurance of faith, having our hearts SPRINKLED from an evil CONSCIENCE." Oh, we cannot press this truth—the blood of Jesus and the sinner's conscience—too earnestly! What thousands are wandering, Cain-like, over the earth, bemoaning their transgressions, burdened with a sin-distressed, sin-accusing conscience, filled with self-reproach and horror of the coming judgment, who see not that the only remedy is, *the atoning blood of Jesus,* one drop of which—so divine and sovereign is its efficacy—will allay the storm, remove the guilt, and diffuse over it a heavenly serenity and a divine sunshine!

And notice how gracefully and skillfully Joseph leads them away from all *second causes* to the purpose and end of God in the marvelous events of his personal history—events in which they had acted so sad and signal a part. "GOD sent me before you to preserve life, to preserve you a posterity in the earth, and to save your lives by a great deliverance. So now it was not *you* that sent me hither, but GOD." Such is the light in which we must study our redemption by Christ. Looking beyond the disciple who betrayed Him, the judge who convicted Him, the Jews who slew Him, we must trace up all to the eternal purpose and sovereign will of Jehovah.

Thus Peter reasoned, while charging home upon the murderers the crime of His death: "Him, being delivered by the determinate counsel and foreknowledge of God, ye have taken, and by wicked hands have crucified and slain." Thus, too, must we, in all the afflictive, trying, and mysterious events of life, rise above immediate and second causes, and trace them up to Him who "worketh all things after the counsel of his own will." There is no anchorage for the tempest-tossed soul but here. The anchor must be cast within the veil. Combating with second causes, looking only at the natural antecedents of an event, calamitous and overwhelming, striving to understand its *rationale* by a scrutiny of human and proximate reasons, we shall but render more dark the event we seek to elucidate, and more entangled and perplexed the mystery we endeavor to unravel.

Beloved and afflicted child of God, cease from reflecting upon yourself for a calamity you could not prevent, from indulging in vain regrets at an event you could not control. It was not *you* who commanded, nor *you* who could have prevented it; it was GOD. Be still, and know that He is God. Oh, the moment that your faith can rest in Him, referring the event enshrouded in such gloom, and entailing such anguish to His eternal decree and good pleasure, and His righteous and wise government, you cease from a battle in which no victory is won, no laurels gained, and your heart is at rest in God! "God himself hath done it;" and, "shall not the Judge of all the earth do right?"

It is thus Jesus would comfort His brethren in all their self-reproaches, in the multitude of their thoughts within them, in the tremblings and forebodings which conscious sin produces. Truly is He the "Brother born for adversity"—His brethren's adversities, the sad, conflicting thoughts of whose mind He alone can read, the deeply-seated sorrow of whose heart He alone can reach. If such the skill and tenderness of Joseph to his brethren, oh, what must Christ's be to His brethren?

How spiritually instructive, too, the fact that Joseph was raised up by God for the special salvation of his family. How clearly he states this—"God sent me before you to preserve your posterity in the earth, and to save your lives by a great deliverance." What were all the families of Egypt compared with this one? For them Joseph was preserved alive—for them he was exalted in the land—for them all the corn in Egypt was placed in his hands—and for their sakes, indirectly, all the families of Egypt were blest.

The first truth illustrated is, that Christ was raised up by God for the special salvation of His Church, to save it by a great deliverance. That the Atonement of the Son of God is an *indirect* blessing to the world admits not of a doubt. In this view its benevolent and beneficial influence is universal; for, but for the death and sacrifice of the Son of God, the world would not stand, nor human society exist as it does for a moment. In this sense we are to interpret the words of the apostle, "Who is the Saviour *of all men*, SPECIALLY of those that believe."

But, for the Church of God alone, the chosen of God, the gift to Christ of the Father, His special treasure, everlastingly loved and eternally elected, did the Son of God die upon the cross. On their behalf obedience was given to the law, satisfaction was offered to justice, the righteousness of God's government was upheld—its honor and dignity vindicated and maintained—"the Church of God which he hath purchased with his own blood." Is God unrighteous in this? Who are you who replies against Him?—a worm— a moth—a vapor—sinful dust and ashes daring to impugn the holiness, the equity, the wisdom, the goodness of Jehovah! Believer in Christ! for you our true Joseph was raised up—for you the food in Egypt was provided to keep your soul alive in famine, and to save it everlastingly—by a great and glorious deliverance.

Make your *calling* sure, and you can safely leave your *election* in His hands to whom alone secret things belong. Election is not the truth that you are either to settle or to sound. Jehovah has already settled it, and there are depths in it you cannot fathom. But you can and may understand what it is to be *called* by grace, to feel yourself a poor, lost sinner, to trample your own righteousness beneath your feet, and to come believingly to the blood and righteousness of Jesus, and accept it as all your desire, all your salvation, and all your hope. Taking hold of this the lowest link in the chain of God's salvation—your *calling* by grace—you will by and by rise to the highest—your election of God; and when your faith grasps this—your *election* of God—your soul will be filled with adoration, wonder, love, and praise.

Let us close with the glorious declaration, "Ho, everyone that thirsteth, come ye to the waters, and he that hath no money; come ye, buy, and eat; yea, come, buy wine and milk without money and without price." Come to Jesus and He will not cast you out. Come just as you are—come without demur—come today—come *now*—

> "With all your sins against your God,
>   All your sins against His laws,
>   All your sins against His blood,
>   All your sins against His cause—
>   Sins as boundless as the sea!—
>   And hide them in Gethsemane!"

"ALL THAT THE FATHER GIVETH ME SHALL COME TO ME, AND HIM THAT COMETH TO ME I WILL IN NO WISE CAST OUT."

Joseph's Exaltation in Egypt

THE GLORY OF CHRIST IN HEAVEN

Haste ye, and go up to my father, and say unto him, Thus saith
thy son Joseph, God hath made me lord of all Egypt: come
down unto me, tarry not: and thou shalt dwell in the land of
Goshen, and thou shalt be near unto me, thou, and thy children, and thy children's children, and thy flocks, and thy herds,
and all that thou hast....And ye shall tell my father of all my
glory in Egypt, and of all that ye have seen. GENESIS 45:9-13

THE reflective reader of this narrative will not fail to have
remarked the sagacious wisdom and true delicacy of Joseph,
in adopting a gradual rather than a premature development
of his entrancing story. Nothing could have been more
consummate in skill, exquisite in taste, or perfect in
execution. It was not by a sudden and immediate revelation
that all the links in the chain of events tracing his marvelous
history were uplifted from the sea of mystery that submerged
them, and made to pass before his brethren. A disclosure
so unpremeditated and abrupt would have failed in awaking
those reflections, producing those impressions, and securing
that moral discipline in his brethren which he, once their
victim, now their deliverer and teacher, sought to
accomplish. Their minds stunned by surprise, and their
feelings petrified with fear—the incidents of the past
crowding upon their memory with startling vividness, and

135

the just consequences of their conduct in ghastly horror
flitting before their eye—the details, too, of the history so
astounding and touching, would have conspired to disarm
them of all mental power of examining and weighing the
facts and evidences of the case, and thus they would have
been incapable of recognizing his person, and of accepting
his statement. They might have ignored the story as a myth,
and have denounced the man as an impostor.

The Christian student of his Bible will trace a striking
analogy in this to a peculiarity in the mode of our Lord's
instruction of His disciples. His revelations were then, as
His teaching is, for the most part, now, gradual and
progressive. In His personal instructions He seldom declared
His Messiahship, or revealed His truth instantaneously. A
few select instances alone occurred, as rare as they were
striking, when, to illustrate the greatness and condescension
of His grace, He, as in a moment, uplifted the veil, and
declared His Messiahship, and, by a sudden flash of light,
filled the mind with truth, and the heart with love.

How much of Christ, of His glory and kingdom, did
the penitent malefactor learn in that hour of lingering agony
on the cross! Ah! no marvel! he was *so near* the Divine Sun
of Truth and Righteousness and Love, as to bathe his soul
in the full beams of its setting glory! But our Lord's
instruction of His disciples, generally, was elementary and
gradual. In the words of the evangelist, "He spake the word
unto them, *as they were able to hear it.*" He saw that their
minds were not prepared to receive instantaneously, and in
its perfect revelation, all that He had to teach them;
therefore, by a process which graduated the new and
marvelous truths He inculcated to their opening
understanding, and by which one doctrine of the gospel
evolved another, He gently instructed them in the fact of

His Messiahship, in the nature of His kingdom, and in the truths, principles, and precepts of His religion.

Such is still the mode of our Lord's teaching. The seal of divine truth gradually is broken, and its light, like the day-dawn, deepening in effulgence to its meridian glory, slowly, yet steadily advances, until, from the babe in knowledge, we reach the stature of the fullness of Christ. Pause, admire and adore the wisdom, gentleness, and skill of Jesus here. He remembers how unlike all other truth is Divine revelation; that, while there is much that transcends the loftiest grasp of the human understanding to comprehend, it yet demands the fullest belief of the heart.

Remembering, then, the infinite vastness of truth, and the dwarfed faculties of the human mind, the dullness of the understanding to perceive, and the slowness of the heart to believe the great things of His Word, He teaches with a skill, a patience, and a gentleness that has no parallel, and which renders His truth so glorious, His discipline so welcome, Himself so precious to those who become His humble and willing disciples. "Lord, in Your school let me be taught—at Your feet would I sit—the lessons of Your love and the truths of Your word let me humbly, believingly, and fully receive, for who teaches like You?"

We reach another stage in Joseph's history, and glorious is its shadow of Christ and His Church—the EXALTATION and GLORY to which he was advanced in Egypt: "Haste ye, and go up to my father, and say unto him, Thus saith thy son Joseph, God hath made me lord of all Egypt...And ye shall tell my father of all *my glory* in Egypt." This was no vain boast, no exaggerated description of Joseph's condition; it was an accomplished fact that Joseph was all that he now portrayed himself to be, and the announcement of his exaltation and glory was to calm their minds and command their confidence, confirm their faith and inspire their hopes.

We see a marvelous display of tact, wisdom, and goodness, in placing the fact of his exaltation, dignity, and power in the very foreground of his story. But for this, how could he have reassured their timid minds, have quelled their rising fears, and have established them in the truth which it was his great object to impress? Had he simply told them the story of his abasement, describing his poverty, delineating the perils, temptations, and sorrows through which he had passed, he would not have quelled a single fear, or have inspired one ray of hope. But when he laid before them his personal dignity, his unmistakable glory and power, the fact became palpable, inspiriting, and confirming to their minds that he was in very deed Joseph, their brother.

But, beloved, a greater than Joseph is here. To Him let me now direct your believing eyes. It is our dear Lord's purpose that His Church should have scriptural, spiritual, and enlarged views of what He is, what His possessions are, and what is the extent of His power. And I do not hesitate to say that scriptural, stable views of the dignity of Christ's person, of the glory of our Emmanuel, of what His wealth is, of what His power is, form the very foundation of our faith in Him. I receive the salvation of Christ, I rest in the atonement of Christ, I accept the promises of Christ, I believe in the coming of Christ, just in proportion as my faith believes that He is actually all that His revealed word describes Him to be.

If my views of the glory of Christ are defective, if my faith in the measureless power of Christ is contracted, there will be a consequent and corresponding feebleness in the realization I have of Christ. But let my faith firmly grasp the truth that He is what He declares Himself to be—that all this honor, all this glory, all this dignity, all this power belong to Him—then, without hesitation and doubt, I can draw from His fullness, receive His assurances, and look forward with confidence to the blessed day when Christ who is my life shall appear, and I shall appear also with Him in glory.

Let us, then, for a moment, turn our attention to two views of Christ illustrated by this part of Joseph's history. And, first, how did Joseph reach this elevation, the announcement of which he now makes to his brethren, and through them to his father? He reached that glory, dignity, and power along the gloomy, rugged path of the deepest abasement and sorrow. Look at the abasement of Christ, the humiliation through which He passed to His present glory. The mediatorial exaltation and glory to which our Lord has arrived in heaven, was reached only by a pathway never before trodden by human feet—the profoundest abasement, humiliation, and grief. I truly believe that the saints of God meditate too little on the *humiliation* of Christ. The humiliation of Christ involved all that would have involved us but for His voluntary suretyship.

The bearing of sin, the exhausting of the curse, the endurance of every form of indignity, the wrath of Jehovah, the sorrow of His soul, the agonies of the cross, the assaults of hell, the conquest of death—all met in the humiliation and abasement of Jesus. But it is necessary for our high appreciation of what Christ has done for us, and of the glory to which He himself has arrived, that we linger much in the valley of His humiliation. Our views of His glory, our conception of His exaltation, our faith in His love, will be graduated by the spiritual, deep, vivid conceptions we have of what He passed through to save us. Oh, then, I do beseech you, beloved, do not slightly scan, superficially study the path of gloom and sorrow, abasement and temptation, your Lord and Savior trod, to deliver you therefrom.

Remember, our dear Lord Jesus was a bondservant; think what that means. He was tempted, oh, how fearfully, by the Evil One of this ungodly world. He was betrayed, belied, slandered, and imprisoned. But what picture of humiliation can your imagination paint, or tongue describe, that the Lord Jesus did not pass through to bring us to glory? Link with this view of Christ's abasement the disciplinary process through which every follower of Christ must, in some degree, pass to reach the glory that awaits him. There must be the emptying, the humbling, the abasing of our natural pride, the subjection of our rebellious will, the prostration of all our fond conceit of personal goodness and righteousness before we know what the true glory is.

Have you trod this valley of abasement? Has the pride of your heart been humbled? the rebellion of your will subdued? the opposition of your nature to God and His holy law vanquished and overcome? Oh, has the Spirit of God emptied you, taught you your sinfulness, nothingness, and led you to God's pardoning mercy, and Christ's justifying righteousness, through the deep, dark valley of soul humiliation and abasement? No man can spring to the apex of God's glory but from the base of his own natural vileness, emptiness, and poverty; and when God brings him low, lays him in the dust, empties him from vessel to vessel, oh, it is the sure and certain prelude to an uplifting, an exalting, and glory infinitely beyond all conception!

Job strikingly says, "When men are *cast down*, then thou shalt say, There is *lifting up*." Observe that in your personal history. When the Lord by some overwhelming providence, some humiliating and trying circumstance in your history, casts you down, infer not that all these things are against you; it is the very process God is taking to lift you up; and as the darkest period of the night ushers in the dawn of day, so the gloomiest stage of the believer's life is often that which precedes the bursting upon him of the sun of God's goodness, mercy, and love, in all its effulgence. It was through this process of humiliation that Jesus passed to the glories of which I will now speak. What expressive words are these, "Ye shall tell my father of *all my glory* in Egypt!" But a greater glory than Joseph's is here—the glory, the eternal glory, of our blessed Jesus; of which glory, if you have a vital union with Christ, you are now, and shall be more completely hereafter, the sharer.

Beloved, for a moment, let us dwell on this glory of our Jesus. He has now forever passed the valley of humiliation. For Him there is no more soul-sorrow, or mental gloom, no more sighing or tears, no more human insult or Satanic assault; He has passed beyond the reach of His humiliation. And where is He? Let faith plume her pinions and endeavor to reach His blest abode. For a moment contemplate the place and scene of this glory; it is heaven, heaven itself. The apostle in his beautiful argument in the Hebrews, illustrating the superiority of Christ's priesthood, is anxious to enforce this truth on the minds of his readers, that Christ had entered "into heaven itself," into the highest heaven, the paradise of God, the place where Jehovah Himself dwells. "For Christ is not entered into the holy places made with hands, which are the figures of the true; *but into heaven itself.*" There Jesus has entered.

The scene of His glory is where the Father resides, where holy angels congregate, where the spirits of just men made perfect dwell, where all is perfect purity, and perfect love, and perfect light, and perfect glory. There is no danger, I apprehend, of trespassing on the region of fancy, in our most glowing anticipation of heaven. It will infinitely transcend the most poetic, the most sublime, the most transcendently glowing pictures the mind has ever conceived. We should make ourselves more familiar with the nature, employments, and glory of heaven, since we are, through grace, traveling there, and shall soon be there. We should know something of the home we are to occupy, the society with which we shall mingle, and the scene in which we shall be employed. Oh, could our thoughts and affections travel there more frequently, fervently, and hopefully, methinks we should come back to earth realizing what poor, contemptible things those are who constantly seek to veil faith's eye to our future, to limit the scope of our minds, and chain us down to these inferior objects so soon and forever to be relinquished! Yes, the place, the theater of Christ's exaltation and glory is heaven, the heaven of heavens; there is His throne, there are His saints who have gone to glory, and there soon we all shall be.

In connection with this scene of His glory, contemplate *His position of dignity.* He is at the right hand of God. Great stress is laid on this in the Bible. "Having purged our sins, he is for ever set down on the right hand of God." Do not think that this description of Christ's position in heaven is given without special and deep significance. There is nothing revealed in the Bible, especially relating to our Lord, that is not of infinite moment, and worthy of the profoundest study. Why are we expressly told that the Lord and Savior sat down at the right hand of God the Father? That we might realize the resources of grace and power we have in heaven, and that this is the dignity and glory for which we should be constantly training, and to which we should be constantly aspiring.

We participate, in virtue of our covenant relation, in all the dignity, glory, and wealth of Christ. As He is exalted, so are we. As He is honored, so are we. As He is at the right hand of the Majesty on high, so, virtually, are we. Oh, beloved, Christ and His saints are one. The Bridegroom has raised the Bride to His highest rank, wealth, and power. All things are ours, because we are Christ's. Think of this when the world hates, maligns, and persecutes you. Think of this in your poverty, obscurity, and earthly lowliness. Think of this when the world ridicules your saintship, and the saints themselves either question or disown it because you see not as they see, and accept not what they accept. Think that you are identified with Christ in His exaltation and glory. Remember that the Premier of Heaven, the Governor, not of all Egypt, but of the Universe, is your Head, your Redeemer, your Brother; that He wears your nature still; and that though He now dwells in glory resplendent, encircled by celestial spirits hymning His high praise, yet He has a human heart, a human sympathy; and that there beams from His eye not one glance of love less tender, that there breathes from His lips not one word of sympathy less soothing; and that all the power He possesses, and the scepter He sways, and the resources He commands are possessed, and exerted over all flesh, that He might give you eternal life.

And what is He doing there? How is He occupied? He is incessantly pleading on your behalf, interceding for your well-being with a love that never falters, with uplifted hands that never weary, bending upon you a glance infinitely more tender and wakeful than the mother watching her sick and suffering babe. "He ever liveth to make intercession for us."

In addition to this, we must think of "the riches of his glory," or, His *glorious* riches. Were all the treasures and wealth of Egypt at the command of Joseph? Could he not only fill the empty sacks of his brethren with the food they needed, but also with gold and silver? Could he give them more than they required, or even asked, because his possessions were so vast, his generosity as boundless as his affluence?

Forget not the mediatorial possessions of our glorified Christ, the illimitable extent of His wealth, the inexhaustibleness of His resources. The Head of creation—all creation's wealth is His. The Head of the Church—all the Church's fullness is His. The Elder Brother of His Father's family—all worlds constitute His estate. "The earth is the Lord's, and the fulness thereof." All the riches of wisdom, all the riches of grace, all the riches of love, all the riches of glory are in Christ's hands, held by Him on behalf of His brethren. God has raised Him up for us, to keep us alive in famine. Why need we be cast down when the cruse of oil and the barrel of meal fails, seeing Jesus can either remove the poverty or supply the necessity? When there is no food, He can take away our hunger, or meet the hunger with an ample supply. He can either avert a necessity, or provide for it when it arises. He can prevent a famine of any one good in our experience, or when the famine comes, unlock the granary of His boundless wealth, and fill our sacks, not with corn only, but also with silver and gold, always giving us more—never less—than we either asked or expected.

Jesus delights to show us how rich we are in Him—that all things are ours because His is ours, and we are His. Oh, why, then, should we permit our faith to succumb to trying circumstances, as though our Jesus was not alive, having all the treasures of the everlasting covenant, all the fullness of the Godhead, all the resources of the universe in His keeping, and at His disposal? Look at the starry sky—Jesus strewed it with its jewelry. Look at that enchanting landscape—Jesus enameled it with its loveliness. Look at that cloud-capped mountain—Jesus reared it. Look at that beautiful lily—Jesus painted it. Look at that soaring bird—

Jesus feeds it. He, with whom is all this strength and beauty, is your Brother. Are not you—loved and chosen from all eternity, ransomed with His blood, inhabited by His Spirit, His own brother—better and dearer than these? Why, then, these fears? why this distrust? Arise and open your sack's mouth, and see what is there—food for earth's pilgrimage, and gold and silver for heaven's blessedness; GRACE and GLORY are given you.

Take heart, then, and exercise simple faith in this great and precious truth, and it will relieve you from many a perplexity and feeling of despondency by which you may be assailed. Try and realize, "I have but to go to Jesus to ask for my present requirements; He has all temporal and spiritual wealth at His disposal, and holds it as the Mediator of the Church." Do you think that if you come to Him with your burden of sin, with the dark veil of sorrow on your spirit, with the crushing weight of earthly care on your mind, and humbly bend the knee before His mercy-seat, and ask Him who is exalted at the right hand of all power, authority, and glory, that He will refuse you? Then He must cease to be your Brother, must vacate His seat in heaven, renounce His authority, and change from what He is!

But while He is there, and until He appears again, all He requires of you is to bring to His fullness your emptiness, to His sympathy your grief, to His unerring wisdom your embarrassment, and to His sheltering wing your temptations and trials. All He asks is that you honor Him by recognizing His exaltation, glory, and authority, and by spreading your case before Him in the humble confidence of a child. Listen to His words—"I am the Lord thy God, which brought thee out of the land of Egypt; open thy mouth wide, and I will fill it."

There is another feature in this part of our narrative that strikingly and beautifully illustrates the ruling providence of God in human history. How beautifully Joseph brings out this truth—"God hath made me lord of all Egypt!" Beloved, God is in history—in every man's history—is in *your* history. He is in every event, and circumstance, and incident of life. Whatever that history be, God arranged it, shaped it, and tinted it. Is it dark? He penciled it, with its somber hues. Is it bright? He has thrown upon the canvas those beauteous colors. Are they blended? He mingled and harmonized them. Recognize and acknowledge, adore, love, trust, and glorify Him for all, and in all. "In all thy ways acknowledge him." Beware of that practical atheism that excludes God from His own world—that excludes Him from your individual history. He is not only in national and social, but He is as much in personal events of life, shaping, guiding, overruling each and all.

But there is a vital and spiritual truth taught us here. I refer to the union of the Father with Christ in the grand redemption of the Church, as illustrated by those words of Joseph to his brethren, "GOD hath made me lord of all Egypt." There was a perfect concurrence of the Father's will, and mind, and heart, with the work, abasement, and glory of Jesus. It was by the determinate counsel and foreknowledge of the Father that Jesus was delivered unto death. The Father bruised Him, put Him to grief; it was by the power of the Father that He was raised from the dead; and as the reward of faithful service, of an accomplished mission, He was exalted by the Father at His own right hand, far above principalities and powers. Thus there was a perfect unity of mind and heart between the Father and the Son in the great work Christ has accomplished; and consequently the exalted and endeared views you have of Jesus should be associated with like views of God; every high conception you have of the love and glory of the Son, ought equally to be a high conception of the love and glory of the Father.

Never forget, beloved, that every step the Lord Jesus Christ took—from the moment He left the Divine bosom of ineffable love, to the moment He re-ascended from Tabor's mount back to His heavenly home, the Father went with Him. Therein we trace the love, the grace, the glory of our Heavenly Father, and can read in a new light, and interpret with increased meaning and brightness, our Lord's own precious words, "He that hath seen me hath seen the Father."

But we reach in the *second* point of the narrative the JOYOUS MESSAGE that Joseph sends to his aged father. What was this? "Haste ye, and go up to my father, and say unto him, Thus saith thy son Joseph, God hath made me lord of all Egypt: come down unto me, tarry not: And thou shalt dwell in the land of Goshen, and thou shalt be near unto me,…and there will I nourish thee." Goshen was that part of the land of Egypt that lay the nearest to Canaan; it was a fat land, a land of plenty and of peace; it was the best of the land to which Joseph intended that his father and his brethren should emigrate. He would not give them the worst; he had it in his power to give them the best, and the best they should have.

The Lord Jesus, our Brother, is prepared to give us, His dear people, the *best* inheritance it is in His power to bestow. He gives us the best in this life of spiritual blessing, and the best of glory in the life that is to come. It is a good land, the true Goshen, into which the Lord Jesus Christ brings His brethren. Shall I cite the "glorious *Gospel* of the blessed God," beloved, as illustrating this? Oh, what a feast of fat things, what a banquet costly and rich, plentiful and free, is the gospel of Christ! In bringing you into experience of the gospel, into what a spiritual Goshen does the Lord bring

you! Consider the glorious *doctrines* of grace—full pardon—
free justification—adoption—sanctification. Consider, too,
the Divine *precepts* of the gospel, regulating, controlling,
sanctifying our walk and conversation in this life.

Consider the exceedingly great and precious *promises*
of the gospel, soothing, cheering, comforting us in this vale
of tears. Truly it is into a good and rich land we are led
when by the Eternal Spirit we are led into a heartfelt
acquaintance with the riches and fullness of the gospel.
There is no spiritual need of the soul which the provisions
of the gospel of Jesus do not meet. For our wounds it is a
balm; for our fears it is a cordial; for our battles it is an
armor; for our soul's hunger and thirst it is manna from
heaven and water from the Rock. "O Lord, we bless You
for the gospel! It is a feast of fat things, a mine of
inexhaustible wealth, a spring of all consolation, a good
and pleasant land, bathed in the sunshine and laden with
the fruit of eternal summer."

And then, O beloved, into what a rich, spiritual Goshen
Jesus brings us when He brings us into experimental
acquaintance *with Himself!* Oh, to know Jesus; to have the
least degree of spiritual and heartfelt acquaintance with
Christ—a full Christ, a present Christ, a compassionate
Christ, a powerful Christ—is what an angel's tongue never
can unfold! Our own silence is, perhaps, the most eloquent
expression of our feelings. I believe that the deepest views
of this truth, and the most intense throbbings of the divine
life within us, are those that the tongue can but feebly utter.
They are too sacred, vast, and glorious, to be idly and lightly
spoken of.

But, beloved, we would have you know into what a
land of spiritual wealth, plenty, and peace you are brought
when in the least degree you are enabled to realize what
Christ is to you. Do you, amid life's trials and earth's cares,

consider the possessions you have in Jesus? What a Savior, what a Kinsman! what a Brother! what a Friend! what an Advocate, what a Counselor! what a loving heart loves you, what a sleepless eye watches over you, what a full hand supplies you!

Remember, too, what a God and Father God is to you; what a present help in every time of need. Realize this in your sorrows, difficulties, and perplexities, and then you will be enabled to say, "What are you, O great mountain? before my glorious Zerubbabel you shall become a plain; for my Savior, my Joseph, is at the right hand of the Father, having all authority, wealth, and power."

Nor must I fail to remind you into what a land of Goshen Christ our Brother soon will bring you, when He shall have delivered you from out of this Egypt, this iron furnace, this land of toil and bondage, service and sorrow. In a little while He will send the chariot, all laden and furnished for the journey, and with it a celestial convoy to bear your spirit home. Yes, believer, there awaits you in heaven the best inheritance—"incorruptible, undefiled, and that fadeth not away." The best of our Goshen is on high. We dwell here but in its suburbs, the outskirts of glory; we wait with patience, yet with ardent longing, our full return from present exile—for our present spiritual Goshen is still in Egypt—and our abundant entrance into that glory and blessedness, the first-fruits of whose vintage, faith often gathers and presses into our cup as the pledge and token of the fullness of joy that is at God's right hand, and of the pleasures that are evermore.

Pilgrim of Zion! child of weariness and sorrow! cheer up! a few more milestones passed, a few more stages traveled, a few more battles fought, and Jesus will say to you, "Come up hither," and then you shall exchange the earthly for the heavenly Goshen. You will no longer dwell within its borders and eat of its fruit by hard labor, but shall inherit the kingdom prepared for you from before the foundation of the world—and be AT HOME with God.

One feature more yet awaits our study—Joseph's FILIAL LOVE: "Thou shalt dwell in the land of Goshen, and thou shalt be near unto me…And there will I nourish thee." Such were the words of Joseph addressed to his aged father. What a beautiful and touching picture of filial affection and piety! Here was the least of his father's house raised up by God to be the savior of his brethren, and that father's benefactor in his old age. Let us who have parents—aged parents—learn a lesson here. Be very tender and gentle towards them. Reverence their gray hairs. It will be but a little while that the privilege and honor will be given of comforting and soothing their trembling descent to the tomb. Let your filial piety and love deepen and intensify as their sun declines. Be as patient and gentle towards the *infirmities* of their *age*, as they were towards the *frivolities* of your *youth*. Rock gently the cradle of their decrepitude, and give them the best it is in your power to bestow; and God will bless you for it when they are gathered to their fathers. Who can tell but that God has spared your life and raised you up for this special office and mission of filial piety and love!

Study these two promises in their *spiritual* import: "Thou shalt be near unto me, and there will I nourish thee." Beloved, the Lord Jesus intends that His brethren—His Father's house—shall be near to Him in heaven. His satisfaction of soul will not be complete until He clusters around Him in glory all for whom that soul travailed in suffering on earth. Nothing shall separate Him from His people. Not a jewel from His crown, not a lamb from the fold, shall be missing then. If you have the weakest throb of spiritual life, the faintest spark of Divine love in your soul now, Jesus, who inspired that life and kindled that love, will send for you to glory, "and so you shall be for ever with the Lord."

The second promise is—"And there will I nourish thee." The nourishment of heaven! oh, what is it? It is to drink of the pure river of the water of life, clear as crystal, flowing from the throne of God and of the Lamb. It is to eat of the fruit of the tree of life in the midst of the paradise of God, yielding its fruit every month. It is to behold Christ in His glory, to enjoy God forever, to be perfected in purity, and to swim in the ocean of infinite and eternal blessedness. There Jesus will nourish you, dear saints of God; and there shall be no more exile, no more sorrow, no more neediness, no more parting, no more sickness, no more death, and no more sin. You will be luxuriating forever amid the glories and plenitude of the new Jerusalem!

> "Oh yes, we shall behold the day
>   When Zion's children shall return;
> Our sorrows then shall flee away,
>   And we shall never, never mourn.

> "The hope that such a day will come
>   Makes e'en the captive's portion sweet;
> Though now we're distant far from home,
>   In glory soon we all shall meet."

The Patriarch's Emigration to Egypt

THE CHRISTIAN'S JOURNEY

And the famine thereof was heard in Pharaoh's house, saying, Joseph's brethren are come: and it pleased Pharaoh well, and his servants. And Pharaoh said unto Joseph, Say unto thy brethren, This do ye; lade your beasts, and go, get you unto the land of Canaan; And take your father and your households, and come unto me: and I will give you the good of the land of Egypt, and ye shall eat the fat of the land," &c.
GENESIS 45:16-23

THIS is not the first occasion, as the reader will have noticed, that the patriarch Jacob, the father of Joseph, is introduced in the narrative. We have seen him, amid accumulating and deepening sorrows, bend like a mighty oak before the storm, in bitterness and anguish of soul exclaiming, "All these things are against me!" It is in another and a happier point of light we view him now—summoned to go down into Egypt to see and embrace the son whose supposed death he had so long and so sorely deplored.

Beloved, there is a bright light in every dark cloud of the Christian's pilgrimage from earth to glory. It is not all gloom and dreariness—simple, unmingled, and unmitigated woe. The path is variegated, the stones that pave it are of many colors, the mosaic so exquisite in its combination and form as none but a Divine hand could

152

have laid. Thus was it with Jacob, and thus is it with all the "sons of Jacob." If the Lord breaks up our earthly resting-place, as the eagle stirs up her nest, it is but to lead us by a way we knew not, into a deeper experience of His love, a closer acquaintance with Himself, and a more perfect fitness in grace and holiness for heaven. Thus was it with the patriarch whose history we are now to consider. The three points in this stage of the narrative illustrating Christ and His people are—the JOURNEY, the PROVISION for the journey, and the COMMAND.

What a new and unexpected chapter in Jacob's history was this! At an advanced period of life, at a time when its sun seemed touching the horizon, when, as one would suppose, all his thoughts and arrangements and feelings would cluster around the last, the final, the most solemn stage of his pilgrimage, lo! he is summoned by the providence of God to leave his country, relinquish his home, and set out upon a long, tedious, and perilous journey. We must suppose, too, that there would be much in this step that was trying to his faith; much that would depress, grieve, and sadden him. It was no light matter for Jacob to abandon this sacred and beloved spot, with all its fond, hallowed associations, and, at his time of life, undertake this long and tiresome journey.

But, beloved, we know not what God may call us to, just at the very time we are supposing that life's weary pilgrimage is about to terminate. Well, be it so; God will not summon you at the close of life, at a period, perchance, when you are sighing for repose, longing for perfect quietude, to any service, mission, or trial, in which He has not purposes of love, and thoughts of peace to accomplish in your history and experience, and for which He will not prove "the Almighty God"—*God all-sufficient.*

What is our Christian course but a journey? Jacob's was from Canaan into Egypt, but the Christian's is from Egypt into Canaan; and this makes all the difference. God, by His sovereign grace, has brought us out of our moral Egypt, delivered us from the iron furnace, the tyranny of Satan, the bond-service of sin, in which by nature we are involved. By a mighty and strong arm, He has rescued us, and set our face fully towards Canaan, into which blessed land He will ultimately and certainly bring us.

The time of setting out on this spiritual journey differs. Some enter upon it *early* in life. Blessed, thrice blessed, are those who, through grace, turn their back on this world, its pleasures, its vanities, its joys, its seductions, its sins, and set out on the Christian journey; who in the season of youth are led to taste that earth's sweets are bitter, that all the world's promises are false, and that there is nothing in its most attractive joys that can satisfy the craving of the soul; who, by the blessed Spirit, have been led to see the depravity of their nature, the plague of their heart, the utter worthlessness of their own righteousness, and have gone to the altar of consecration, and dedicated the first, and the best, and the sweetest of their life to God, "Choosing rather to suffer affliction with the people of God, than to enjoy the pleasures of sin for a season; esteeming the reproach of Christ greater riches than the treasures in Egypt!"

Others set out on this great journey heavenward later in life. They are called in *middle age*, immersed, though they are, in life's cares and avocations; yet we do find that, by Divine and sovereign grace, the Lord can, in spite of all the worldliness, turmoil, and excitement by which they are surrounded, seek them out, and bring them to see the utter emptiness and insufficiency of their worldly pursuits to make them truly happy.

Others are led to enter on this new and blessed course in *old age*. After many long years of unregeneracy, of living to self, to the world, and to sin, electing love and sovereign grace has sought and found its object. Just as the sun of human life was near its setting, the man of seventy or eighty winters has taken the first step towards Zion, setting out on that journey which, though commenced at the eleventh hour, will end in eternal glory. Oh the infinite patience of God! Yet all whom the Father has given to Christ in an everlasting covenant *shall* come to Him! Long years of rebellion, gray hairs stained with many a sin, a heart petrified with long-persisted impenitence, unbelief, and worldliness, shall not rob Jesus of one of His crown jewels. He will search them out and bring them home, though the object of His love and the subject of His grace be the "sinner of a hundred years old." He can make a father in sin, a babe in Christ.

Then, beloved, what a view does this present to us of our pathway homeward! It is not through a paradise of beauty that we are traveling to heaven, but it is through a "waste-howling wilderness." God found us in it, and through it He leads us home to Himself, and He will make us to know, by daily experience, that the world is but a desert. Not one sentence would I utter calculated to convey a false or gloomy idea of the religion of Christ. I believe that no individual knows what true happiness or real joy is until he knows Christ; and that no individual really enjoys God's temporal blessings, the beauties of creation, the marvelous works of His hands, until his spiritual eye has been opened; and then that new-created soul sees more glory in the works of God, more beauty in nature, more wonder in the marvelous operations of God's hands, than the most profound philosopher with the film of spiritual darkness still on his mental eye. The man who has not an eye, a spiritual eye, to see the beauties of revelation, the glory of Christ, and the kingdom of God, has a veil on his soul, and cannot trace, admire, and adore the wisdom and power, goodness and beauty of God, even in nature.

And yet, beloved, our God will make us see daily that the world through which we are passing is but a waste-howling wilderness, a land of drought and peril, in which often the weary pilgrim longs for the wings of a dove that he may fly away and be at rest. It is a wearisome and perilous journey, and the soul of God's children is often discouraged because of the way. Oh, how often are you cast down because of the difficulties and straitness of the path. You find every path a strait and narrow one! The path of truth is strait; the path of Christian obedience is difficult; the path of Christian duty is ofttimes intricate and perplexing; the path of your domestic duties is often a very trying one.

I pity the professed Christian pilgrim who does not find the world a desert, the path a narrow and strait one, and who is not led day by day to learn it out from deep experience that he is coming up out of a wilderness, yet leaning on his Beloved. Be suspicious of yourself, examine your own heart in the light of God's Word if you find the Christian way to be an easy one, if you find the path to be a smooth one, if you find the world smiling on you, cheering you onward, seeking your fellowship, courting your society; suspect the real state of your own heart, and look well to your way; for, be assured of this, the more a man grows in grace and advances in the path of glory, the more will he learn that the world is a desert, the worldling a trifler, the way is perplexing; his own utter weakness and insufficiency, and that the resources of strength, wisdom, and grace which God has provided for him are all laid up in the Lord Jesus Christ.

Another view of this part of the subject. Although the journey of Jacob was a long, wearisome, and perchance a perilous one, yet there was much to look forward to at its termination. The thought of meeting Joseph, of feeling the warm embrace of his son, the prospect of exchanging a land smitten with famine for a land luxuriating in plenty, must have flung many a gleam of sunshine on that dreary road, irradiating it with hope, and cheering it with the melody of song. Beloved; look to *the end* of the Christian journey. Look not at the roughness of the way; be not swallowed up with its difficulties; do not despond because of its privations. Oh, look to *the end* of the journey, especially you aged saints. There is a glorious life at the termination of the Christian course; there is "hope in thine end:" it is the hope of being with Jesus; it is the prospect of seeing your beloved Lord; it is the glorious anticipation of feeling the embrace of His love; it is the blessed hope, the glorious hope, the certain hope, that when you have crossed the desert, and made the last stage of your journey, you will be forever with the Lord.

Oh, let the prospect, then, cheer and strengthen you! You will be less desponding, less depressed and discouraged by reason of the way, if you dwell more on its glorious, blessed, and sublime termination. Soon you will emerge from an arid desert into a beautiful garden, from a wilderness of storm into a paradise of beauty, from a land of scarceness and famine into a land of luxuriant richness and eternal sunshine. "For the Lord your God bringeth thee into a good land, a land of brooks of water, of fountains and depths that spring out of valleys and hills; a land of wheat, and barley, and vines, and fig trees, and pomegranates; a land of oil olive, and honey; a land wherein thou shalt eat bread without scarceness, thou shalt not lack any thing in it."

Observe, now, the PROVISION that Joseph made for this journey of his father and brethren. Let us just take two or three of the prominent points illustrative of the spiritual truths we wish to place before you. You will observe, in the first place, that Pharaoh commands Joseph to send *conveyances* for his father and his household from Canaan to Egypt. "Take you wagons out of the land of Egypt…And Joseph gave them wagons, according to the commandment of Pharaoh." These were conveyances by which his father and his household were to be conducted in safety and comfort in their transit from Canaan into Egypt.

Beloved, God has provided every conveyance for the journey of the soul from earth to heaven; He has anticipated all its exigencies, and has supplied all the spiritual helps by which we cross this desert world, and arrive safe in glory. Do not, I beseech you, overlook this wondrous unfolding of God's love to, and His care for, His Church. He has not left us to our own resources. In other words, He has not unkindly left us to find our way homeward by our own ingenuity or self-sustaining power. He has provided for the safe, the certain journey of your soul out of this Egypt, across this waste-howling wilderness, into the celestial Canaan that the Lord has promised.

Shall I remind you, in the first place, what a divine help, what a powerful conveyance is His OWN WORD? God has given you this blessed Book to be the chart, the guide of your soul, passing to eternity. We do not need the light, the wisdom, the teaching of man to conduct us through the darkness, perils, and temptations of our course. Let us be diligent students of God's revealed Word, become more conversant with its glorious contents, dive deeper into its divine instructions, and we shall not then need the crude, diluted views of truth that emanate from human pens, perchance ofttimes bewildering, misguiding, and alluring us by teaching fatal to our spiritual advance, holiness, and comfort.

Oh, that God might make us better acquainted with this precious truth, that the BIBLE, His revealed Word, is our divinely provided and complete guide to heaven! He that has the truths of this Book written on his heart, inwrought in his soul's experience, shall not miss the way. The Holy Spirit his teacher, he shall not err in the path of holiness, nor be left to his own blind understanding, nor be tossed about "by the sleight of men and cunning craftiness whereby they lie in wait to deceive;" but, committing himself to the light, teaching, and guidance of this inspired volume, he will find that his spiritual Joseph has supplied him with a safe conveyance from earth to heaven in the blessed instructions, doctrines, precepts, and promises of God's own revealed Word.

THE MINISTRY OF THE GOSPEL is another divinely appointed conveyance for our souls' advance homeward. The Christian ministry is an ordained institution of Christ. It is appointed for the instruction of the Church of God in truth, righteousness, and holiness, and for the calling in of God's people; and he who would willfully and knowingly ignore this institution of God, would ignore any ordinance or doctrine of the Bible, and would take from the Church in her homeward march one of her most powerful auxiliaries and aids. We read, "And he gave some, apostles; and some, prophets; and some, evangelists; and some, pastors and teachers; for the perfecting of the saints, *for the work of the ministry,* for the edifying of the body of Christ."

Oh, yes, beloved, I need not appeal to your experience how often you have had occasion to thank God for a living, Christ-exalting, holy ministry; how often you have praised Him for the instruction conveyed to your mind, the consolation distilled into your heart, the sunshine reflected on your dark and gloomy way, through this divinely-appointed channel and blessed agency. And thus the Christian ministry, originating with God, given to the Church by her great Head, has proved one of the divine conveyances for the spiritual transit of the believer across the desert into the glorious Canaan to which God has promised to bring His people.

Demonstrate your gratitude for its appointment, and show your estimate of its value, by sustaining it with your fervent, believing prayers; remembering that your progress in spiritual knowledge and grace will be in the same ratio with that of your minister. He can only instruct and aid you as he himself is taught and enriched of God. Therefore, let both him and his ministry be the constant burden of your prayers. Remember that "a *praying people* makes a *preaching minister.*" And, oh, how deeply does he need your most fervent and continuous intercessions! He has infirmities and temptations, trials and sorrows, which, perhaps, the deep sanctity of his office veils from nearly every eye. Because he preaches so gloriously of the love of Christ, we think that his own love is never chilled. Because he expatiates so earnestly on the mighty power of faith, we deem that his own is never tried. Because he pours forth such strong consolations, we imagine that his own heart is a stranger to sorrow. Ah! he treads a path of which his flock but little know. For them he is tempted, for them he is tried, for them he is comforted: yes, for their sakes and his own, he is often accounted as a sheep for the slaughter— prepared to sacrifice health, wealth, ease, fame, in a word, his own self, if he might present them as his joy and crown in the day of the Lord. Pray, then, for your minister!

And let me add, what a divinely appointed and blessed conveyance is THE CHURCH of God itself! This may seem a paradox, but it is true. The Church can help the Church, saint can help saint, brother can help brother; and this is one of the wise arrangements of Christ. He has not appointed angels to support, and teach, and strengthen, and sympathize with His saints; but fellow-saints, fellow-believers, fellow-sinners ransomed by grace. Now, the Church is a most powerful agent for the advancement of its members. When the saints of God are walking closely with their heavenly Father, are living in near communion with eternity, and are living under much of the anointing of the Holy Spirit, oh, what powerful helpers are they of the saints; and how often God strengthens, supports, and comforts one weak, timid, desponding, sorrowing brother, by the strength, the grace, the sympathy of another!

Never forget, beloved, what a help you may be to some poor weary traveler across this sandy desert, often desponding and cast down by the weariness of the way—how much, by kindness and sympathy, you may comfort, sustain, and soothe him, and thus smooth and speed him heavenward. The Church of God is to be nourished *by* the Church of God. Every joint is to supply some ministry for the whole body, every member is to sympathize with the other members, each contributing to the vigor, healthfulness, and advancement of the whole; so that there is not a member of the body, the lowest, the weakest and most insignificant, who may not, and does not, contribute something to the upholding, the strengthening, and the advancement of the Church of God in its transit from this desert home to heaven. "But speaking the truth in love, may grow up into him in all things, which is the head, even Christ: from whom the whole body fitly joined together and compacted by that which every joint supplieth, according to the effectual working in the measure of every part, maketh increase of the body, unto the edifying of itself in love," (Eph. 4:15, 16.)

And yet another and a powerful conveyance to heaven is a THRONE OF GRACE. Nothing so advances, I had almost said wafts, the soul towards heaven as *prayer*. Praise is a mighty help, and when we are full of real praise, we approximate nearer to what our employment in heaven will be than when in prayer. But, nevertheless, prayer is the more appropriate engagement of the Church on earth; and when this divine breath expands its sails, our bark is borne rapidly and safely forward to the celestial haven. Poor, weak, timid brother! God has given you the conveyance of a throne of grace; make great use of it. Often get into this heavenly chariot, with all your burdens, and cares, and griefs, and see how swiftly and gently it will waft your sour towards God. Your prayers will come up to his holy habitation, even into heaven. Your true Joseph has sent it to uplift your mind, your heart, your soul often to Himself; and, ascending in this conveyance, your breathings will touch the throne. The Lord waits to be gracious; and you have but to plead the name of Jesus, to enter into the holiest by His blood, and you will have power with God, and shall prevail.

Oh, what a mighty strengthener and uplifter of the soul is prayer! "As the naturally weak ivy, which, if it had no support, would only grovel on the earth, by adhering to some neighboring tree or building, or entwining itself about it, thus grows and flourishes, and rises higher and higher, and the more the winds blow and the tempest beats against it, the closer it adheres, and the nearer it clings, and the faster its fibers embrace that which supports it, and it remains uninjured; so the Christian, naturally weak, by prayer connects himself with the Almighty, and the more dangers and difficulties beset him, the more closely they unite him to his God; he reaches towards, and bears upon, and clings to, the throne of grace, and is strengthened with divine strength."

We come to the PROVISION for the way; it is stated in the 23d verse what that provision was: "To all of them he gave each man changes of raiment; but to Benjamin he gave three hundred pieces of silver, and five changes of raiment. And to his father he sent after this manner; ten asses laden with the good things of Egypt, and ten she asses laden with corn and bread and meat for his father by the way." It was very considerate and kind of Joseph to make this ample provision for the temporal necessities and needs of the whole house.

Is *our* Joseph less thoughtful, less careful and considerate? Oh, no! Christ has provided for every step of our journey home to His glorified self. You shall not find a difficulty in your path, a peril in your way, there shall not spring up a new need, trial, or affliction, but God will have provided for it in the fullness of his dear Son, and in the supplies of His everlasting covenant of grace. Oh, how should this cheer, strengthen, and animate us; how should it keep you calm, cheerful, and trustful! Leave your future all with Christ, who has anticipated it all.

Suppose tomorrow you meet some new exigency, confront some new trial, face some new foe; be it so—you will find that your Joseph has gone before you in it all. When trouble comes, the grace will come that sustains it; when perplexity comes, the counsel will come that guides it; when grief comes, the soothing will come that allays it. You will find, beloved, that Christ has gone before you; that He has provided an ample supply for all the spiritual exigencies that may spring up at each step of your journey.

Once more would I remind you of the "good things" which God has provided for the maintenance of His Church in her travel through the wilderness—for the sustenance of each individual saint. Well may we exclaim with the Psalmist, "Oh, how great is thy goodness which thou hast laid up for them that fear thee!" All the wealth of the eternal covenant of grace is ours—all the fullness that is in Christ Jesus is ours—all the treasures of the everlasting gospel are ours—all the promises of God are ours. These are our "provisions for the way"—"laden with corn and bread and meat."

Why, then, should we faint, despond, or despair? Shall we in our daily march, in our conflict with new trials, new temptations, new exigencies, succumb to our circumstances, when faith, looking at its inexhaustible resources, may confront them without a fear? "My God shall supply all your need according to his riches in glory," (or, His glorious riches,) "by Christ Jesus." There is bread in our Father's house, and to spare—plenty of corn in Egypt—all strength, all restraining grace, all constraining love, all human sympathy, and all divine power in our Immanuel, God ever with us, our exalted, enthroned, and glorified Joseph. He who is leading us to heaven will bring us there at His own charge and beneath His own convoy.

But Joseph not only supplied maintenance, but also *clothing*. This illustrates a very precious and glorious spiritual provision of Christ. Joseph was a liberal man, and he devised liberal things; a wealthy man, and he gave affluently; he was a prince, and he provided in a princely way. Our true Joseph supplies ample clothing for the souls of His saints in their homeward journey; He has provided not one clothing only, but varied raiments; and it is well for us to know what they are, that we may put them on and wear them. The first He has provided is the *robe of righteousness*, which covers, beautifies, and fully justifies the saints of the Most High; that glorious and perfect righteousness in which we stand forever accepted, and in which, were we to die at this moment, we should appear before God, not only "unblameable" (that is not a good translation, for we are blamable, but *unblamed*) "and unreproveable" (or, *unreproved*) "in his sight," there being against us nothing whatever that the law, justice, or sin can possibly allege.

Now, this is the righteousness that exonerates you if you believe. Christ has provided it, the Spirit invests you with it, faith receives it, and God justifies you through it. "It is God that justifieth." Realizing your investiture in this divine clothing, you may pursue your journey through life with the peace of God ruling in your heart, and the hope of glory shedding a bright halo around its close. No doubt or fear respecting the future need disturb your mind while your faith can enfold itself in the "righteousness of Christ, which is unto all and upon all them that believe." Justified by faith in Christ, you shall surely enter heaven, and be found in Him, "the Lord our Righteousness."

There is another garment provided by our glorious Joseph. Christ freely supplies, not only the robe of righteousness, but the garment of *sanctification*. Christ himself is our sanctification. As Christ by the Spirit grows in us, and we become conformed to the image of Christ, He becomes our sanctification. We grow holy only as we approximate to the nature, the spirit, and image of Christ. This is true holiness, and nothing else is. Holiness does not consist in fastings, in prayers, in religious duties, rites, and ceremonies. How many there are in the present day who are religiously and rigidly observing all these external things, dreaming of holiness and fitness for heaven, without one particle of real sanctification! What a fearful and fatal delusion! Your sanctification, beloved, is Christ—Christ growing in you, "who of God is made unto us wisdom, righteousness, *sanctification*, and redemption."

This is the holy clothing Christ has provided for your journey homeward. You have to battle with indwelling sin, and to conflict with outward temptation. But never forget that you are to live upon Christ as much for your sanctification as for your justification; that His grace is pledged to subdue your iniquities, to arm you in the conflict,

to give you skill in the holy fight, and the final victory over
all your enemies; and in proportion as Christ grows in you,
you will grow in a true hatred of sin, in a deepening love of
holiness, and thus in real, gospel sanctification.

In addition to the robe of righteousness, and the
garment of sanctification, with which the believer is
invested, there are the adornments of the Spirit, the
ornaments of the Christian character, the divine graces that
ever accompany the righteousness of the saints, evidencing
and illustrating their high and holy relationship to God.
Lovely spectacle!—a sinner clothed with the righteousness
of Christ, all glorious within through the renewing of the
Holy Spirit, and in his external and visible walk exhibiting,
in their beautiful combination, the different graces and fruits
of the Spirit. Well may the believer exclaim, "I will greatly
rejoice in the LORD, my soul shall be joyful in my God; for
he hath clothed me with the *garments of salvation,* he hath
covered me with *the robe of righteousness,* as a bridegroom
decketh himself *with ornaments,* and as a bride adorneth
herself *with jewels.*"

Are these sacred graces of the Spirit exhibited in our
life, beloved? Is our religion lovely? is our Christian life
thus adorned? Are we walking in the Spirit, and not fulfilling
the lusts of the flesh? Is Christ's robe of righteousness girdled
around us by the Spirit's graces, thus walking with Jesus in
white, and in the joy and comfort of the Holy Spirit? Oh,
you temples of God through the Spirit, how holily, and
softly, and warily should you walk! A temple of the Holy
Spirit!—heaven has not a more sacred and God-loved
structure! Yet how shall we preserve it from defilement, or
cleanse it when defiled, but by a constant application of
the "blood of sprinkling?"

Indwelling sin there must be, outward sin there will be;
but the Fountain is *open,* and in it we must daily wash. His

blood alone will keep the conscience clean, the mind peaceful, and the heart in close, filial communion with God.

We thus reach the COMMAND of Joseph to his brethren—"Also regard not your stuff, for the good of all the land of Egypt is yours." This command was imperative. They were not to allow their eye to spare any of the earthly possessions they were now relinquishing. Nor were they to repine or regret that they were abandoning their country, homestead, and property, since the land to which they were emigrating, with all its wealth and abundance, was theirs. The injunction was wise. To have burdened themselves with the things they were leaving would but have increased their anxieties and care—have slowed their progress and prolonged their journey. One thought was to shed its sunshine upon their way—the thought of seeing Joseph, and of perfect immunity from neediness and toil amid the abundance and repose of Egypt.

Beloved, how deep the spiritual teaching here! How holy and unearthly the precept it enjoins upon heaven's emigrant! We are passing through this world to glory. And the command of our Lord is, that we be constantly forgetting the things that are seen and temporal, nor regard the world, its possessions and attractions, in the anticipation of the world of glory that is before us. Our Jesus says, "Lay not up for yourselves treasures upon earth. Take no thought for your life, what ye shall eat, or what ye shall drink; nor yet for your body, what ye shall put on." The follower of Christ is to consider earth's wealth and glory, this world's pleasures and politics, as nothing to him; and constantly detaching himself from the things that are earthly and temporal, he is to be pressing forward to things heavenly and eternal.

How many a child of God, who should be growing in grace and advancing in heavenliness, is constantly clogging his feet with earth's clay, weaving around him the net and the mesh of earthly, carnal, sensual engagements, thus impeding his spiritual progress! How can he grow in grace and heavenly-mindedness if this be so?—it is utterly impossible. You must become more dead to earth, more crucified to the world, and realize more the power of Christ's resurrection in your soul. This is the apostolic exhortation, "If you then be risen with Christ, seek those things which are above, where Christ sitteth on the right hand of God. Set your affection on things above, not on things on the earth. For ye are dead, and your life is hid with Christ in God....Mortify therefore your members which are upon the earth."

Your true Joseph, your blessed Jesus, says to you emphatically, "Regard not your earthly possessions, your belongings, your worldly advantage; regret not the loss and sacrifice of home, friends, and property that you make for your attachment to me, my service, and my cause; count it all as vanity and dross; gird up your mind to endure my shame, to share my reproach, yes, to deny all ungodliness, to come out of the world and be my cross-bearing disciples. I have laid up for you treasure in heaven, infinite wealth, an inheritance that is incorruptible, riches that perish not, joys that glut not, a crown of glory that fades not away. Count the world as loss, all created good as dross, and the creature itself as vanity, for the glory, and honor, and immortality that will soon be yours."

Thus would our blessed Lord teach, cheer, and animate us in our heavenly journey, by bidding us cease from needless earthly care, and cultivate the spirit, the mind, and the hopes of pilgrims traveling to the celestial city! Consonant with this is the whole tenor of God's Word. How impressive and emphatic its exhortations! "Depart ye, depart ye, go ye out from thence, touch no unclean thing; go ye out of the midst of her; be ye clean, that bear the vessels of the Lord." "Let us go forth therefore unto him without the camp, bearing his reproach." "Let us lay aside every weight, and the sin which doth so easily beset us, and let us run with patience the race that is set before us, looking unto Jesus." God give us grace to lay to heart these exhortations to heavenly-mindedness! We are but crossing a desert land on our way home to Christ. He has promised that our bread and our water shall be sure, and that we shall lack no good thing. Upon Him, then, let us cast our care, anxious for nothing except how we may so walk as to please Him in all things.

This life of faith, by which thus we become dead to the world, will soon conduct us to the last stage of our homeward journey. He who was with us in all its preceding stages, will be with us in this its last and closing, its most solemn and eventful one. Think not, O weary, trembling pilgrim, that He will abandon you then to resources of your own. Oh no! Jesus has provided for the hour and details of His people's departure. He will send with the conveyance that is to bear you home to glory, grace, strength, and hope for the solemn transit. Christ will be with you then; and, Christ with you, all will be well—seeing JESUS, you "shall not see *death*."

> "When my last hour is close at hand,
>   My last sad journey taken,
> Do Thou, Lord Jesus, by me stand,
>   Let me not be forsaken.
> Lord! my spirit I resign
> Into Thy loving hands divine,
>   'Tis safe within thy keeping.

"Countless as sands upon the shore,
  My sins may then appall me;
Yet, though my conscience vex me sore,
  Despair shall not enthrall me,—
For, as I draw my latest breath,
I'll think, Lord Jesus, upon Thy death,
  And there find consolation.

"Limb of Thy body, Lord, am I,
  This makes me joyful-hearted;
In death's dark gloom and misery,
  From Thee I am not parted.
And when I die, I die to Thee,—
Eternal Life was won for me
  By Thy last hour of anguish.

"I shall not in the grave remain,
  Since Thou death's bonds have sever'd;
By hope with Thee to rise again,
  From fear of death delivered,
I'll come to Thee, where'er thou art,
Live with Thee, never from Thee part;
  Therefore to die is rapture.

"And so to Jesus Christ I'll go,
  My longing arms extending;
So fall asleep in slumber deep,
  Slumber that knows no ending;
Until Jesus Christ, God's only Son,
Opens the gates of bliss—leads on
  To heaven, to life eternal!"—*Nicholas Hermann*

Joseph's Exhortation to Unity

CHRISTIAN LOVE

So he sent his brethren away, and they departed: and he said unto them, See that ye fall not out by the way. GENESIS 45:24

SUCH was the appropriate charge with which Joseph dismissed his brethren on their return to their father, bearing with them the evidences of his greatness, and the expressions of his love. He well knew the necessity for such an exhortation to unity as this. He remembered that the elements of evil which led to his own abduction from his father's family, with all its dire, yet strangely overruled results, still dwelt in their nature; and that although time and adversity may have subdued and softened that evil, yet, nevertheless, its root still was there, and that without a caution on his part, and strict vigilance on theirs, in all probability before they reached their home, the smoldering embers would break forth again in envy, strife, and division, and sad and disastrous might be the consequences.

Holy and important is the spiritual instruction here conveyed! That the children of God are not exempt from the necessity of a similar charge, is clear from the many and constant exhortations to brotherly love and Christian union with which the Word of God abounds. Perhaps there is no precept of which we need to be more perpetually reminded, and to whose violation and neglect we are more constantly exposed than this one—the precept of *Christian love*. A striking confirmation of the tendency of the Lord's brethren to "fall out by the way," occurs as early as the history of the apostles. It took place between Paul and Barnabas, and arose from a difference of opinion as to the expediency of being accompanied in their apostolic visitation of the churches by Mark. Barnabas, influenced, perhaps, by his relationship to Mark, who was his nephew, proposed it, but "Paul thought it not good to take him with them." This dissonance of judgment led to a separation of these apostles the one from the other, and is thus narrated—"And the contention was so sharp between them, that they departed asunder one from the other." (Acts 15:36–39.) And so they quarreled along the way!

Another instance, so gently chided and skillfully improved by our Lord, implicated the whole college of apostles. Thus Mark records it: "And he came to Capernaum: and being in the house, he asked them, What was it that ye disputed among yourselves by the way? But they held their peace: for by the way they had disputed among themselves, who should be the greatest." (Mark 9:33, 34.) And thus they quarreled along the way!

We learn that our nature, even in its renewed state, is still carnal, and exhibits the same marks of innate corruption, and needs the same holy exhortations of God's word that the Church of God ever did. Dismissing the original application of this exhortation to brotherly unity, we propose to ground upon it a few observations enforcing the holy and much-needed precept of Christian love among the brethren of Christ. For who that is spiritually and intelligently acquainted with the Church of God is not solemnly convinced of the necessity of a higher and holier standard of Christian union and love among the members of the body of Christ, the children of the one family of God, than at present exists?

Beloved, "God is love." And Jesus Christ was the incarnation of love to our world. He was love living, speaking, acting, toiling among men. His birth was the nativity of love; His sermons, the words of love; His miracles, the wonders of love; His tears, the meltings of love; His crucifixion, the agonies of love; His resurrection, the triumph of love. All that He did, and said, and commanded, was the embodiment and the expression of Divine love. In the further prosecution of this delightful subject, we shall consider the *nature* of Christian love—its *features*—and the *exhortation* to its culture.

Now with regard to the NATURE of Christian love—in what does it consist? It differs essentially from all other feelings embraced under the general term love. The natural affection of families, the friendship that has its foundation in assimilation of mind and taste, the feeling of benevolence that prompts us to acts of kindness to our fellows, and that denominational or party feeling cherished by those who profess the same ecclesiastical polity and adopt the same mode of worship, all differ essentially from the love that unites the one Church of Jesus Christ. All these modifications of love may exist, real, intense, warm, and yet true Christian love may have no place in the soul. There may be the warmest natural affection, the profoundest feelings of benevolence, the most zealous party attachment, and yet the individual may be utterly destitute of the divine and sacred affection of which we speak. In what, then, consists this Christian love, thus standing apart so distinctly from every other form and modification of love?

Surely there must be something unique, peculiar, and lofty to invest it with this marked and lovely character! For a few moments look at the *origin*, and this will illustrate the *nature*, of that Christian love, which finds its home in every regenerate, Christ-loving heart. In the first place, I would remark that it has its origin in our *new nature*. When we are born again of the Spirit, divine love is born in us. There is with the advent of the divine nature, the advent of divine love. The nature of God is *love;* and if we become partakers of the divine nature, we necessarily become partakers of the love that dwells in God. The heavenly birth and divine love are coexistent properties in our spiritual regeneration. I emphatically repeat that, a partaker of the divine nature, I am necessarily a partaker of divine love.

Then, again, it has its origin *in the indwelling of the Holy Spirit in the heart*. Every child of God is a temple of the Holy Spirit, consequently there is in him the very inspiration of divine, spiritual love. "The fruit of the Spirit is *love*." If you have the Holy Spirit dwelling in you, making you His temple, there dwells in you the principle of love—a love that emanates from God, which entwines itself with all who are God's, and that ascends again in holy affections to God. The indwelling of the Spirit is the indwelling of love in your heart; and this it is that should make us prompt to recognize a saint wherever we find him, be his nation, his complexion, his dialect, or the section of the Church to which he belongs, what it may. If I see in him unmistakable marks of the Spirit of God; if I see, clustering in his life and conversation, the fruits of the Spirit, and yet I refuse to recognize him as a Christian brother, to receive him as a child of God, to have fellowship with him as one of the sacred brotherhood, I deny and grieve and wound the self-same Spirit dwelling in me.

Again, we may understand the nature, and trace the origin of this divine principle of love, if we remember that it is the grand moral feature that assimilates the whole family of God. It is, if I may so express myself, the family likeness.

Nothing more strikingly brings out the unity of the divine nature in all God's people, the indwelling of the same Spirit thus establishing their membership with the family of God, than the feature of *love*. Let me see in a Christian man real love, true spiritual affection, affection flowing towards me because I am a brother in Christ—love recognizing my discipleship, my saintship, my sonship—I see in that brother the family likeness, the image of the Father, and the image of all the brethren. Yes, beloved, in a few words, the love of which we speak is a divine, unearthly, spiritual principle. It is not of the flesh fleshly, it is not born with us; it proves its origin and nature by the divine and spiritual fruits that it brings forth. It is from God, it ascends to God, and all its operations are godlike and divine. He who discovers in his heart no other evidence of his filial relation to God, of his discipleship to Christ, of his membership with the one brotherhood, than the existence of this divine, holy principle of love, has sufficient warrant to put in a humble claim to be a disciple of Christ, a child of God, and an heir of glory. "By this shall all men know that ye are my disciples, if ye have love one to another." "By this we know we have passed from death unto life, because we love the brethren."

The day may come when you may thank God for this one and simple evidence of your salvation. All other evidence of your membership with Christ, and of your adoption into the family of God, may be, not extinguished, but beclouded; and one remains, and one only, to shed its luster, like the lone star of evening, upon your dying pillow—love to the brethren, love to the holy ones because they are holy, love to the saints because they are saints. Beloved, with that one evidence you may tread the valley of the shadow of death, fearing no evil, and you shall have an abundant entrance into the everlasting kingdom of our Lord and Savior Jesus Christ.

Having thus briefly explained its nature, let us for a few moments specify some of the GROUNDS on which Christian love should be exhibited. There occur analogies in the narrative that will be our guide. On what grounds may we suppose Joseph exhorts his brethren not to quarrel along the way, on their return home to their father? Would he not naturally remind them, in the first place, that they were the children, the sons of one father, and being so, there existed a strong bond of union between them? Most assuredly he would. Beloved, the Church of God acknowledges one God and Father: "One God and Father of all." One Father loves all—has predestinated all to the adoption of children—has given all alike His beloved Son— embraced all alike in His one heart—and lends His ear alike to all clustering around His mercy-seat and addressing Him as, "*Our Father* which art in heaven."

Find the sons of God where you may, belonging to what religious section of the Church they may, kneel with them in prayer, bend with them before the one mercy-seat, and you will be at no loss to ascertain who is their Father. Oh, there is nothing so convincing of the essential unity of God's family, or which constitutes so beautiful and touching a manifestation of that unity, as the clustering together of the Lord's people from their various communions around God's throne of grace. It is the most true, sacred, and sublime visible exhibition of the unity of the Church of God found on this side of glory—the unity of worship—the unity of prayer.

Listen to the language of each—of all: "Our Father which art in heaven." In this sublime utterance who can fail to see the three essential elements of union—the PARENTAGE of God—the BROTHERHOOD of the saints— the HOME of the Church: FATHER—OUR Father—in HEAVEN! Oh, see how the renewed nature of man travels back to the *Fatherhood* of God! See how man travels in fraternal affection towards the *Brotherhood* of man! See how the child of God seeks the *Home* from which he has wandered—the point of his departure—the place of his return. And when they assemble at their Father's feet, confessing like sins, deploring like infirmities, breathing like sorrows, unveiling like needs, and supplicating like mercy, oh, how true, beautiful, and holy appears the essential unity of the family of God!

> "The saints in prayer appear *as one*,
> In word, and deed, and mind,
> While with the Father and the Son
> Sweet fellowship they find."

Would not Joseph also remind them that, thus belonging to one father, *they were brethren?* What are all the saints of God but brethren in the Lord Jesus Christ? "Ye are all the children of God by faith in Christ Jesus." "One is your Master, and *all ye are brethren*." The Church of God is one holy brotherhood. Every child of God, be the depth of his experience, or the strength of his faith, or the measure of his attainments what it may, stands in fraternal relation to the one brotherhood of which Jesus is the First-born. Beloved, wherever you thus meet with a child of God, a believer in Christ, one who acknowledges his relation to Jesus, you meet a brother in Christ, and in giving to him a fraternal recognition, you but recognize and exhibit your own personal union with the sacred brotherhood.

This is the only real fraternity. Sin has broken up the human family. By detaching our nature from its Center, it has detached it from itself. The human race has nothing of its original brotherhood remaining but the name, and even this finds often an unwilling recognition. The hate of races and the caste of society are proverbial. As if our common

Father had not "made of *one blood* all nations of men for to dwell on all the face of the earth," race disowns race, and class denounces class, and caste scorns caste. "The Celt swears vengeance against the Saxon; the Slavonic cannot fraternize with the German stock. The dim repositories of the past are ransacked for missiles and watchwords that may serve as firebrands to rekindle the old hereditary feuds of alien and rival lineages. The Italian thinks himself scarcely a creature of the same blood and of the same God with the Austrian. Now the gospel goes forth as the great, the peaceful, but unappeasable revolutionist; but its watchword is a fraternity broad as humanity. And when men learn to feel these ties and claims of brotherhood, the needy and the lowly are soothed and elevated; the savage puts on dignity, and the bondsman hope; and the woman glides from the prison where barbarism had immured her. So, on the other hand, the mighty, and the intelligent, and the rich, thus instructed, forget their transient and skin-deep distinctions of caste and culture; and feel, in the view of a common sin, and salvation, and judgment-seat, the sense of stewardship casting out the odious spirit of self-gratification. Literal equality, no change in man's power can bring about. There would remain, on the day after an equal distribution of all goods and lands to all earth's inhabitants, the eternal and irremovable distinctions of sex and age, and mental talent and bodily endowment. You might as well propose to equalize the whole body of the man into an eye, clear but defenseless, or into a cheek, earless and eyeless and browless, as to make the body politic, in all its members and all its circumstances, one. But give the feeling of true Christian fraternity; and, while each member retains its individuality and its distinct offices, and its fitting peculiarities, the good of one member would become the good of all. The hand would toil in the light of the guiding eye; and the eye travel in the strength of the adventurous and patient foot." (W. R. Williams, D.D.)

But the religion of Jesus wins back our divided and hating race to its original brotherhood. It has been remarked that, "One touch of nature makes the whole world kin." But one touch of grace does more. It unites the kin into Christian brotherhood; it introduces it into the family of God. This is the only true, sacred, and permanent fraternity; the republican and the democrat, the peer and the peasant, the sovereign and the subject, the bond and the free, are in Christ Jesus one sacred brotherhood, bound in filial relation to God, and, in virtue of this union, in fraternal relation to each other.

Another uniting element is our union with, and the reception of all our blessings from, the Lord Jesus Christ. Here is a strong basis of union, a holy bond of love and sympathy. These brethren of Joseph were returning to Canaan, all richly laden with wealth through the kindness of Joseph. They were all alike furnished with provision, with clothing, and every comfort necessary for the journey. Thus they had a common bond of sympathy and union in the blessings all richly and freely received alike from Joseph. What gospel teaching is here!

Are we not all of us, as saints of God, dependent upon Jesus? are not all of us hanging upon Jesus? do we not all receive from Jesus? The blood that cleanses us, the righteousness that justifies us, the grace that sanctifies us, the sympathy that comforts us, the hope that cheers us—is it not all derived from the fullness that is in Christ? Are not all clinging to that one dear Savior, depending on His finished work, and all drawing from His infinite resources? Oh, yes! Where do the saints of God the most frequently meet? Is it not at the feet of Jesus? Modes of worship may sunder us outwardly. A Liturgy may divide in form those who in heart draw near to the same God and Father. But *here* we all in spirit meet. The fountain from where we draw our stores of strength and grace, comfort, joy, and peace, attracts and unites us at the Savior's feet.

This ought to draw closer together in affection and sympathy the scattered, divided members of Christ's body, since they are all living on Jesus, drawing from Jesus, and alike indebted to Jesus. Thus, if through prejudice or preference, ecclesiastical polity or modes of religious worship sunder the saints of God from each other, here is that which attracts them to one spot, and binds them in one holy fellowship—a full Christ to whom all repair, and from whom all alike receive supplies, and who loves and blesses all alike. Journeying to one heavenly home, wearing the same robe of righteousness, clad in the same garments of salvation, sustained and nourished by the same spiritual supplies, should not these considerations raise us superior to sectarianism, prejudice, and harsh judgment? What have we that we have not received? Why should one brother boast against or judge another? "Of his fulness have *all we* received;" and all alike living upon Christ's fullness, nourished by His grace, kept by His power, soothed by His love, fed by His hand, guided by His counsel, and bound together in the same heart of God, supplies us with one of the strongest and most persuasive motives why we should love one another, and see that we "fall not out by the way."

I thus anticipate another ground of Christian love— our individual membership with the one body of Christ. It is a beautiful illustration of the Church, the human body. Perfect in itself, it yet has different members; one organization, yet several parts. How masterfully does the apostle work out this illustration, bringing us to the conclusion that one part cannot dispense with another; that no member can say to another member, "I have no need of you;"—all are useful and sympathetic in the body. So in the Church of Christ: it is essentially one spiritual corporate Body. Every believer in Christ is a member of that Body, and the Church of God is not perfect without that member. And thus members of Christ's body are members one of another. "For as the body is one, and hath many members, and all the members of that one body, being many, are one body: so also is Christ. For by one Spirit are we all baptized into one body, whether we be Jews or Gentiles, whether we be bond or free; and have been all made to drink into one Spirit."

And here let me remark, what a bond of union is found in the existence of the same trials and temptations! Infirmities and necessities are common to all the children of God. This is a touching, tender argument for Christian love and sympathy in the one Church of Christ. Are not our trials ofttimes the same? our temptations and infirmities, our adversities and sorrows? Have we not, too, the same spiritual exercises, the same mental operations? are we not perpetually exhibiting the same stumblings, falls, and backslidings? Oh, how this ought to knit and unite more closely together the saints of God! In view of this truth, how should ecclesiastical distinctions vanish and disappear!

What! has my brother of the Establishment, has my Nonconformist brother the same temptations and corruptions to combat with as *I?* Is he conscious of the same frailties, infirmities, and suffering? Does he walk in the same spiritual darkness, despondency, and distress? Then do I not see that which should draw my heart to him, which should make me forget external distinctions and separations, and which should rouse my sympathy, prayer, and love, and prompt me to go to him and endeavor to distill comfort into his sorrowful spirit; to speak a word of consolation to his grieved heart, a divine promise to his distressed mind? What are the things that sunder me, externally, compared with this touching, tender bond of union, that ought to unite in closer sympathy the living, spiritual members of the Church of God?

Would not Joseph, too, in exhorting his brethren not to fall out by the way, remind them that they were journeying towards one home and to one father? What a sweet thought is this, that the Church of God is on its way to one blessed, glorious inheritance! The family of God are all traveling to one loving Father. In a little while, these dear saints of God, who now, through infirmity, and often under the temptation of the wicked one, contend and wrangle for their external differences, minor and petty in comparison with the great and momentous one in which they substantially agree, will meet together in a better land, in a better home, in their Father's house. Oh, if shame could crimson the cheek, if tears could gush from the eye in heaven, it would be in the recollection that on earth we allowed these non-essential things to create heart-burnings, rivalries, jealousies, divisions, hard thoughts, speeches, and actions, before the world; thus wounding our blessed Savior, impeding His cause, injuring His truth, and crucifying Him afresh!

Beloved, the saints of God are journeying towards one promised land, going home to one eternal inheritance, traveling to one heavenly Father; and this alone, did no other argument or bond of union exist, should knit and blend in love, sympathy, kindness, and prayer, the different members of the ONE body of Christ, the ONE family of God. "The ransomed of the Lord shall return, and come to Zion with songs and everlasting joy upon their heads: they shall obtain joy and gladness, and sorrow and sighing shall flee away." With the prospect of a termination of the journey so glorious, and with the assurance that then every parti-colored standard will be lost in the blaze of light, and every jarring note, in the song of heaven, let us cultivate the union that will then exist, and by love, service, and worship on earth, antedate and anticipate the bliss of glory.

> "Lord, may our union form a part
> Of that thrice-happy whole,
> Derive its pulse from Thee the Heart,
> Its life from Thee the Soul."

We propose, in the further prosecution of this subject, to present a few FEATURES characteristic of Christian love. And the first we adduce is, its *nonsectarian character.* Christian love is essentially so. It may indeed cherish a warmer glow, and exhibit greater confidence and freeness of expression in that Christian communion where its fellowship, from a more perfect harmony of sentiment, is recognized; nevertheless, it is essentially nonsectarian, since it embraces all who love Christ and walk in His commandments, and is as expansive as the length and breadth of the Church universal. If I only love a Christian brother because he belongs to my branch of the Christian Church, or holds my distinctive principles, my love in this case is sectarian, and not Christian. If I love him merely because he is a Conformist, or because he is a Nonconformist, because he holds believers' baptism, or because he holds infant baptism, this is not a genuine, spiritual, divine love, but a love of party, a love of denomination, a love of self.

I must love my brother because he is a brother in the Lord. I must love him because he is a saint of God. I must love him because I see in him the image of my Father, the Spirit of my Savior; and if I thus see in him the Divine image, hear him speak in the language of Canaan, and trace in him the likeness of a loving, lowly, unearthly Christ, my affection leaps over the walls of ecclesiastical separation, and embraces him as a brother in Christ. Beloved, the only love that truly authenticates your discipleship to Christ, and your adoption into the family of God, is nondenominational and nonsectarian.

It is not called upon to give up what God's Word enjoins, or conscience feels to be right. It does not say to a brother, "I will believe what you believe, because I love you;" but it says, "I cannot be all that you are; but, because I see in you the image of my Father and the Spirit of my Savior, I love you. Though I cannot see eye to eye with you in all things, though my judgment differs from yours in some; yet, tracing in you the indwelling of the divine nature, the anointing of the Holy Spirit, the likeness of Christ, I love and recognize you as a brother beloved of God."

It was a noble remark of Wesley—"Is your heart right with God? If it is, give me your hand. I do not mean, 'Be of my opinion;' you need not. Neither do I mean, 'I will be of your opinion;' I cannot. Let all opinions alone; only give me your hand." Oh! it is a tragic thing to stand aloof from a holy man of God because he is not in all things of our own opinion! Such a violation of the first law of Christianity does despite to the Spirit of grace, the Spirit of love, the Spirit of God, and either proves our own utter destitution of the Spirit, or must result in the withdrawal of His sensible presence, and a consequent spiritual leanness, darkness, and desertion of soul.

Another feature of Christian love *is its studied avoidance of all cause of offense.* True brotherly love will not needlessly offend a brother; it will endeavor to steer a course that will prevent those occasions of painful, unhappy collision, that so much stir up the natural corruption of the human heart. One of the sweet characteristics of real spiritual love is, that it endeavors so to deport itself as not needlessly to wound and grieve a brother; it will not go out of its way to speak unkindly of or to misjudge a Christian. It will endeavor to refrain from injuring and giving offense, avoiding those things that tend to stir up what is carnal in a Christian brother's heart.

We are reminded in God's Word that offenses, through misunderstanding and infirmity, will come; there will be those collisions of judgment or of action in the Church of God which frequently call forth hasty expressions, injured and angered feelings; a spirit is shown, and words are spoken, that may leave a long and fretting wound. But true love will ever stand ready to forgive the offense, when the offense is repented and deplored. It will not cherish malice, hatred, and revenge in the heart, but, God-like, it is ever ready to forgive, even to the "seventy times seven." Our Lord's injunction respecting giving offense is explicit and clear— "Whoso shall offend one of these little ones which believe in me, it were better for him that a millstone were hanged about his neck, and that he were drowned in the depth of the sea." "Woe to that man by whom the offence cometh."

Oh, if this divine precept had a deeper lodgment in the hearts of Christ's brethren, how much charity, gentleness and forbearance would be exhibited—how tender would they be of each other's feelings—how jealous of each other's reputation—how kind in word and action—how careful lest even a momentary wound might be inflicted, regarding the least disciple of Christ as dear to Him as the apple of the eye!

Another and most lovely essential feature of Christian love is that of *forgiveness*. Flowing from the forgiving love of God, it partakes of the nature where it springs. Christian *love* approaches the nearest of all the graces of the Spirit in the regenerate soul to the divine nature. God is love, and love is of God, and he who loves the holy because they are holy, and who *forgives* the wrong done by friend or foe, approaches the nearest in imitation of God. Nothing seems more to becloud or even to invalidate our Christian character, to annihilate all evidence of our being a child of God, as cherishing a malicious, unrelenting, *unforgiving* spirit. How can we go to God and say, "And *forgive* us our sins; for we also forgive every one that is indebted to us," while we are cherishing in our hearts an *unforgiving* feeling towards a brother who has grieved, wounded, or offended us?

What if God took you at your word when bending at His throne offering this prayer? Terrible thought! Condemnation, just and eternal wrath, unmitigated and endless—the banishment of the outer darkness until the last mite were paid, would be your most fearful and righteous doom! But go and *forgive* your brother; tell him that, yourself forgiven of God the ten thousand offenses, you forgive him the one; that love only is in your heart toward him; and that forgiving all, you forget all. *Then* go and offer your prayer to your Heavenly Father for His forgiveness!

One of the loveliest, most precious unfoldings of God's love towards us is that He has pardoned all our sins, has forgiven us all our transgressions, and having blotted them all out, will remember them no more forever. "Be ye therefore followers of God, as dear children," and ever keep in view the divine precept teaching the forgiving of offenses—"Let all bitterness, and wrath, and anger, and clamour, and evil speaking, be put away from you, with all malice: and be ye kind one to another, tenderhearted, *forgiving* one another, *even as* God for Christ's sake hath *forgiven* you." Instead of sitting down and brooding over an injustice and a wronged, wounded sensibility, or slighted affection, until the imagination has augmented the injury from a molehill into a mountain, the little rivulet that one step of love might have crossed into an impassable gulf, see if there has been any real cause of offense, any intended injury; and if there dwells in the offender the spirit of Christ, and in you, the offended one, the love of God, both will be prepared, on a mutual understanding, the one to confess the fault and the other as ready to forgive it. Oh, let the dying prayer of Jesus ever linger in our ear amid the assaults of enemies and the woundings of friends—"Father, FORGIVE them!"

Forbearance is another feature of true Christian love. "*Forbearing* one another in love." This feeling is frequently called into exercise. How constantly we are under the necessity of bearing with one another's failings, frailties, and actions! All do not think and feel and act alike. If we really loved, as we ought, in the spirit of kind, Christian forbearance, we should make all allowance for each other's different modes of thought and peculiar frailties, constitutional infirmities and tendencies. It may demand peculiar and no little degree of grace to bear with our brother's constitutional temperament and weaknesses, his uncouthness of manner, his disposition to look at the dark side of the picture, his crotchets and fault-finding spirit, and other infirmities which inspire our dislike if not disgust; nevertheless, if I love as my Lord and Master loves me and loves my brother, I ought to *forbear* in love; not to censure or condemn, but casting over him the mantle of charity, cherish that "love which suffereth long and is kind."

It is another operation of brotherly love that it *avoids rash judgments and harsh interpretations.* True love is not judicial, it is fraternal. It avoids the judgment-seat. How tempted we often are to sit in judgment on a brother's actions, motives, and opinions; just as if we possessed the divine attribute of reading his heart, and fathoming the secret principles and motives that influence him. If we love that brother as we ought, we should avoid those judgments, which almost invariably bring us to rash and wrong conclusions, censuring and condemning when, had we a perfect knowledge of his heart, we would probably admire and approve. Rather let us ever aim to put a kind and charitable construction upon actions, the circumstances and motives of which, we are profoundly ignorant.

Nor must I forget to remind you that *sympathy* is a striking characteristic and feature of Christian and brotherly love. It will prompt us to compassion and kindness towards brothers and sisters who are in distress, trial, and suffering; it will make us willing to bear one another's burdens, to weep with those who weep, and rejoice with those who rejoice; it will constrain us to do all we can to soothe, soften, and ameliorate, and shed the sunshine of gladness on the gloomy path of some tried, lonely child of God.

Faithfulness is another of its essential characteristics. It does not shrink from tender, loving, yet wise and holy admonition. It is faithful to conscience, to God's Word, to Christ's honor, and to the brethren. "Faithful are the wounds of a friend." To be thus faithful—to show our love by our fidelity—to rebuke, reprove, and exhort; not allowing sin or error in a Christian brother, but, in the meek, lowly, gentle, yet firm, faithful spirit of the Master, to warn and rebuke—oh, this is love indeed! In nothing do we require more tenderness, lowliness, and love; and in the discharge of no duty is Jesus more prepared to give us all the wisdom, grace, and love demanded. Never let us rebuke or reprove a loving brother until we first repair to Jesus, and get our hearts replenished with His love.

In conclusion, how needed and forcible the *exhortation*, "See that ye fall not out by the way." How like the words of our Lord Jesus to the disciples, "A new commandment I give unto you, *that ye love one another.*" Let us aim to walk in this divine, Christ-like precept. Let our conduct, our communion, our whole spirit and carriage, be influenced and governed by *love.* Let us show how superior is Christian unity and love to denominational distinctions, ecclesiastical polity, and outward forms. Let us not fall out with other Christians by the way because we differ in judgment on some minor points, or worship God in different ways. Let us not renounce or denounce a Christian brother, who loves the same Savior, is of the same Father, is engaged in the same holy fight, because he wears a different uniform, belongs to a different battalion, or lays his offering of love upon another altar than our own. This would be grieving to the Spirit and dishonoring to the Captain of our salvation.

> "Shall I ask the brave soldier, that fights at my side
>   The cause of mankind, if our creeds do agree?
> Shall I give up the friend I have valued and tried,
>   If he kneels not before the same altar with me?"

No! if his creed is essentially correct, if his life is divinely holy, if his altar is sprinkled with the blood of Christ's atonement, and if, in the spirit of adoption, that altar is inscribed to the One Father in heaven, and he bends, and loves, and worships there as a humble believer in the Savior, as a loving child of God, as a true soldier of the Cross, then I must ignore my own Christianity and deny my Lord if I refuse to hail him as a beloved brother, or to join him in the holy strife of reducing the kingdoms of this world to the reign and supremacy of Christ.

Cultivating Christian and brotherly love, we shall antedate and anticipate the happiness and employment of heaven, where love reigns in every breast. There, in those pure and blissful regions, where the God of love dwells, and the Savior of love is enthroned, and the Spirit of love breathes, there are no strifes or dissensions, no jarrings or discords. The music is of love, the songs are of love, and all hearts beat in unison with love; the tree of life that bends over the river of joy, and the bowers of bliss, fanned by spicy breezes, all are vocal with the melody and embalmed in the fragrance of LOVE.

"Love is the golden chain that binds the happy souls above,
  And he's an heir of heaven who finds his bosom glow with LOVE."

"WE KNOW THAT WE HAVE PASSED FROM DEATH UNTO LIFE, BECAUSE WE LOVE THE BRETHREN. HEREBY PERCEIVE WE THE LOVE OF GOD, BECAUSE HE LAID DOWN HIS LIFE FOR US: AND WE OUGHT TO LAY DOWN OUR LIVES FOR THE BRETHREN."

"SEE THAT YE FALL NOT OUT BY THE WAY."

Joseph Alive

A LIVING CHRIST THE LIFE OF THE CHRISTIAN

And they went up out of Egypt, and came into the land of Canaan unto Jacob their father, and told him, saying, Joseph is yet alive, and he is governor over all the land of Egypt. And Jacob's heart fainted, for he believed them not...and when he saw the wagons which Joseph had sent to carry him, the spirit of Jacob revived. GENESIS 45:25-27

THERE is not to the Christian, and to the Christian philosopher, a more interesting and instructive study than the varied spiritual and mental exercises of the renewed soul. Nothing takes so deep and powerful a hold upon the intellect, or penetrates so deeply the heart's hidden springs of feeling, as the grace of God in the soul of man. We hesitate not to say that man is an inexplicable mystery apart from revealed and vital religion. He is more than a material, or even intellectual being. He possesses, in addition to this, a *moral* nature, and as a moral being he must be studied, if his nature, history, and destiny are to be understood.

He may be a subject of inquiry ethnologically, physiologically, and intellectually—that is, in relation to his species, his material and rational organism; but until he is studied as a *spiritual* being, the wonders and powers of his complicated and glorious nature are still deeply veiled in their lonely grandeur from the eye, and man remains the profoundest mystery of the intelligent creation.

But Christianity places man in a new point of light, and constitutes him altogether a new object of study. The secret of this is in possession of the Christian student. It is this—The soul of man has been brought into vital contact with God, the great and holy Lord God, and *this* solves the mystery. Instinct with spiritual life, a partaker of the divine nature, a temple of the Holy Spirit, in a word, an entire new creature, he unfolds and exhibits powers of mind, and sensibilities of soul, a grandeur and sublimity of being, which the religion of Jesus and the grace of God alone could unveil, develop, and call into play.

The present incident of our narrative has suggested this train of thought. The joyous tidings are brought to Jacob that Joseph is really alive. He is overpowered by the information. The first announcement staggers his faith, and his heart dies within him. As doubt gives place to conviction, and conviction deepens into assurance, the spirit of Jacob revives, and he braces himself to meet the occasion. What a rich and instructive page in the believer's experience does this incident unfold! The fact that Christ is alive, the conflicting feelings which that fact produces, the varied emotions—unbelief and its reaction, the swooning and the reviving—are points of profound interest. May the Holy Spirit be our Teacher! I take them in their order—the TIDINGS—the FAINTING—the REVIVING.

With regard to the TIDINGS, there appears to have been three things involved in it of a most interesting and touching character—First, that Joseph was alive; second, that being alive, he was exalted to great dignity and power; and third, that, though thus exalted, he still remembered with affection and regarded with kindness his father's house. We shall pursue briefly these three points as illustrating some of the most vital, precious, sanctifying truths ever uttered in the ears of the believer in Jesus.

The first fact that this joyous intelligence conveyed to the aged patriarch was, that Joseph was alive: "Joseph is yet alive!" The image of his death—a death which to his mind had been attended with circumstances of such brutality—still flung its dark shadow on the spirit of Jacob; but in a moment, like an electric flash, the information is brought to him that his son, long lost, and, to his mind, long dead, was alive—actually living—and that he was now confronted by the witnesses of the astounding and thrilling truth. Beloved, what is the grand central truth of the gospel, the fact around which all its other facts revolve, and from which all other truths derive their vitality? Is it not that Jesus, our true Joseph, is *alive?*

Alas! we have to do in our present condition so much with *death*—death within, death without, death all around us, and the grim tyrant, with uplifted dart, standing at the very termination of our pilgrimage—how soothing and delightful it is for a child of God to turn from its contemplation, and find himself dealing with *life!* And what is the grand, quickening truth of the Bible—the great and precious fact that transmits its vitality to every part? It is a living Savior—a living Christ—a living Intercessor—in a word, that Jesus lives. When the first builders of the glorious temple of truth went forth to build the sacred fabric, like master workmen they laid the broad basis of the edifice in the glorious announcement, in the indisputable fact, that *Jesus was alive.* Could they but make good and demonstrate this one fact, the whole fabric of Christianity stood firm on a rock that no power could overthrow. We therefore find that the grand truth upon which the early preachers of Christianity everywhere dwelt was, not the Death of Christ, marvelous and precious as that fact was, but, the RESURRECTION of Christ, the confirmation and groundwork of His death. It was not so much that Christ was crucified, as that He was *risen*, that they testified; and for their testimony to this truth they were willing to endure scorn and ridicule, contempt and persecution, no, a martyr's death. Thus we read, "Wherefore of these men which have companied with us all the time that the Lord Jesus went in and out among us…must one be ordained to be a *witness with us of his resurrection*." "And with great power gave the apostles witness of the *resurrection* of the Lord Jesus." "Jesus, which was dead, whom Paul affirmed to be *alive*."

In these touching words Paul refers to the persecutions he endured for this truth:—"Persecuted, but not forsaken; cast down, but not destroyed; always bearing about in the body the dying of the Lord Jesus, that *the life* also of Jesus might be made manifest in our body." The daily persecution was the *dying* of the Lord Jesus; the daily succor and support was the manifestation of the *life* of the Lord Jesus. The very scars of the Lord Jesus that they bore were so many evidences that Christ was *alive*. Had not Christ risen from the dead, they had then been exempt from the hatred and persecution of the Sanhedrin, all whose power had been exerted to disprove and invalidate this one fact of Christianity, and this central doctrine of their preaching. But every epithet of scorn with which they were denounced, and every form of persecution through which they passed, but confirmed the fact that Jesus was alive. It was not likely that, simpleminded and feeble men as they were, they would be willing to endure all they did in testifying to what they knew to be false. No man will heroically sacrifice his life, or endure a moral martyrdom in support of a known *lie;* but when conscious that he is testifying to *a truth,* that he is witnessing to and ratifying *a fact,* if he is a man of integrity, honesty, and courage, he will be ready to seal his testimony with a martyr's death. Thus did the apostles—so important and precious to their heart was the truth that Jesus was *alive*.

And is the doctrine less sweet, precious, and blessed to us? Ah, no! Rob me of the truth that Jesus lives, take from me the great fact that Christ is alive at the right hand of God, and oh, you have thrown the pall of eternal death over all the bright hopes of my soul. But let my faith realize that Jesus lives, and that I live in Jesus, that I have a life from Jesus, that my eternal life is bound up with Jesus, that a living Christ supports and sustains me moment by moment, and that because Jesus lives I shall live also, and you have given me an object of hope that will bear me cheerfully onward through all the changing scenes and sufferings of life, painting its brilliant bow upon each dark cloud of my earthly pilgrimage; you have, in a word, thrown open to me the very portal of heaven. Let but this precious truth, by the power of the Spirit, be brought home to your heart when it is low, struggling with sin, fighting with temptation, battling with the world, when difficulties, trials, and depressions weave their web around your path—let but the blessed Spirit testify to your soul that Jesus lives, and lives to sustain you, to pray for you, to deliver you, and in a moment you are conscious of a new-born energy, you float in calmness and security upon the crest of the highest billow.

The touching incident of a little child sitting in the lap of its widowed, weeping mother, and looking up earnestly into her face, asked, "Mamma, is Jesus *dead?*" will be familiar to the reader. Gentle chiding! precious soothing from a babe's lips! Yes! God can teach and comfort us by a little child, if *this* be but the truth brought home in simple, touching earnestness to our sorrow-stricken heart. Jesus is not dead, but lives to bind up the broken heart, to dry the tear, and supply the needs of His saints—to cause the widow's heart to leap for joy, and to befriend, and guide, and comfort the orphan.

What though some human hopes are fled, what though some earthly friends are gone, what though some cherished joys are withered, Jesus lives, and you shall live through all life's trials, and through all eternity's glories—your life forever entwined with Christ in God.

But Joseph was not only alive, he was also exalted to great dignity, power, and wealth. He might have been alive, but still the slave for which his brethren sold him. He might indeed have been alive, but in great poverty, lowliness, and obscurity. So far from this being the case, he was not only alive, but he was advanced to be the chief man of the realm, second only to the king upon the throne. This fact must have imparted additional confidence and solace to the mind of the aged patriarch. Is it less a joyous, less a satisfying, less a precious fact to you to know that Jesus Christ has—as we have shown in the preceding chapter—passed through all the dark stages of His abasement and suffering, and is now enshrined in the glory which He had with the Father before the world was, with the added glory of mediatorial supremacy and government, sitting at the right hand of the Father, holding the scepter of universal empire, all powers and principalities subject to Him, and "waiting until his enemies be made his footstool?"

Oh, we ask, is it not a glorious and precious announcement to the Church that her Savior not only lives, but that He fills the central throne in heaven, that all beings bend before His majesty, and that He has power over all flesh? Is it not a precious truth to you that Jesus, once "a man of sorrows and acquainted with grief," once spit upon, insulted, tempted, crucified, is now exalted a Prince and a Savior, the triumphant Head of the Church, and is preparing to appear again in His glorified kingdom? Yes! it is a precious truth, that "him hath God highly exalted," and that in that exaltation and glory you who believe shall share.

There is another feature in this announcement that must have been precious, I had almost said, the most precious, because it was the most touching: it was, not only that Joseph was alive, and that he was exalted to great dignity, power, and wealth, but that he loved his father and that he remembered his brethren still, that he had purposes and thoughts of kindness and mercy towards those who his heart yearned to unfold. Beloved, not only is Jesus alive, not only is He exalted to great dignity, clothed with boundless power, and is possessed of endless wealth—all of which He exercises on your behalf—but He loves you, has purposes of mercy, and thoughts of peace, and feelings of compassion towards you, thinks of you, prays for you, is perpetually guarding your person and consulting your highest interests, until He sends His chariot to bear you home to Himself. "I go to prepare a place for you...I will come again to receive you unto myself; that where I am, there ye may be also." "I have prayed for thee, that thy faith fail not." Realize this precious truth, and it will shed many a bright gleam on your dreary way, and uplift your thoughts, affections, and hopes, from earth to heaven.

Let us now observe the effect of these tidings on Jacob's heart. How was the first information of this gladsome announcement received by the patriarch? Jacob's heart fainted through unbelief. The tidings seemed too great and joyous to be true. "And Jacob's heart fainted, for he believed them not." What an impressive and instructive illustration of that unbelief which marks our Christian course in some of its circumstances and stages in life—unbelief awakened by the very vastness, the very preciousness, the very joyousness of the truths of the gospel, of the words, the invitations, and promises of Jesus. In common language, it seems "too good to be true," too vast for *faith* to credit, too overpowering for the mind to grasp, too precious for the heart to receive.

Beloved, it is astonishing how faith and unbelief operate here. How diverse and opposite are their actings! For example, *faith* always looks at the *bright* side of a dark picture; *unbelief* always looks at the *dark* side of a bright picture. Unbelief often discards a fact because it is too vast and precious to believe; but faith can extract ofttimes from a dispensation that is gloomy and threatening, the sweetest joy and the brightest hope. Faith can transform a curse into a blessing; while unbelief will often turn a blessing into a curse. Do we not find something like this in our spiritual experience—unbelief not giving full, unquestioning, prompt credence to the revelation of God's Word, especially the announcements respecting a living Christ?

We might cite a Scripture instance of this. You are aware that when the first announcement was made to the Church of the resurrection of Christ, they could not believe, actually did not credit, the fact that the Lord was really alive, because of the overpowering joy that the tidings produced. And even when the fact that He was risen from the dead was confirmed by His actual and personal appearance among them, they still doubted! *"And while they believed not for joy, and wondered,* he said unto them, Have ye here any meat?" Mark the significant words, "they *believed not for joy."*

We now turn to our own Christian experience, as illustrating a few of the exercises of unbelief. In the first place, we cite the fact, the faint hold we have of the truth that Jesus is *alive* at the right hand of God, bearing our name on His heart, our burden on His shoulder, and with uplifted and pierced hands making intercession for us in

heaven. Does not the working of unbelief often rob you of
the power, the preciousness, and influence of this truth—
that Jesus is *alive?* Is not your faith's grasp of it often weak,
wavering, unrealizing? Oh! had we a stronger faith in the
fact that Jesus is actually alive, we should not be so often
and so deeply cast down as we are—succumbing to fears
within, and to conflicts without, to the dark and trying
providences which shade and sadden our path. We would
not believe that some day our enemy would prevail, that
we would at last come short of heaven. We would never
inquire, "Who shall roll us away the stone?" or, "Can God
furnish a table in the wilderness?" No! the reason why our
hands droop and our knees tremble in this glorious and
spiritual life is because our faith has such a vague, uncertain,
tremulous grasp of this gospel, vital truth—a risen, living,
loving, and interceding Christ. Oh, we are but half believers
in what the Bible says of Jesus, and in what Jesus himself
says.

Then, with regard to the *Promises* of God, see how our
faith is constantly at fault. The promises of God are the
divine affirmations and pledges of His faithfulness and love
to His saints. These "exceeding great and precious promises"
are God's promissory notes—to speak commercially—
which He has given us, assuring us that if we plead and
present these promissory notes in faith and prayer, He will
acknowledge, honor, and make them good. And yet, such
is the working of unbelief, that our hearts faint within us
under new trials and reverses, although we have these
precious promises of God to rely upon and to plead—all
pledging the unchanging love, the covenant faithfulness,
and the infinite power of God on our behalf; as if He had
not said, "For the mountains shall depart, and the hills be
removed: but my kindness shall not depart from thee,
neither shall the covenant of my peace be removed, saith

the Lord that hath mercy on thee." May we not, in view of this feeble, fluctuating faith that we have in the promises of God, and in the God of the promises, repeat the statement we have just made, that we do but *half* believe what we profess fully to believe!

How faint and dim, too, is our faith's realization of the eternal glory that awaits us! How little do we live on that precious truth—the certain salvation of every believer in Jesus, and the eternal glorification of every child of God? Did we more vividly realize it, we should be less desponding and discouraged by reason of the difficulties we meet, the inbred sins we combat, our own shortcomings, and Satan's constant suggestions. Did our faith more firmly believe that the Lord's flock, "the flock of the slaughter," shall never be plucked from the Shepherd's hand, that not one of them shall perish, that the weakest believer and the lowliest saint of God, the soul that has but touched in faith the border of the Savior's robe, shall finally and certainly be brought to glory, would it not enable us to enter more fully into the experience of the apostle, "Our light affliction, which is but for a moment, worketh for us a far more exceeding and eternal weight of glory"?

I will only refer to what ought to humble us very much, the weakness of our faith in the great and glorious fact of a *coming Lord*. Oh, how little does our faith deal with the glorious truth of the second personal advent of our Lord Jesus Christ! Beloved, the promise of a coming Savior has ever been the hope of God's Church. It was the hope of the Church of old. They saw His star in the dim, distant vista of time, believed and rejoiced. "Your father Abraham *saw my day*, and was glad." Faith in a promised and coming Messiah sustained them in persecution, bore them through trials, tuned their harps, inspired their prophecies, and shed the faint beams of the Sun of Righteousness upon their departing hours. The coming Christ, the glorious appearing of the Lord, is still the pole star of the saints of God, who are described as *"looking for* that BLESSED HOPE, and the *glorious appearing of the great God and our Savior Jesus Christ."*

My reader, if you are a believer in Jesus, you will be one of the blissful throng who will cluster around the descending form of the Son of God, when He comes in the clouds of heaven "to be glorified in his saints, and to be admired in all them that believe." He is coming to raise us from corruption, to perfect us in His own likeness, to reunite us to those who sleep in Him, to give us the victory over all our enemies, and to associate us with His glorious and eternal reign. "Wherefore, comfort one another with these words." Embrace this hope with stronger faith, and you will realize one of the most soothing, animating, sanctifying doctrines of revelation. "I will come again and receive you unto myself." Sweet words! "Come, Lord Jesus, come quickly," be your heart's response. Prophets sang of it, evangelists portrayed it, apostles wrote of it; let your faith embrace it, living and dying in the blessed hope of the personal advent of the Lord to consummate the glory and bliss of His saints. "Believe in the Lord your God, so shall ye be established; believe His prophets, so shall ye prosper."

We now reach the last part of the subject of the present chapter—*the reviving* of Jacob's faith. The depression of the aged patriarch was but momentary. There is just this difference between a regenerate and an unregenerate man— the unbelief of the unregenerate man is continuous, that of the child of God is but momentary. He may be greatly depressed because of unbelief, his heart sorrowing within him; but such is the divine nature, the indestructible energy of real faith, it ever emerges from the darkest cloud, floats upon the highest billow, and comes out of the battle bearing in its hand the spoils and the laurels of victory. See it illustrated in the history of Jacob; the depression was but momentary. Now came the uplifting, the revival of his drooping faith. What was it that roused its pulse, and restored him, as it were, to life? The first thing was, "they told him all *the words of Joseph;*" and these words were the first inspiration of his depressed and dejected spirit.

Beloved, what is it that truly and effectually revives the drooping faith, and uplifts the disconsolate spirit of the child of God—rolls off the melancholy that crushed his mind, and disperses the dark cloud that hung over his soul? Oh, it is *the words of Jesus!* Are there any words to you like His? When Christ comes and speaks a promise, and says to you, "Be not depressed, 'My grace is sufficient for thee;' be not cast down, 'My strength is made perfect in weakness;' be not disconsolate, 'I will come again and receive you unto myself;'" oh, what words so reviving, so quickening, and so cheering to the child of God as these words of Jesus? And when the Eternal Spirit brings the very words, statements, promises, and assurances of Jesus, unfolds them to the eye, whispers them to the ear, reveals them to the mind, engraves them on the heart, I ask you whether it has not been like an inspiration direct from heaven? Has it not been like a cordial to your fainting spirit? Has it not infused new life into your soul?

See how the angels at the tomb revived and cheered the drooping hearts of those holy women, who came with their spices early to the sepulcher, by the words of Jesus!—"And it came to pass, as they were much perplexed thereabout, behold, two men stood by them in shining garments: and as they were afraid, and bowed down their faces to the earth, they said unto them, Why seek ye the living among the dead? He is not here, but is risen: *remember how he spake unto you* when he was yet in Galilee, saying, The Son of man must be delivered into the hands of sinful men, and be crucified, and the third day rise again. *And they remembered his words.*"

And thus it is the Holy Spirit the Comforter revives and cheers the fainting hearts of God's people, by bringing to their remembrance and speaking to their hearts *the very words of comfort and promise and guidance which Jesus himself has spoken.* "But the Comforter," says Christ, "which is the Holy Ghost, whom the Father will send in my name, he shall teach you all things, *and bring all things to your remembrance, whatsoever I have said unto you.*" There are no words like those of Jesus for the nourishment of faith, for the quieting of conscience, for the guidance of our perplexities, and the reassuring of our confidence and hope. That one saying of Jesus is worth untold worlds, "Him that cometh to me I will in no wise cast out." Oh, cling to the revealed words of Christ, and esteem them more precious than gold, and sweeter than honey.

But we trace the reviving of the patriarch's faith to another cause, the power of *evidence:*—"And when *he saw the wagons* which Joseph had sent to carry him, the spirit of Jacob their father revived." Now, here was clearly the acting of faith, aided by the operation of sight. Seeing the wagons that Joseph had sent to carry him to Egypt, laden as they were with provision for the journey, there was evidence clear and unmistakable on which his drooping faith could rest. Here mark the condescension of the Lord to the weak and fainting faith of His disciples. I do not for a moment ignore the idea that the Lord may at times revive the heart of the drooping believer by sight as well as by faith, or, in other words, that faith is aided by sight. Were this idea rejected, we must ignore the institution of the Lord's Supper itself, for most assuredly, our faith in the death and atoning sacrifice of Jesus is essentially aided by these visible and expressive symbols.

And was it not so with Gideon? He was summoned to a great work, but his faith staggered, and he asked God for some evidence that He was true in what He promised, and God gave it to him. He asked that the fleece might be saturated with the dew of heaven, and God granted his request. Still his faith staggered, and he asked another evidence of His faithfulness, that the fleece might be all night on the earth and remain dry, and in the morning it was so; and thus God strengthened his faith by the evidence of sight.

We select a case in point from the New Testament— that of the unbelieving disciple, Thomas. He would not believe the evidence of the disciples that Jesus was alive. "Except I see in his hands the print of the nails, and put my finger into the print of the nails, and thrust my hand into his side, I will not believe." Jesus knew it. Presenting Himself in the midst of His assembled disciples, He singled out Thomas from the group, and said, "Reach hither thy finger, and behold my hands; and reach hither thy hand, and thrust it into my side: and be not faithless, but believing." As if He had said, "I will stoop to your weak faith, and will give you the evidence of *sight*; you shall see, and handle, and know that I am indeed your risen, living Lord."

Oh, the condescension of Jesus to weak faith! And when the eye of faith is dim, Christ will come and give you some sensible token or evidence that He is yours, that His word of promise, on which He has caused your soul to hope, shall be made good. God will have you *look* to your mercies, to your blessings, to all His dealings with your life, in order that your faith in Him may be revived and strengthened. He will have you throw back a glance on the past of your journey, trace all His providential interpositions on your behalf, and remember the time when your heart was

sorrowful, and how He comforted it; when your mind was
desponding, and how He sustained it; when your path was
dreary, and how cheered it; when your needs were pressing,
and how He supplied them; and when the cloud was dark,
and your trouble threatened and your foe was ready to
devour you, how He appeared for your help and deliverance.

Yes, God will have you look at these witnesses that He
is faithful to His promises and faithful to His saints. Listen
to the Psalmist—"I had *fainted*, unless I had *believed* to SEE
the goodness of the Lord in the land of the living. Wait on
the Lord: be of good courage, and he shall strengthen thine
heart, wait, I say, on the LORD." Thus may our soul be
found in holy waiting *upon*, and waiting *for* the Lord! The
wagons laden with tokens and pledges of heaven have come.
"Christ is risen from the dead, and become the *firstfruits* of
them that sleep." "And not only they, but ourselves…have
the *firstfruits* of the Spirit." Let us look at the promises and
the providences and the unspeakable Gift of God, and our
faith, so ready to fail, and our spirit, so prone to faint, will
be strengthened and revived, and we shall be preparing to
take our last stage home to God. "Faint, yet pursuing," will
be our motto, until faith is turned into sight, and we wake
up in glory perfected in His likeness, satisfied with all the
way by which the Lord our God conducted us there.

The Patriarch's Contentment and Resolve

THE SATISFACTION AND ANTICIPATION
OF FAITH

And Israel said, It is enough! Joseph my son is yet alive. I will go
and see him before I die. GENESIS 45:28

IF ever a plant was known by its flower, or a tree by its fruit,
it is the principle of *faith* implanted in the heart of man by
the Spirit of God. We considered in the last chapter the
swooning of faith through the excessive joy produced by
the tidings that Joseph was yet alive. We then glanced at
the revival of that drooping faith by the visible, tangible
evidence of the fact. "When he saw the wagons…the spirit
of Jacob their father revived." His faith was, as it were,
turned into sight, and this brought his mind into perfect
contentment and repose. We are, in the present chapter, to
meditate on a marvelous result of that revived faith—
perhaps one of the most striking and instructive illustrations
of this divine principle in the soul. What was it? And Israel
said, *"It is enough;* Joseph my son Joseph is yet alive. I will
go and see him before I die." This marks the highest point
of faith, the loveliest, and most fragrant fruit borne on that
divine plant—contentment and repose, amid all the dealings
of God. There are two points to which we would direct the

206

reader's attention—the PERFECT SATISFACTION, and the ANTICIPATED DEPARTURE.

The PERFECT SATISFACTION. And Israel said, "*It is enough.*" There is but one class of our race from whose lips, in truth and emphasis, this sentiment could breathe, and that is *the renewed and sanctified man.* Take the other and probably the largest portion of our species, and where will you find language corresponding with this, indicating the perfect repose and full satisfaction of the soul? Is not the cry of our unregenerate humanity that of the horseleech, "Give, give, give"? Is there not, as we have shown in the former part of this volume, a restlessness, marking every individual we meet, the language of which is, if properly interpreted, "Who will shew us any good?" No, our nature will never arrive at anything like perfect satisfaction until it finds its way back to God, drinks its happiness and draws its bliss from Him. Then it will adopt the language of the patriarch, "It is enough. I have obtained the chief good; I have found the jewel for which I have excavated earth's mine; I have plucked the flower that never dies, and have partaken of the fruit that never gluts, have drunk of the stream that has quenched my desire, and I shall thirst no more."

But these are only general observations; let us descend to a few particulars. What is implied in this language of the patriarch, "It is enough?" As I have already hinted, it expresses the feeling of full satisfaction: "It is *enough.*" Israel was now satisfied with all the government of God, satisfied with all that had transpired, satisfied with the present, and, as we shall show you presently, fully satisfied with regard to the future. Beloved, does not this feeling of full satisfaction find its corresponding experience in the bosom of every child of God? Most assuredly! The soul that has found God in Christ, that has been brought to rest in Jesus, that has tasted what is divine, spiritual, and heavenly, has in it an element, a feeling of perfect satisfaction.

Are you not satisfied with the Lord's gracious dealings with your soul, in choosing you to be His from all eternity? in directing all your course during your unconverted years? in effectually calling you by His sovereign grace to a knowledge of Himself? Are you not satisfied to rest your salvation on the one offering, the one atonement, the one sacrifice of the Lord Jesus? Are you not willing to accept Christ's righteousness as your justification, Christ's merit as your pardon, and Christ's work as the sole ground of your everlasting hope? Ah, yes! I anticipate your reply: "Heavenly Father, with such a Savior, with such a salvation, I am satisfied! It is enough, I want no more. I renounce my own righteousness, I cast from me my own merits, I utterly renounce my own works. I am satisfied to be saved as a poor, empty, self-condemned sinner, by faith in the atonement of Your dear Son, and go to heaven clad in no other robe, saved by no other merits, washed in no other fountain, than that which my Lord and Savior has graciously provided; and with Your salvation, from its beginning in eternity past to its consummation in eternity to come, blessed Lord, I am satisfied; it is enough!"

In connection with this feeling is the believer's perfect satisfaction *with all the conduct of God's providence*. During the process that God is providentially dealing with His people, there is often much that seems to ruffle the surface of the soul, disturbing its repose with a wavelet here, a billow there, and the swelling yonder. His providential dealings are sometimes so inexplicable, painful, and dark, that for a moment the child of God is, as it were, unbalanced. He begins to think that all these circumstances and events are about to militate against his best interests; and there cannot be, while that is transpiring, the feeling of perfect satisfaction. But let him calmly wait and trustfully hope until God Himself interprets these mystic symbols, gives him light on what now is so shaded, perfects the thing concerning him, and then, as he takes a retrospect on the past, he will say, "Lord, it is enough; I am perfectly satisfied with all Your dealings with me. I thought that stroke severe, I felt that burden crushing; I trembled as I entered into that cloud; my unbelieving heart murmured; but now, my God, my Father, in clearer light I can see it was a divine plan, a complete whole, a discipline of love, and my soul bows to the perfect rectitude of Your government, and my heart exclaims, It is enough, You have done all things well."

But, oh! the blessed period awaits us when we shall, with deeper emphasis of meaning, and more prolonged melody of song, exclaim, "It is enough; I shall be *satisfied* when I awake in thy likeness." The full, the perfect satisfaction is reserved when we enter glory, and look back on all the past, and see how wise, how loving, how holy, was the whole arrangement of God's gracious and providential dealings with us. "I shall be satisfied"—fully, forever *satisfied*—and exclaim, "It is enough!"

> "Enough, my gracious Lord,
> Let faith triumphant cry;
> My heart can on this promise live,
> Can on this promise die."

But these words are not only the expression of satisfaction, but they are *the reasoning and conclusion of faith*. It is faith traveling through dark and trying dispensations, and arriving at this its blessed goal—"It is enough." Whatever may be the trials and temptations of our faith, whatever the assaults made upon it by the subtle foe of God's people, whatever its depressions and becloudings, its soundings and strugglings, the ultimate conclusion to which the true believer arrives is this, "Lord, it is enough! I am perfectly content with the process You have taken to separate my faith from its foil, to purify it from its dross, though it has been as by fire. It is enough!" Does this page address one whose faith is severely assailed, painfully tried, perhaps deeply depressed? Let me remind you that whatever may be the present battle, temptation, or despondency of this principle, the issue will be triumphant. The language of Israel breathing from your lips will proclaim your victory, "It is enough. Every trial of my life has been more precious than gold; and now that the storm has passed, and I can calmly view all the way You have led me, my heart in the depth of its satisfaction exclaims, It is enough!"

Nor must I omit to add that these words of the patriarch express *praiseful gratitude.* The soul of Israel was now touched with the true spirit of praise, in the review of all the past of God's conduct. The harp, so long silent on the willows, plucked from thence, now breathed the softest and sweetest strains of thanksgiving and praise to Him to whom all praise is due. He seems to be brought into similar experience with David, who, after tracing the gracious dealings of God with him, exclaimed, "Return unto thy rest, O my soul; for the Lord hath dealt *bountifully* with thee!" Such was the spirit, if not the language, of Israel: "It is enough, my soul. My past history, painful, chequered, and somber though it has been, rude and thorny though my way, yet the Lord has dealt bountifully with me. He has kept me alive in famine, He has brought up as from the grave my long lost child, He has clothed with sunshine life's closing evening; and now, return unto your rest, O my soul; for the Lord has dealt bountifully with you!" Such, my reader, will be your language, whatever may be the path along which God is conducting you, or whatever may be the landscape of life now unfolding to your eye. Yes; you shall at last be brought to this blessed conclusion, "The Lord my God has dealt liberally and bountifully with me; return unto your rest, O my soul! It is enough."

We reach the second point—the ANTICIPATED DEPARTURE: "I will go and see him before I die." It is quite clear that thoughts of life's close, anticipations of the termination of his long pilgrimage, occupied the mind of Israel. It was natural that it should be so. And yet we sometimes meet with examples of extreme old age, associated, too, with a religious profession, in which there is such an absence of the idea of death, such a faint conception of the nearness of eternity, as presents one of the most affecting and solemn spectacles in human life.

We scarcely can conceive of a more melancholy sight than old age, not only without religion, but without any serious thought of death! With the last enemy almost at the door—with eternity about to burst upon the soul in all its dread reality, its personal scrutiny, its solemn judgment, its final and changeless destiny—and yet to trace the indifference, the worldliness, the covetousness, the scheming, that marks so many standing on the brink of the grave, its very earth crumbling beneath their feet, is a phenomenon in the history of our race over which angels might weep. But not so was it with the aged patriarch. He realized that he was an old man, that life's taper-light was almost extinguished, and he seemed to hear the music of Jordan's waves as they murmured in sweet cadence at his feet. He felt that the time of his departure was at hand; and, in the solemn realization of the fact, he girded himself to meet life's last mission at the bidding of God. "Joseph my son is yet alive: I will go and see him before I die."

An impressive event is referred to in those words, *"I die!"* Whether uttered by youth, by middle age, or by hoary hairs, they are words of solemn import—"I DIE!" Oh, it is an overwhelming thought, that through that portal our spirit must pass. Through that shaded valley, along that gloomy pathway to eternity, *you* must travel. Are you prepared, my reader, *to die?* Have you solemn thoughts of death? Are you taking it into the account? Are you so numbering your days, fast fleeting and few, as to apply your heart to heavenly wisdom?

"*I die.*" Oh, interpret the solemn words, view the impressive truth in the light of the gospel, in the exercise of faith in Jesus, and the whole character of death is changed, the whole scene is transformed. "I do not die," exclaims the believer; "I only sleep in Jesus. I do not die, I languish into life. Mine will be a departure, a translation, a soft slumber in which there are no fitful, fevered dreams. Absent from the body, I shall in one moment be present and forever with the Lord."

But what made the thought of death so pleasant, its prospect so cheerful, its coming so hopeful to the aged saint? It was the sight of Joseph! "Joseph is yet alive: *I will go and see him before I die.*" The living Christ—on whom we repose, as Israel's eye rested on his living son Joseph, is the grand preparation for death. No individual can meet death with dignity, composure, and hope, but as by faith he sees Christ and Christ is in him. We need no other preparation for death but a living faith in a living Savior. Here is your true and only preparation for death, my reader—Christ in you the hope of glory. As we shall return to this thought in a subsequent part of this work, we will be content now simply and briefly to remind you who are all your life subject to bondage through fear of death, that when death comes, a living Christ will come with it; therefore, do not die a thousand deaths in anticipating one. Leave your departure to Him who is the "Resurrection and the Life," who will accompany the "king of terrors," the white-robed messenger; and as the earthly house is being dissolved, beam after beam removed, pin after pin loosened, a living Christ in you will lift you, in calmness, grandeur, and dignity, above the wreck and ruin of your mortality, and you shall sing—

> "Jesus can make a dying bed
> Feel soft as downy pillows are,
> While on His breast I lean my head,
> And breathe my soul out sweetly there."

This suggests our last remark. A living Christ, clung to by faith, will fill the soul with longing desires to depart and be with Jesus. You will say, "Jesus is alive, I will go and see Him, and be with Him forever." Oh, beloved, nothing will make you so long to break from the body of sin and death, to sever even the fondest, sweetest, dearest ties of nature, as having your faith firmly rooted and grounded in the doctrine of a living Christ! It will intensify your desire to depart and be with Jesus. What made Jacob so willing to leave Canaan? Was not his estate there? Was not his pleasant homestead there? Were not all the sweet, fond, sacred associations of birth, of family, and of friendship there? Yes; but Joseph in Egypt eclipsed it all, and he exclaimed, "Joseph my son is yet alive: I will go and see him before I die."

With this I close. Get more of a living Christ in your believing heart, and your heart more deeply enshrined in heaven with Jesus, and then, sweet and fond and precious as are earth's attractions now, you will pant to sunder from them all, and fly away and be forever with the Lord.

The Patriarch's Solemn Sacrifice

THE CHRISTIAN'S DEVOUT
ACKNOWLEDGEMENT OF GOD

And Israel took his journey with all that he had, and came to
Beersheba, and offered sacrifices unto the God of his father
Isaac. And God spake unto Israel in the visions of the night,
and said, Jacob, Jacob. And he said, Here am I. And he said, I
am God, the God of thy father: fear not to go down into
Egypt; for I will there make of thee a great nation: I will go
down with thee into Egypt; and I will also surely bring thee
up again: and Joseph shall put his hand upon thine eyes.
GENESIS 46:1-4

IT is a holy precept, coupled with a divine promise, precious
and priceless above rubies to those who have tested its
value—"In all thy ways acknowledge him, and he shall direct
thy paths." Here is the eye directed to the true pole star of
the believing soul—JEHOVAH. No light other than that
which beams from this source can safely conduct him a
solitary step. All other light is but the spark of a man's own
kindling, in which he shall lie down in sorrow. But how
simple and clear the divine rule, "In all thy ways
acknowledge him." Set Him before you, that He may be
the one object you have in view. Take not a step without
seeking His guidance, consulting His will, studying His
glory. Consider that He is ever present with you, shaping

your course, guiding your steps, and acquainted with all your ways. If His providences are adverse, bow to His sovereignty, be still, and know that He is God. If prosperous, be humble, be praiseful, and ascribe to Him all the honor.

Thus walking in the precept, He will fulfill the promise—"He shall direct thy paths." Those paths, whatever they may be, will be just what He makes them. In things temporal and spiritual, He will order all and provide all—will keep your feet from sliding in the smooth path, and from wounding and weariness in the rough.

Such was the spirit and the conduct of the patriarch. Passing into a new epoch of his history, entering upon the last and most solemn stage of life's march, he would commence as he must close it—*alone with God.* It was, indeed, a new and untraveled path. He had not passed this way before. It was pre-eminently one of faith. True to the God he loved, the religion he had professed, the life of faith he had lived, and the habits of communion he had maintained, before he fully embarks upon the journey, he rears an altar to the God of his father and his own God, and offers upon it a holy and solemn sacrifice. How much we may learn of Christ and His Church in this impressive incident of the patriarch's life! May the Holy Spirit be our Teacher while we meditate upon the SACRIFICE—the VISION—the PROMISE.

"And Israel took his journey with all that he had, and came to Beersheba, *and offered sacrifices unto the God of his father Isaac."*

Here was that which identified unmistakably the child of God, the man of prayer, the man who felt that he had to deal with God in all the places and circumstances of his eventful life. He arrives at Beer-sheba—a sacred and memorable spot in its historic associations, for it was here his father Isaac had once reared an altar and offered sacrifice to Jehovah. It is most refreshing and instructive to mark the elevated sanctity of mind in which this sacrifice originated. God had emptied him from vessel to vessel. He had commanded wave upon wave to surge over him, cloud upon cloud to shade his pilgrimage, until at last his home was broken up, all its hallowed associations buried, as it were, in oblivion; and at his advanced period of life, he was summoned to take a long journey into a strange land.

And yet, though God had thus dealt with him so strangely, mysteriously, shall I say, painfully?—there seemed not one hard thought of God in his mind, not one rebellious feeling in his heart, nothing which betrayed a spirit of opposition and resentment, which, if interpreted, would seem to say, "You have taken from me blessing after blessing; You have rooted up my resting-place, have visited me with bereavement and with famine, and are now, in old age, leading me into a strange land, and I do well to be angry." Ah, no! the very reverse of this was his holy state of mind. On the threshold of his journey, he rears an altar, and offers upon it sacrifice to the Lord God of Jacob—a sacrifice expressive of a perfect justification of Jehovah in all His dealings, and his full satisfaction with all the way God had led him.

But look for a moment at the import of this sacrifice that Israel offered to God in view of his contemplated journey. In the first place, this sacrifice was a recognition of God *as the God of his pious ancestors, and especially the God of his father.* The words of the narrative are expressive, "And offered sacrifices *unto the God of his father Isaac.*" Here was Jacob recognizing the fact that Jehovah had been the covenant God of his forefathers. Beloved, God would have His people ever remember what He has been in years gone by to their pious ancestors. It is good to recount, and gratefully to acknowledge, what He was to those who have gone before us, that we may learn to put our trust in God, and embalm in our memories and hearts His providential and gracious dealings in their history.

But especially is it proper and profitable to remember Him as the God of our *godly parents.* "Thine own friend, and thy father's friend, forsake not." Who was your father's, your mother's friend? Who but the covenant God and Father of all the families of Israel? Is there no blessing to be found, no strengthening of our faith, no comfort in our sorrow, no heart-cheer in our depression, to remember what God was to those so near and dear to us, but who are now with Him in glory; to remember His faithfulness, to call to mind His providential interpositions, how they called upon Him and He answered, how He supplied their needs, how He supported them in adversity, how He lavished upon them tokens of His grace and love? Oh, yes, there is a blessing in the hallowed remembrance; and insensible is that individual to the lovingkindness of the Lord who can retrace the history of His dealings with a godly parent and feel no melting of heart, and no strong emotion of gratitude; who with his sacrifices and offerings to God entwines no filial memories, hallowed, grateful, praiseful.

But Jacob did not forget his father Isaac, nor his father's God. The God of his father was equally his God. All that God was to Isaac, Jacob felt He was to him. There were precious promises, and rich benedictions, and glorious covenants made with his father Isaac, handed down to him, on which his faith could take hold and plead with God as sacred heirlooms and precious legacies bequeathed from the holy sire to the son. It is a delightful thought, beloved, that the same covenant of grace to which our pious parents clung, in which they rested, belongs to us. We who believe in Jesus have the same interest in that covenant that they had, the same covenant God, the same covenant Redeemer.

Oh, is it not encouraging to remember that we are now reaping from their prayers, their wrestlings, their faith in God, a golden harvest of blessing? Oh, endeavor to realize that the God of your fathers is your God too, and that all He was to them in making good His covenant, in fulfilling His promises, in answering their prayers, He is now to you, the child of many a father's holy wrestlings, of many a mother's weeping and prayers. "O LORD, truly I am thy servant, *and the son of thine handmaid;* thou hast loosed my bonds." Yes, God delights in us when we go to His mercy-seat and praisefully remember His faithfulness and lovingkindness to those loved ones who a little while have gone before us to heaven.

This sacrifice that Jacob offered also marked *his personal habit of communion with God.* He walked with God in holy converse; he was a man of prayer, a man who lived as beholding the Invisible. He recognized the Lord God of heaven to be his God, and it was his privilege and delight, as it was his obligation and duty, to hold communion and converse with the Lord God of heaven. And in addressing himself to this journey we find him first addressing himself *to prayer.* There is not, beloved, a stronger characteristic of the real man of God, the true believer in Christ, than that he is a man of *prayer.* Let him be in what circumstances he may, in what part of the world he may, in what troubles, temptations, trials he may, he will always have an altar, and on that altar he will always lay a sacrifice of praise, prayer, and thanksgiving to God.

Prayer with us ought to be an element so natural, communion with God a privilege so familiar, that wherever we are, in whatever society we are thrown, or in whatever circumstances we are placed, there should be this altar and the sacrifice to God. Oh, be assured of this, that the professing Christian who can leave his closet altar, his family altar, his social altar, his public altar at home when he travels abroad, or who can postpone his sacrifice of prayer and praise to a more convenient season, knows but little, if anything, of what it is to *walk* like Enoch and Noah and Israel with God. But a man of God is a man of prayer, a man of converse with God, in any place or circumstance or society. O beloved, let this mark you: be men of God and men of prayer, wherever His providence may place you— at home, on a journey, abroad. Forget not that, like Jacob, it is your privilege to build an altar to the sacrifice of prayer and praise, and maintain close, uninterrupted converse with God.

But above, and more expressive, than all, doubtless, there was in the sacrifice that Israel offered *the foreshadowing of the great sacrifice of the Son of God.* We have no doubt whatever that the patriarch's faith looked down the long vista of future ages, and in the sacrifice that he then offered up on the altar that he reared at Beersheba, his believing heart rose above the sacrifice—beheld and rested in a crucified Savior. And this would impart a character, a fragrance, a solemnity preeminently significant and holy to the sacrifice he then offered to the God of his father. There can be no doubt that the patriarchal faith rested in Christ at that moment. The words of Jesus with regard to Abraham are significant of this, "Abraham *saw my day,* and was glad." Now, if Abraham by faith saw Christ's day, Jacob, who was still nearer its glorious dawn than he, must by faith have caught a yet brighter vision of Him; and the sacrifice he now presented would be a solemn profession of his faith in the diviner sacrifice which the Son of God would offer for his sins on the distant altar of Calvary. Thus Jesus crucified was the substance of all the sacrifices both of the Levitical and of the patriarchal saints. Oh, how delightful to find Him who is "the chief among ten thousand," the joy of the saints on earth, the song of the redeemed in heaven, living and speaking and shining amid these twilight shadows, the object of faith and love to the saints who by faith saw His day and were glad!

Oh, let all your sacrifices be associated in faith and praise with the one atoning sacrifice of Jesus Christ! Let us remember that that which gives perfume to our prayers and melody to our praises, which presents our consecrated person to God with divine acceptance and delight, is the one offering and sacrifice of Jesus. And if the patriarchal saints saw in the dimness of their faith, amid almost darkness, the sacrifice of Christ, embraced it, and died in its blessed hope, how much more clear should be our views, and simple our faith, and intense our love, and deeper our holiness, who live amid the meridian light and effulgence of a dispensation whose distinctive history and signal glory is that Christ has come, and that He has died for our offenses, and is risen again for our justification! May this glorious sacrifice become daily more precious to our hearts and sanctifying to our lives!

Thus much for the sacrifice that Jacob offered in anticipation of this journey. Learn from it one practical truth: embark in no enterprise in life, enter on no stage in your pilgrimage, address yourself to no new epoch in your history, without first rearing an altar, and acknowledging the Lord God of Abraham, of Isaac, and of Jacob, as your God. The divine injunction with which this chapter of our work opens stands like a beacon-light amid the rocks and shoals and breakers of life, illumining the voyager's perilous pathway to eternity. It contains both a *precept* and a *promise*—the precept of *divine acknowledgment*, and the promise of *divine guidance*. Obey the one—God will fulfil the other. Oh, begin your day, your enterprise, your service, your journey with an altar and a sacrifice. ACKNOWLEDGE the LORD! And offer the sacrifice of faith, of love, and of praise. Then may you with confidence trust the Lord to guide, shield, and prosper you. This God of Israel will be your God forever and ever, and He will be your GUIDE even unto death.

Having thus considered the state of mind with which the patriarch addresses himself to his journey, let us now study the HEAVENLY VISION with which he was favored. After he had built an altar, and offered up sacrifice to the God of his father, lo! the heavens opened, and a glorious vision burst upon his view—"And God spake unto Israel in the visions of the night, and said, Jacob, Jacob. And he said, Here am I. And he said, I am God, the God of thy father: fear not to go down into Egypt." Each particular of this divine response to the patriarch's solemn act of worship is replete with deep spiritual truth. It would seem as if this must have transpired, as though it would have been impossible that there should have been no immediate response from God to an act of devotion, of gratitude, of praise, and faith so marked and precious as this.

God did not lose a moment in acknowledging the sacrifice and petition of His servant. The altar had scarcely been reared, the incense of the sacrifice had scarcely ascended, when, lo! a heavenly vision bursts on the soul of the worshiping patriarch. Now, there is much that is spiritually instructive in this heavenly vision, to which for a moment we will turn our thoughts. The first thing that strikes us is the close and intimate nearness into which Israel was brought to God. Jehovah and the patriarch stood face to face. There could not have been the shadow of a doubt on his mind that he was now in solemn audience with God—the God of his father Isaac, and his God. O privileged saint of the Most High! to be so near the Infinite Fountain of light, life, and love. Honored man of God! to be favored with a vision of the Divine glory and power such as angels might have coveted. But is not God as near to His people now? Most assuredly! What does the Lord himself say? "He that loveth me shall be loved of my Father, and I will love him, and will *manifest myself* to him." "My Father will love him, and we will come unto him, and make our *abode* with him."

Oh, we live at too great a distance from God! We forget how close, filial, and precious may be the communion of the believer with the Invisible One. I speak not of visions like those of Jacob or of Paul, bursting with splendor on my eye—I ask not to hear audibly the awful voice of God—but, with the blood of atonement in my hand, I can penetrate the mysterious veil, and enter into the holiest, and talk with God and commune with Him as really—as closely—and as blessedly as when Jacob uplifted his eye and saw heaven open, and God talking with him from His glorious throne.

The way into God's presence is more fully opened by the sacrifice and blood of Jesus than it ever was, even when by vision or dream or voice God spoke to His saints of old. The blood of Christ is so powerful, the atonement of the Son of God is so glorious, the intercession of Christ at the right hand of the Father is so prevailing, and faith is so much more far-seeing an eye than that of sense, that a man of God coming into His presence by the blood of the everlasting covenant may enjoy fellowship and converse with God more close, more filial, more real and holy, than that which marked Abraham, Isaac, and Jacob. Seek, oh, seek it, then. Be not content with standing in the outer courts, when the blood gives you admission into the holiest. "Having therefore, brethren, boldness to enter into the holiest by the blood of Jesus, by a new and living way, which he hath consecrated for us, through the veil, that is to say, his flesh; and having an high priest over the house of God; let us *draw near.*"

And mark the time of this divine vision. It would seem as if God almost invariably selected the *night-season* of their experience for the marvelous manifestations of Himself to His people. Night-visions of God were familiar to Jacob. How vividly would he remember the memorable night when, a fugitive from the vengeance of Esau, and an exile from his home, there appeared to him in his sleep the vision of the ladder, God speaking to him from above it in words of comfort and promise! Would he not, even in that early part of his eventful life, behold in this ladder an impressive symbol of the incarnate Son of God, the Mediator between heaven and earth, on the mystic rounds of which his faith would ascend to God reconciled in Christ?

Yet more vivid and hallowed would be the remembrance of the long night at Peniel, when the Divine Angel, with whom he wrestled and whom he overcame, knighted him as a prince of God, mighty and prevalent in prayer. A third time God appears to His servant in the night, by an extraordinary and gracious vision, at a most important crisis of his history, as if the Lord would close the patriarch's earthly pilgrimage, as He had commenced it, with those glorious and consolatory manifestations of Himself, so timely and so precious to the heart in seasons of sorrow and despondency.

There is much to us that is precious and soothing in this thought. When our mental and spiritual exercises are with us as though it were night; when our path is shaded; when soul-depression and heart-crushing sorrow, loneliness and dreariness, drape the landscape of life; in this night season when most need a word of comfort and a ray of light, the most need some assurance of His faithfulness and love—lo! the gracious vision transpires, and a blessed manifestation takes place, and God in Christ draws near, reveals Himself, or speaks a promise, and so gives a song in the night.

Such was the season in which the Psalmist strengthened himself in the Lord his God. How affecting his language, "In the day of my trouble I sought the Lord: my sore ran *in the night,* and ceased not: my soul refused to be comforted…Thou *holdest mine eyes waking:* I am so troubled that I cannot speak. I call to remembrance my song *in the night.*"

Yes, the sweetest songs that ever flowed from pilgrims' lips are those of the night. The Lord Jesus knows your night sorrow, loneliness, and widowhood; and He will come at that season and graciously manifest Himself to your soul, and you shall know what it is to meditate on your bed in the night watches, and your meditation of Him shall be sweet.

Then mark the divine call: "And God spake unto Israel and said, Jacob, Jacob!" There is something very beautiful and touching in the truth that God has a special knowledge of the personal names, places, and circumstances of His people. "The foundation of God standeth sure, having this seal, *The Lord knoweth them that are his.*" He knows you personally, your position, your individual infirmities, trials, and needs. The names of His people are engraved on the palms of His hands, and are worn upon His heart. Is it not a delightful thought? Do not overlook God's personal transactions with you. Do not lose yourself in the crowd of saints, for your God and Father does not. The child of God, pursuing, perchance, a path that isolates him from his fellow-pilgrims, is as profoundly dear and precious to God as if he were the only being He loved and cared for in the universe. Try and realize that your personal circumstances, your individual needs and heart-sorrows, God takes cognizance of, cares for, and feels an interest in. And often, if the ear of faith is but wakeful to His voice, you will hear Him as if calling you by name, and addressing Himself to you with all the yearning tenderness and loving familiarity of a gracious father to his child.

Now, mark the immediate response of Israel: "And he said, Here am I." God spoke, Jacob answered; God called, Jacob responded. Are we as ready to hear and to respond to God's voice when He speaks to us in instruction, in doctrine, in precept, in rebuke, as in comfort and in guidance? Truly, I fear not. How often has God spoken once, yes, twice, and we have not heard! Oh to have an ear wakeful to the still small voice of His Spirit dwelling in us—an ear so hearkening, so exquisitely harmonized to His voice, that though it may speak in the subdued tones of some overwhelming trial, or in the gentle accents of love, we may hear it! "My sheep *hear* my voice."

Another instructive feature in Jacob's reply was his willingness to do whatever God enjoined. The promptness of his response indicates the willingness of his mind to obey. Let us cultivate, beloved, a willingness to obey the voice of the Lord our God. "Here am I, Lord; what will You have me to do? Speak, for Your servant hears. I stand ready to go where You bid, to stay where You require, to do what You command, to yield what You ask, to suffer what You send; I am Your servant, Your child; Your will is my will, Your pleasure my pleasure." O holy, blessed state of mind! Cultivate it in the spirit of prayer and dependence upon the all-sufficient grace of Christ.

We now reach the DIVINE ASSURANCE: "Fear not to go down to Egypt, for I will there make of thee a great nation. I will go down with thee to Egypt; and I will also surely bring thee up again: and Joseph shall put his hand upon thine eyes." If ever the kindness and love of God towards

His dear saint was manifest and palpable, it is now. Let us gaze upon the picture until our soul melts into love and admiration before it. Here was His aged servant in a new position, begirt with strange and trying circumstances. God appears at the very juncture to succor, support, and assure him of an interest in His faithfulness and love.

Consider the twofold acknowledgment:—First, "I am God." Could Jehovah place before him a higher trust of faith than this? Only let God speak that word to your heart, my beloved, and however low that heart may be, however deeply immersed in sorrow, adversity, and trial, your faith stands upon the Rock that is higher than you, and higher than the highest billow through which you wade. The truth with which Jehovah here met the position of His servant is that with which He would meet yours—His own all-sufficiency. Is He not constantly challenging you, "Is any thing *too hard* for me, saith the LORD God?" Now, take the loftiest mountain that casts its deep, long shadow on your path, or the weightiest stone that seals the grave of some buried blessing, bring it in contact with the infinite sufficiency of God, and, lo! the mountain falls and the stone is rolled away! Oh we deal too little with the *power*, the *infinite sufficiency* of our God! Lord, increase my faith in it! Let me not limit You, Holy One of Israel! Oh, then, let your faith realize that God is your God in Christ, your Father, your Friend, your God all-sufficient, and you shall laugh at impossibilities, you shall overcome all those impediments that seemed to intercept the blessing for which you have long prayed and looked.

The second assurance of God was still more calculated to strengthen the mind of His servant in the anticipation of what was before him: "I am the God of thy father." What touching words are these! Perhaps you are ready to ask, "What connection had this with Isaac? His was a past and bygone victory." True, but though dead, he yet spoke. The interests of Isaac and of Jacob were closely entwined. The promises God had made to Isaac, the prayers Isaac had offered, were now to be fulfilled and answered in Jacob's experience. We have much to do with God's dealings with our pious parents. Their personal and bygone history is a part of our own. They still live in us their children; their good name is entrusted to our keeping; their honor is confided to our hands—it is in our power to preserve undimmed the luster of their lives, and to preserve, embalmed in our holy walk, the fragrance of their memories unimpaired.

Under what responsibility, then, are we placed, and by what solemn obligations are we bound, in consequence of God's dealings with our parents! When God would comfort us, when He would strengthen our drooping faith, and cheer our depressed and desolate heart, is it nothing that He says to us, "Fear not, be not dismayed, my child; I was your father's Father, your mother's God. All that I was to them, will I be to you." Is there nothing for faith to take hold of here? How touchingly does David recognize this truth in his dying charge to his son—his successor to the throne. "And thou, Solomon my son, *know thou the God of thy father,* and serve him with a perfect heart and with a willing mind: for the Lord searcheth all hearts and understandeth all the imaginations of the thoughts: but if thou forsake him, he will cast thee off for ever."

These words of God to His servant were well calculated to allay all his trembling and timidity: "Fear not to go down into Egypt; I will go down with thee into Egypt." Just the timely assurance that he needed. And thus, beloved, does our God seek to prepare us for duty, for trial, for service, by prefacing every new chapter in our history with divine assurances of His faithfulness, power, and love. "Fear not."

What a favorite expression was this of Jesus when He tabernacled in the flesh! How often He breathed it in the ears of His timid disciples! "Fear not, it is I." And still He speaks it to you—this *same* Jesus! Lord, speak these soothing, assuring words to my trembling heart, and my soul shall be quiet and trustful as a weaned child!

> "The billows swell, the winds are high,
>   Clouds overcast my wintry sky;
>   Out of the depths to Thee I call;
>   My fears are great, my strength is small.
>
> "O Lord, the pilot's part perform,
>   And guide and guard me through the storm;
>   Defend me from each threatening ill;
>   Control the waves; say, 'Peace, be still!'
>
> "Amidst the roaring of the sea,
>   My soul still hangs her hope on Thee;
>   Thy constant love, Thy faithful care,
>   Is all that saves me from despair."

Having thus allayed his fears by the assurance that His presence should accompany his emigration into Egypt, God then gives him *a threefold promise:* "I will there make of thee a great nation; I will also surely bring thee up again; Joseph shall put his hand upon thine eyes;"—all of which God literally and faithfully performed. God increased his seed in Egypt greatly; Joseph closed his eyes in death; his bones were borne back to Canaan and interred in Machpelah, and, after four hundred years, his posterity were brought up out of Egypt back to Canaan with a great and glorious deliverance.

Thus—and this shall be the closing lesson of the chapter—however low God may bring His people, though it be as into Egyptian exile, bondage, servitude, He will yet lead them out of this earthly Egypt up to the heavenly

Canaan, into which no "Pharaoh" shall ever enter, and from which no "son of Jacob" shall ever depart. And when the time arrives that you shall be gathered to your fathers, Jesus, your true Joseph, will come, and closing your eyes in death, will gently lay His right hand upon you, saying, "Fear not; I am the first and the last: I am he that liveth, and was dead; and, behold, I am alive for evermore, Amen; and have the keys of hell and of death."

Jacob Sees Joseph and Desires to Die

A SIGHT OF JESUS IN DEATH

And Joseph made ready his chariot, and went up to meet Israel
his father, to Goshen, and presented himself unto him; and
he fell on his neck, and wept on his neck a good while. And
Israel said unto Joseph, Now let me die, since I have seen thy
face, because thou art yet alive. GENESIS 46:29-30

AND still our chief and entrancing theme is Christ and His
people. And as the twilight shades of this exquisite page of
patriarchal history grow more attenuated and luminous,
our portrait assumes more distinctness of outline, beauty
of form, glow and warmth of tint. We reach in the present
stage of the story its most heartfelt and suggestive chapter—
the meeting of the aged patriarch and his long-lost but
recovered son, with the emotion it awakened and the desire
it inspired. Each of these points—the MEETING, the
EMOTION, and the DESIRE will be found highly illustrative
of one of the most interesting stages of the Christian's
spiritual experience.

The MEETING is that of Joseph and his father's house.
The chief figure of the group is the aged sire. They had
been separated widely and long. The victim of a cruel
imposture, for years he had nursed his loss in lonely grief,
and was now approaching that goal of a good man's life,
where "the wicked cease from troubling, and the weary are

230

at rest." But his sun shall not set enshrouded in gloom and sorrow. Happier scenes and brighter hours are in reserve. A resurrection as from the dead awaits him. Crushed and long-buried hopes are about to bloom into life again, scattering flowers of brightness and perfume on his few remaining steps to the tomb.

Pause at this stage of the narrative, and receive the comforting instruction the God of Jacob would send you. The world is full of the divine idea of a *resurrection*. Nothing entirely perishes—nothing is wholly annihilated. Nature teaches it, as the earth throws off her wintry robe, and arrays herself in the vernal life and beauty of spring. Providence teaches it, as it wins back to us blessings we had for a while lost—health restored, wealth recovered, friends found again. Grace teaches it in the comforting and sublime hope of the gospel, that "As in Adam all die, even so in Christ shall all be made alive." Take the consolation of this truth. You are, perchance, mourning the fading of manly vigor, or the loss of earthly substance, or the removal of some object of deep love whom God has taken from you either by the stroke of death, the estrangements of life, or the vicissitudes of time—some being of your heart in whom you had garnered up its best affections and fondest hopes.

Oh! deem not your blessing irrevocably lost—entombed never to rise again. Ah, no! bright angels watch that grave, celestial sentinels guard that treasure. And when God shall have taught you, and you shall have learned the blessed and precious lessons He designed to convey by the discipline, He will utter His majestic, all-commanding, all life-giving voice, "Come forth!" and you shall clasp once more the long-lost, long-buried mercy. Oh! let not the words again escape our lips, "All these things are against me!" Precious Jesus! I would enjoy You in all my blessings, and merge all my blessings in You. If You are my Life, my

Portion, my All, then my interests for time and for eternity are safe.

Let us, then, contemplate the spiritual instruction that the meeting with Joseph conveys. How illustrative is this of the first meeting between Christ and the believing soul, when He comes in the chariot of His *converting grace!* If, in the life of the believer, there is an epoch traced by its solemn momentousness—an event never fading from his memory—a picture upon which he will gaze with deeper wonder throughout eternity—it is that which marks his first espousals to Jesus, that period of his life when Christ met him by the mighty power of His effectual grace, drew him to His feet, and there revealed Himself to him as his Savior. I am now but faintly portraying one of the most entrancing periods of your history.

Can you look back to the time when the Savior brought you to Himself—when His effectual grace called you— when the Divine Spirit quickened you, convinced you of sin and the condemnation you were under by the law— when Christ met you, manifested Himself to you, revealed His great salvation, awoke your heart to joy, inspired hope, and gave you to know that your sins were pardoned, and that your person was accepted? I ask, can you review that period of your personal history, and feel no deep and hallowed emotion? Whatever, then, may be the shadows that have since intervened, whatever may have been the misgivings, doubts, and fears through which you have passed, I do earnestly beseech you to carry back your thoughts to that blessed hour when Christ took you just as you were to be His disciple, and you took Christ just as He is to be your Savior, entering into a covenant with Him, and in that solemn hour you became His. O blessed espousals, when the soul, in the joy of its first love, can exclaim, "I am my Beloved's, and my Beloved is mine!"

This meeting illustrates, too, the interviews between Christ and His brethren—those gracious and special manifestations known only by the Church. It is a distinctive feature of the Christian religion, that it involves the manifestation of the Divine presence. A religion that is lacking in this, as one of its distinctive elements, is at best a dubious religion. It is an essential attribute of the religion of a true believer, that he realizes gracious interviews with Jesus; that he knows what it is to walk in personal converse with God; that at times he basks in the sunshine of God's countenance. His religion is a religion of fellowship with the Father, of communion with the Son. He knows from personal experience what it is for Christ, his Joseph, to ride in the chariot of His love, filling his heart with holy surprise, joy, and delight. Oh! you require no tongue or pen of man to portray to you the blessedness of those interviews, or to describe the happiness of those meetings, when, like Amminadib, your soul is borne by faith and hope heavenward.

Blessed are you who are favored with these gracious visitations and precious manifestations, and who, with the surprise and gratitude of the disciples of old, exclaim, "Lord, how is it that thou dost manifest thyself unto us?" Oh! be not satisfied with a Christless profession of Christianity! Be not content with holding up the empty lamp of religious profession. Seek to obtain from Christ special manifestations of Himself to you. See that this is an essential element of your religion: that you have frequent interviews with your Lord, gracious discoveries of His beauty and love, so that you may know what it is for your true Joseph often to make ready His chariot, and come to meet you, and grant you to feel His warm and loving embrace.

And is there nothing in this meeting of Joseph and his house to remind you of your solemn end, that most gracious and halcyon hour of your life when Jesus will make ready His chariot and come to bear you home to be with Himself forever? Death is not death to you who believe in Jesus. It has lost its name with its character. It is not death to die to him who has a living Christ enshrined in his soul. The mode of our transit to eternity is by a chariot—the chariot of Jesus; for, when the hour of our departure comes, it is Christ who will come for you, and not death—Christ, and not the king of terrors. It will be the true Joseph, conducting hence His brethren and His Father's house.

Why, then, turn pale, and tremble, when you think of death? Why do you shrink from the final dissolution? Why are you all your lifetime in bondage to its fears? Oh! fear not. Beloved, when the hour of your departure comes, you will find Jesus in His chariot of love, waiting beside your dying bed, and in that chariot He will bear you to glory. He will give you in that solemn hour of departure such longings and pantings to be gone, such views of the coming bliss as shall make you exclaim, "Why do the wheels of His chariot tarry? Why does He not come to take my soul to be with His blessed self?" I beseech you then, dishonor not Him who has conquered death for you; grieve not His loving heart who is your resurrection and your life, by dwelling so much on death, forgetting in these sad musings Him who is your life, and who has conquered and triumphed over death for you. Oh! what will be the bliss, the glory of that moment, when Christ's chariot stands at your door, waiting to waft you home to be with Him forever!

But there is in this simple and affecting interview between Joseph and his family a chapter in the final history of Christ's kinsmen after the flesh, to which I must for a moment direct the reader's attention. A spiritual and intelligent mind will not find it difficult to trace a striking analogy here between the history of Joseph and his brethren, and the history of Christ and the Jewish nation. A very great glory is deepening for the Jew, a "life from the dead" awaits that ancient and extraordinary nation. It will be in striking harmony with the history of Joseph. They will be a people who had sold their Brother into bondage; who had scorned, despised, and rejected Him; who, in consequence of that act, had been brought into a condition of famine, a state of moral destitution, suffering, and need. But lo! the tidings reach them that their Messiah has actually come— that He is appointed Ruler and Judge of the earth. What will be the astonishment of the whole house of Israel—the brethren of Christ after the flesh—when the astounding fact is announced, when surmise deepens into conviction, and conviction matures into certainty, that He whom their fathers slew, whom for centuries they had scorned and rejected, is really alive! Oh, what will be their wonder, grief, and joy!

Methinks I see the hoary-headed Israelite just on the verge of eternity receiving the information that his Messiah has actually come, and is alive; and when he beholds the "wagons and provisions" which Messiah has sent to bring home to Himself His scattered brethren—in the preaching of the gospel, in the multiplication of Christian missionaries, in the wondrous movement of His providence on the mind of his nation, and in the outpouring of the Spirit of grace and supplication—how will the conviction and glory of the fact fasten upon and overwhelm his mind?

What, too, will be the mingled emotions of the whole Jewish nation, the gladness and sorrow of the people of Israel, when they thus shall rush into the embrace of their long looked-for Messiah—shall "look upon him whom they have pierced, and shall mourn?" And mark, this feature will distinctly characterize the final restoration of the Jews: it will not be the Jew seeking the Messiah—it will be the

Messiah first seeking the Jew, just as Joseph first recognized his brethren, and revealed himself to them. Famine, indeed, will have prepared them for Jesus. The pressure of spiritual need and destitution will impel them to the Savior; but when they are brought into that state to receive Christ, Christ will then manifest Himself to them as their Messiah.

And all this will illustrate the grace, mercy, and love of Jesus, who, notwithstanding all the wrong that He received from His brethren—their hands imbrued in His blood, sold into slavery, and at last crucified—yet notwithstanding these wrongs and injuries, all is fully, freely forgiven, and He condescends to uplift the veil and manifest Himself to them as their long-lost Messiah.

One of their own poets, with singular beauty, has embodied in verse the hope and expectation of his nation. Interpreted in the light of Messiah's *Second Coming*, a beauty, and a meaning yet more exquisite and expressive, attaches to the sentiments thus touchingly expressed:—

"Messiah's coming, and the tidings are rolling wide and far,
As light flows out in gladness from yon fair morning star.
He is coming! and the tidings sweep through the willing air,
With hope that ends for ever time's ages of despair.
This old earth from dreams and slumbers wakes up, and says,
    Amen;
Land and ocean bid Him welcome, flood and forest join the
    strain.

"He is coming, and the mountains of Judea ring again,
Jerusalem awakens, and shouts her glad Amen.
He is coming, wastes of Horeb, awaken and rejoice;
Hills of Moab, cliffs of Edom, lift the long silent voice,
He is coming, sea of Sodom, to heal thy leprous brine,
To give back palm and myrtle, the olive and the vine.

"He is coming, blighted Carmel, to restore thine olive bowers;
He is coming, faded Sharon, to give thee back thy flowers;

Sons of Gentile-trodden Judah, awake! behold, He comes!
Landless and kingless exiles, reseek your long-lost homes;
Back to your ancient valleys, which your fathers loved so well,
In their now crumbled cities, let their children's children dwell.
"Drink the last drop of wormwood from your nation's bitter
 cup,
The bitterest, but the latest, make haste and drink it up;
For He, thy true Messias, thine own anointed King,
He comes in love and glory, thine endless joy to bring.
Yes, He thy King is coming, to end thy woes and wrongs,
 To give thee joy for mourning, to turn thy sighs to songs."
            (*Jewish Chronicle.*)

Nor must I fail to refer to the promised and expectant day when Christ shall make ready the chariot of His glory and come the second time to meet His Church. I think no intelligent, spiritual mind can study the signs of the times, the state of the world, and not feel an overwhelming conviction that Jesus is already preparing the chariot of His *second advent*. All the events in the present history of the world indicate that the coming of the Lord draws near, yes, that He is at hand, and that to those who look for Him He will soon appear "without sin unto salvation." Those who are waiting for the redemption that shall be accomplished in the spiritual Jerusalem, who, with outstretched necks, are looking and longing for His appearing, shall be the foremost among the gladsome ones who will lift up their heads and say,—"My redemption draweth nigh."

I would ask the unconverted reader of this page—Where will you be when the Savior shall thus come in the chariot of His glory and receive the Church to Himself? Oh, remember, if He has not come to you riding in the chariot of His converting saving grace, you will be found among the multitude who shall wail with inconceivable grief in that awful hour, and will cry to the rocks and to the mountains to fall on them and hide them from the wrath of the Lamb. "Behold, he cometh with clouds; and every eye shall see him, and they also which pierced him: and all kindreds of the earth shall wail because of him. Even so, Amen." God grant that when your eye beholds Him, your heart, like that of Joseph's brethren, may bound with gladness, transport, and hope!

The second point for consideration is the EMOTION expressed. Joseph wept on the bosom of his father. "And he fell on his neck, and wept on his neck a good while." We have had occasion, in the process of this story, to remark upon the deep sensibility of Joseph's nature. God evidently fitted him, both by nature and grace, for the high mission he was to discharge. He had passed through a much-chequered history, yet no adversity, no vicissitude, no sorrow had annihilated, or even had impaired, the fine sensibilities of his nature. In this particular he was an eminent type of the Lord Jesus Christ. We doubt not that Joseph was the most loving, tender, and sympathizing of all his father's house; that his was a heart of deeper sensibility, and his nature one of more exquisite tenderness, love, and sympathy, than all the rest combined. Thus God fitted him for the high and peculiar position he was to occupy in the history of his family.

Our Jesus, the Elder Brother, centers in Himself infinitely more than all the tender love and sympathy found in His whole Church. It was necessary that by every possible human sensibility He should be qualified to be the gracious, sympathizing Head of a suffering body; and no truth is brought out in the history of Joseph more luminously, or exquisitely touching and beautiful, as portraying the Lord Jesus Christ, than the deep sensibility of Joseph's nature.

But as we have touched upon this subject in previous parts of this volume, and have discussed it at length in a separate treatise, we content ourselves with this passing reference, and hasten to conduct the reader to a consideration of the DESIRE of the patriarch—"Now let me die, since I have seen thy face, because thou art yet alive." What a touching part of our picture is this! Methinks I see the aged patriarch clasping his beloved Joseph to his bosom, and with uplifted eyes exclaiming, "I have now no more attraction to earth, nothing more to bind me here; my cup of bliss is full; let me die, for I have seen your face, and am satisfied."

Such is the influence of a believing sight of Jesus upon the soul. The sight of Christ weans from the creature, detaches from earth, disarms the mind of its fearful apprehension of dissolution, and inspires it with ardent longings to depart. It is not wrong to wish to die if that wish is prompted by weariness with sin, a panting for perfect holiness, and a longing desire to be with Jesus. This was the experience of Paul, "Having a desire to depart and to be with Christ, which is far better." Cherish this desire meekly, patiently, prayerfully, yet ardently, as a holy thing nestling in your bosom. It will tend to smooth the rugged way, to cheer the lonesome way, to illumine the darksome way— the desire and the expectation of soon seeing Jesus. It will render you prayerful and watchful—will preserve your heart from settling down in creature comforts, building its nest below God and heaven—and will keep it in expectation of the blissful moment when Jesus shall beckon the spirit home.

What a spiritually instructive picture this! Death had no terror for Jacob. Not a fear disturbed his serenity; not a cloud dimmed his hope; not a vapor veiled his prospect. Such will be the experience of the departing Christian. When the hour actually comes—when heart and flesh are failing—when the damp sweat of death is upon the brow, and the glazed eye is fixing, and the pulse is sinking, and eternity is opening to the soul—the utterance faintly breathed from those pale lips will be, "Let me go, for the day breaks. Let me die, for I have Christ in my arms, the hope of glory."

Thus was it with good old Simeon, as he clasped the infant Savior in his arms—"Now, Lord, lettest thou thy servant depart in peace, for mine eyes have seen thy salvation." And thus, too, was it with the proto-martyr, Stephen. What was it that gave to his death a fascination so great? What imparted to him such tranquillity and composure amid the storm of stones, the shouts of his infuriated murderers, and the agonies of his mangled body? We read, "He, being full of the Holy Ghost, looked stedfastly into heaven, and saw the glory of God, *and Jesus standing on the right hand of God*, and said, Behold, I see the heavens opened, and the Son of man standing on the right hand of God!" And with this vision of Jesus streaming in glory around his departing spirit, he laid his bleeding brow on the bosom of his Lord, and gently fell asleep. "Let me die the death of the righteous, and let my last end be like his."

> "Jesus, the vision of Thy face
>   Has overpowering charms;
> Scarce shall I feel death's cold embrace,
>   If Christ be in my arms."

Joseph's Introduction of His Brethren to Pharaoh

CHRIST'S PRRESENTATION OF HIS CHURCH TO GOD

Then Joseph came and told Pharaoh, and said, My father and
my brethren...are come out of the land of Canaan...And he
took some of his brethren, even five men, and presented them
unto Pharaoh. GENESIS 47:1-6

WE reach, in the course of this interesting narrative, so
replete with shadowings of Christ and His brethren, a new
phase in Joseph's history. Up to this time, a veil of
comparative secrecy appears to have concealed both his
personal and domestic history from the knowledge of
Pharaoh. A new era commences with the introduction of
his father and his brethren, little knowing what might be
the nature of the reception on the part of the king of Egypt.
We thus reach a most interesting and striking illustration
of Christ and His people—the future withdrawal of the
veil of secrecy which had hitherto concealed His Church,
and her visible appearance and final presentation to the
Father.

The Church in her present state is not a visible Church,
as Romanism teaches. She is an invisible body; her
visibility yet awaits revealment, and the time is coming

when the Lord Jesus Christ will gather together His scattered and hidden people from the four winds of heaven into one united, undivided body, and will present them to His Father, and then shall her visibility and glory be revealed. This is the truth that we propose to illustrate in the present chapter. The three points contained in the narrative are, the PRESENTATION—the DWELLING-PLACE—and the EMPLOYMENT.

First, we have the PRESENTATION by Joseph of his brethren to Pharaoh. In no previous incident of his history does he assume an attitude so commanding, so noble, so truly great, as when he stands before the king of Egypt, encircled by his brethren, and presents them as his father's house to the king. Does this picture of filial and fraternal affection move you to sensibility and admiration, my reader? Is there something touching, something grand, in the spectacle of this man, once a despised, injured, long-lost brother, but now elevated to such a position of dignity and power as to present his household with honor and favor to Pharaoh?

Transfer your thoughts for a moment to another and yet more glorious spectacle, which will be exhibited when the Lord Jesus Christ shall gather together His elect from the four winds of heaven, and shall present them unto God. Methinks He will then appear before celestial intelligences, yes, before the eyes of the universe, in an attitude of dignity, power, and glory such as He never before occupied. Look at this truth in two or three points of light, for it is an inconceivably precious and glorious prospect to the believer— the day when the veil of secrecy will be withdrawn, and the Church, no longer hidden and despised, but emerging from her obscurity and humiliation, shall be presented a glorious Church before the Father.

There are *two* presentations of the Church by Christ. There is a *present* presentation of the Church by Christ to God. Christ is in heaven the Representative of His people. He has entered heaven; has passed within the veil as the Forerunner of His Church; He is now there, presenting us every moment to God. He presents our persons with acceptance in His righteousness; He presents our petitions, praises, and offerings with acceptance through His merits. There is not a moment that you are not represented and presented in heaven. Christ represents your persons, and thus there is not a moment in which you do not stand complete and accepted before God. Christ presents your sacrifices, and thus there breathes not from your lips an utterance of prayer or an ascription of praise that ascends not to God with acceptance, presented by the Great High Priest and Intercessor within the veil. Oh, do not lose sight of this precious truth, so replete with present comfort and encouragement!

Doubtless you are often led to inquire with yourself, "Is it possible that I, who see so much defilement and imperfection within, so much infirmity and frailty in all I do for God, can be an object of His delight? Can this stammering prayer, this imperfect ascription of praise; possibly find acceptance with the Holy One?" Beloved, there is not a moment in which Christ is not representing you in heaven, presenting your person with acceptance in His righteousness, and your lowliest, feeblest offerings with fragrance, loveliness, and acceptance to God.

But there is another presentation by Christ—a *future*—and a more complete, visible, and glorious one. It is that blessed presentation which the apostle in various passages speaks of: "And you, that were sometime alienated and enemies in your mind by wicked works, yet now hath he reconciled in the body of his flesh through death, to present you holy and unblameable, [*unblamed,*] and unreproveable, [*unreproved,*] in his sight." Again: "Christ loved the church, and gave himself for it; that he might sanctity and cleanse it with the washing of water by the word; that he might *present* it to himself a glorious church." Once more: "Now unto him that is able to keep you from falling, and to *present* you faultless before the presence of his glory with exceeding joy."

We need not multiply these proofs, for it is quite clear from God's Word that there is to be *a future presentation* of the whole Church by Christ Jesus unto the Father. And on what grounds will Christ thus present us to God? In the first place, He will present His Church to God as His own chosen and loved people. He will present them to the Father as His own peculiar treasure. The Church of God was given to Christ to be redeemed. When Christ will present His Church to the Father, He will be able to say, "Here are those whom You have given me; not one of them is lost. Here is Your cabinet of precious jewels for whose recovery I went down into that world; I have brought them home to You." Oh, what a presentation will that be, when the elect of God, eternally loved by the Father, shall by the Son be brought home and presented to Him—a *glorious* Church!

He will also present them as the fruit, the precious fruit, of His obedience and death; as those on whose behalf He obeyed the law, for whose sins He suffered, bled, and died upon the cross. He shall present them as the "travail of His soul," as the reward of His sufferings, as the glorious harvest of that seed of blood that He sowed. What an appropriate crown and consummation will this be of His mediatorial work! Not one for whom He died will then be missing.

There will also remarkably appear in this perfect presentation *the power of Christ in preserving His Church.* Oh, what a crown of glory will Christ have in that day when He presents His people, whom He not only *redeemed* and bought with His precious blood, but *kept* by His power! We need as much the power of Christ to *keep* us, and finally to preserve us to eternal life, as we need the atonement of Christ to *save* us. What a glory will there be in this presentation in that day when His power shall appear conspicuous in having kept His Church, preserved His people, and upheld them through all their sufferings, temptations, and backslidings!

With the combined power of Satan, of sin, and of the world to thwart Him, yet He brought them through, and shall present them, a perfect and complete Church, to God. He will be able to say, "Here am I, and the Church You gave me: Satan strove hard to pluck them from my hand; the world sought hard to engulf them in its vortex; their indwelling sin sought hard to consume them; but here they are! I have kept them by my omnipotence, I have watched them with my sleepless eye of love, I have guarded them moment by moment, and not one of them is lost." Let this truth comfort you who are ofttimes led to fear lest, after all, you should fail to arrive at heaven. Forget not that He who had the power to *redeem* has also the power to *keep* you; and He will keep unto the end all those for whom He travailed in His agony and death upon the cross.

View this presentation of His Church to God in the light of a recompense and reward. The crown of Jesus, for all He has done, will be the Church He has redeemed by His blood. He is to wear many crowns on that day, but the brightest and the choicest will be the diadem of His Church—and a glorious diadem will that Church be. What a reward for all He has endured will it be to present His ransomed to God, all washed from every stain; not a spot, nor wrinkle, nor any such thing marring their perfect and peerless beauty. "Thou shalt also be a *crown of glory* in the hand of the Lord, and a *royal diadem* in the hand of thy God." May we, my reader, be jewels in that crown. Oh! the joy that Christ will feel at that moment! This will be the highest elevation of the joy that was set before Him—the joy, first of ransoming, and then the joy of presenting His ransomed to His Father! May we form a part of that assembly, and participate in that joy!

Observe, too, there was not only the presentation with acceptance to Pharaoh, but there was also his appointing to them a PLACE OF ABODE in the best portion of the land: "And Pharaoh spake unto Joseph,...In the BEST of the land make thy father and brethren to dwell; in the land of Goshen let them dwell." Beloved, what is heaven? what is the final glory of the saints? Is it not the best place, the richest inheritance provided by the Father for the people ransomed and brought home to glory by His Son? Our Lord reminded His disciples of this. When the two brethren sought a place, the one on His right hand, and the other on His left, in His kingdom, He thus met their blindly-offered petition: "To sit on my right hand and on my left, is not mine to give, but *it shall be given to them for whom it is prepared of my Father.*" It is our Father in heaven who appoints the place where the Church shall finally repose. Heaven is a place designated by God, chosen and consecrated by Him for the Church redeemed by the precious blood of His dear Son.

And when we enter there, it will not be as intruders in an unknown and unvisited place, but we shall enter as children welcomed to a Father's home. It will be *the best* that God can give us! He has ever bestowed upon us, who deserved the least, the best in His power to bestow—the best Savior, the best robe, the best banquet, the best inheritance. In the new heaven and the new earth there will be nothing more to taint, nothing more to sully, nothing more to embitter, nothing more to wound; no serpent to beguile, no Eve to ensnare, no spoiler to destroy, no sin to defile, no adversity to sadden, no misunderstanding to alienate, no tongue to defame, no suspicion to chill, no tear, nor sickness, nor death, nor parting. It will be the best part of the pure, radiant, glorified universe that God will assign to His people.

But Joseph's brethren were not to dwell in Egypt in inglorious indolence. "And if thou knowest any men of activity among them, then make them rulers over my cattle." Thus spoke Pharaoh. Beloved, heaven is not a place or scene of inactivity. God never made man to be idle. Even in his paradisaical state, He sent him into the garden to keep it. So that labor is coequal with man's state of innocence. And will heaven be a place of inglorious repose? Never! One of the most inviting anticipations to a renewed mind is, that it will be a place of enlarged faculties, of perfected powers. But will these perfected faculties and powers find in that sphere of perfection an appropriate range of employment? Oh yes! In heaven there is full and unceasing employment for all the glorified. They *serve God* day and night in His temple. We know not exactly what that employment is; we know that they are constantly praising God, beholding Christ, contemplating the Divine glory, and studying the mysteries of God's government.

For anything that we know, they may be messengers of God to distant spheres; for anything that we know, they may be permitted, invisibly to us, to revisit our world on some high behest of Jehovah. Be this as it may, we believe that when we shall enter on our glorified state, and our mental faculties and spiritual powers are fully developed and perfected, we shall be fully and eternally employed in a service that will be for the honor and glory of God.

And now, my reader, what will be your presentation in that solemn day? Have you a well-grounded hope that you will form part of that blessed throng whom Christ will present to His Father, all washed in His blood, and clothed with His righteousness? Have you the witness of the Spirit that you are accepted in the Beloved—that you have already been presented in a justified state to God? Have you truly repented of sin, and do you sincerely believe in the Lord Jesus Christ? If not, what will be your true and solemn position in that day? It will be banishment, eternal banishment from God, from Christ, and from heaven. If you are not found among the blessed ones of whom Christ will say, "Here am I and the children, the ransomed ones, whom thou hast given me," you must be found among those to whom He will say, "Depart, ye cursed, into everlasting fire!"

Saints of the Most High! let the prospect cheer, sanctify, and comfort you, that it will not be long that you are to labor and battle here on earth. It is but a little while that you are to occupy your present sphere of conflict, of trial, and of sorrow. The time is coming; oh, how fast it speeds! when the Lord Jesus Christ will bring you home to heaven, and will present you a part of His glorious Church to His Father! Oh, then, *then*, will come the reward of grace which Christ will give to all those who have confessed Him here on earth—who have witnessed for His truth, endured suffering on His behalf, and have proved faithful unto death. The Lord grant that in that day we may be found among the presented ones, to whom He will say, "Come, ye blessed of my Father, inherit the kingdom prepared for you from the foundation of the world!"

"He will present our souls,
 Unblemished and complete,
Before the glory of His face,
 With joy divinely great."

"Then all the chosen seed
 Shall meet around the throne,
Shall bless the conduct of His grace,
 And make His wonders known."

Jacob's Pilgrimage

THE AGED CHRISTIAN

> And Joseph brought in Jacob his father, and set him before
> Pharaoh: and Jacob blessed Pharaoh. And Pharaoh said unto
> Jacob, How old art thou? And Jacob said unto Pharaoh, The
> days of the years of my pilgrimage are an hundred and thirty
> years: few and evil have the days of the years of my life been.
> GENESIS 47:7-9

WHAT a magnificent study does this group present for the
pencil of the spiritual painter! Here is a powerful monarch,
an aged pilgrim, and an affectionate son; and from the
history and character of each, ample material might be
gathered well calculated to richly furnish our minds with
the most impressive and instructive lessons and facts in
relation to our present and future state of being. But it is
more specially around the central object of this picture—
the aged patriarch Jacob—that the peculiar interest gathers.
There are three or four suggestive features in the portrait;
may the Spirit of truth make our meditation of them
instructive and sanctifying!

The first is the PILGRIMAGE of the patriarch. The aged
saint selects one of the most striking figures with which to
depict his own and all life—"the days of the years of *my
pilgrimage.*" He stands before the king of Egypt in the
character of a pilgrim. His life, if we examine it with care,

will be found literally and strikingly to have exemplified this idea. He seemed to have no permanent resting. His life was migratory. God saw fit to lead His servant about in the wilderness, thus perfecting his character as a Christian pilgrim. He first dwelt in Canaan, from thence he removed to Padan-aram, and again he returned to Canaan. For some time he dwelt in Succoth, and then at Shechem, and after that at Hebron; and now in his old age, when we might suppose perfect repose would be vouchsafed to the aged saint, we find him, under God's special direction, emigrating into Egypt; and from there, as you will see by the sequel of his history, his remains were carried back again, and at last found their final resting-place in Canaan, the place from where he first set out.

Thus God is constantly teaching His saints that this cosmos is not their rest—that the world is but an inn, and life a journey to another and a distant environment. It is recorded of the ancient worthies that "they confessed that they were strangers and pilgrims on the earth;" they were not ashamed to acknowledge that this was their character. Let us now see how this character applies to all believers, and ascertain if in any feature it corresponds with us.

What are some of the elements, or rather characteristics of the Christian pilgrimage? In the first place, there is this characteristic—the Christian pilgrim *is not at home here in this world*. A pilgrim is never supposed to be so; he is traveling to a distant place. If ever this characteristic finds a truthful application, it is in the life of the child of God. He is not at home in this world; he does not feel so, and he is day by day made to realize that he is a stranger here, and that he experiences the heart of a stranger. Is this characteristic of the Christian pilgrimage ours? Oh, do we feel that earth is but a lodge, a sojourn as for a night? If so, then give grateful utterance to the sentiment: "My heart is a stranger here; I feel myself homeless in this world; my witness is above, my abode is on high; and if God sees fit to plant the thorn in my earthly nest, that my life should in this respect be felt to be that of a pilgrim, I will praise Him for the discipline into which it brings me, for the deepening conviction it imparts to my soul that my home is in heaven."

Another feature or characteristic of the Christian pilgrim is—*indifference to present objects, scenes, and events*. A traveler, passing through a strange city to another and distant place, feels but little or no interest in the affairs of that city, its local administration, and its party strifes. There is an emphatic and solemn sense in which we as Christians ought to be indifferent to what is transpiring around us. We say 'a sense'. We do not think that God would have His people pass blindfolded through life, abjuring their intelligent and observant faculties, taking no note of His administrative government of the world. A true child of God cannot be totally indifferent to the mode by which his heavenly Father conducts His providential government. God's providence is the handmaid of His grace; and events in the divine administration of the world that often confound the statesman, baffle the diplomatist, and revolutionize the nations of the earth, are but the awful footsteps of Jehovah preparing the way for the advancement and consolidation of His kingdom.

Our Lord, in His gentle rebuke of His disciples for not studying the "signs of the times," recognized the duty of all His followers to make themselves intelligent, interested, and prayerful students of His dealings with individuals, with families, and with nations. Beyond this we are to be Christian pilgrims, feeling no more interest or regard for these things than as though they were not. Ah, many a Christian professor merges his religion in his politics, loses the spirituality of his heavenly, in the deadening influence of his earthly calling. Beware, as a Christian man, of the politics of the world; beware of a too absorbing interest in worldly scenes; beware, oh, beware, of having the affections, thoughts, and powers of your soul swept onward by the tide of political, commercial, and scientific excitement, which drowns so many souls in perdition. As a believer in Jesus, you are a pilgrim on earth; and a denizen of heaven— you are the citizen of a better, that is, a heavenly country.

Another characteristic of the Christian's pilgrimage is— *the life of faith that he lives.* This is an essential element of the Christian pilgrimage—a life of faith in God. It is a blessed life to live. Some of our sweetest moments are those in which we trace the blessing bestowed immediately to God's hand and to God's heart, when it comes to us, so detached from what is human, and from what is the result of our own planning, scheming, forethought, and anticipation, as compels the grateful acknowledgment— "This is from my Father's love; in this I trace my Father's hand; it comes to me in answer to prayer, and as the fruit of filial, believing trust in God." If, then, we are true to our confession, the life we live must be one of faith, day by day, on the fullness of Christ, on the life of the Spirit, on a Father's care, protection, and counsel. O sweet and blessed life! it is the most God-honoring, Christ-crowning, holy life the Christian pilgrim can live. It is the happiest life too. What a pressure of anxious care it uplifts from the mind, what fears it removes, what confidence it inspires, and what peace it imparts!

A pilgrim's life must also, in a great measure, be a life of privation and vicissitude, a chequered and changeful life. It must be one of trial and disappointment. He has often a thorny path to tread, dreary, desolate, and lonely. Were it otherwise, it would be lacking in much that renders a Christian pilgrim's life blessed and enviable—a life above the ordinary beings around him. To prevent him from sliding, God often makes the believer's path flinty; to allure him into closer communion with Himself, He makes it solitary; to bring him into the deeper experience of His love and sympathy, He makes it trying and sorrowful. Thus the Christian pilgrim's path homeward is just what his heavenly Father makes it—a truth well calculated to bring us into perfect and cheerful contentedness with all God's ways.

But let us not paint the Christian pilgrim's path in hues too somber. It is not *all* loneliness and straitness; it is not *all* darkness and sorrow. Oh, no! We partake in our earthly pilgrimage ofttimes of the luscious grapes of Canaan. We often have in faith the firstfruits of glory. David speaks of *music* in his pilgrimage: "Thy statutes have been *my songs* in the house of my pilgrimage." The Christian can sing in the ways of the Lord—traveling to Zion with the songs of Zion floating from his lips. Oh! it is a slander upon the gospel of Jesus to suppose that it inculcates a religion of gloom and despondency, a religion rayless, cheerless, joyless.

Even in the deepest and most painful soul-exercises of the believer, there is more of real happiness than in the entire world combined. One would rather have the tears of the Christian than the smiles of the worldling, the mourning of the saint than the laughter of the sinner. To sing in the Lord's ways—His trying ways, His disappointing ways, His darksome ways, His chastening ways—to sing in the ways of His truth, and obedience, and love—oh, there is infinitely more sweetness and melody in those songs which wake their echoes along the Christian pilgrim's lonely, tearful, weary path, than ever breathes from the world's harp of gladness and of song. To sing of a precious Savior, of a full Christ, of a Father's dealings, of a coming glory, of an eternal heaven—

oh! who will say that the Christian pilgrim is not a joyous, happy man?

Our Christian pilgrimage, too, has its special supports, succourings, and consolations. The Lord does not leave us to tread this pilgrimage at our own cost, relying upon our own resources. Ah, no! you do not take a step in your homeward march but you are surrounded by the presence of your Savior. Jesus is with you; He knows all your sorrows, He sees all your battlings, your misgivings, your infirmities, trials, and needs. Jesus is with you in the pilgrimage, and you cannot be alone.

Nor would we forget to remind you that the Christian pilgrimage has a glorious termination. We must keep this fully in view. We seek a city that is to come; we are not journeying to any uncertain, imaginary place. We are going to our heavenly mansion; we are traveling to the celestial city; we are wending our way to our glorious inheritance, and in a little while—O solemn thought! God give us to realize it!—it will burst upon us in its glory, blessed, indescribable, inconceivable glory, and we shall exchange an earthly yet Christian pilgrimage, for the heavenly and eternal rest that awaits the people of God—the *end* of our pilgrimage!

Now, observe the CHARACTER of this pilgrimage as depicted by the patriarch—it is emphatic and striking: "And Jacob said, Few and evil have the days of the years of my pilgrimage been." This is its character—"*few and evil.*" Here is a good man's estimate of life. You will only obtain such an estimate from a child of God. It is only a Christian man, a believer in Jesus, one who lives as seeing Him who is invisible, who can form a proper estimate of life. How impressive are these words! Let us consider them for a moment.

First, the *duration* of our Christian pilgrimage—"*Few* have the days of the years of my life been." He does not compute his life by years, but by *days*. At the longest, they are but few. Ask the most aged saint, as he throws back a glance on the past, if that retrospect does not appear to be like a little speck in the horizon of his existence. At the longest, our days are but few. Compare the days of our years with the thoughts, the plans, the enterprises appertaining to our present existence. How full of thought, of enterprise, of plan is human life! How much the mind is contemplating, how much the hands are expecting to achieve! And yet, compared with what we actually accomplish, and with what we leave unfinished, how brief is our present existence!

Look at those teeming thoughts in the busy brain of man! Look at those extensive schemes he is meditating! Look at those vast enterprises he has embarked in! Why, those thoughts, those schemes, those enterprises, were they to be actually achieved and completed, would require the years of Methuselah! How contemptible, then, as to its duration, does the present life appear in contrast with the teeming, enterprising thoughts of man! His days are but *few*. "He giveth up the ghost, and in that very day his thoughts perish." All his worldly thoughts, all his ambitious thoughts, all his miserly thoughts, all his selfish thoughts, all his sinful and self-righteous thoughts perish in that day when God extinguishes his candle.

But the most impressive point of light in which we can view the brief duration of human existence is in its relation to the soul's preparation for eternity. The work of salvation is a mighty—the mightiest work, wrought in man. When we think, then, of the great work that is to be accomplished for eternity, the salvation of the soul, the preparation for a state of being that is fixed and eternal—when we remember how much is to be done in the soul before it is fit for heaven—when we think how much is to be crowded into the few days of this short and fleeting life—the soul quickened—sins pardoned—the person justified—the heart sanctified—God loved—Christ accepted—oh, it is truly but a few days that man has to prepare for an endless eternity!

My reader, are you neglecting the great salvation? Are you postponing to another and more convenient season the work of repentance? I tell you that the one work of saving your soul is the work of a life! You have no time to lose. Your hours are fleeting, your days are numbered—the sands of time are flowing fast. Onward, then, in this great work, and do not rest until you have "made your calling and election sure." Remember that salvation is of God, and that the essential work is all finished and perfected by Christ; that the work to be wrought in you by the power of the Holy Spirit is the necessary work of repentance towards God and faith in the Lord Jesus Christ—the new, divine, and heavenly birth, apart from which there can be no place for you in the new heavens and the new earth. Christ must make all things new—the heavens new—the earth new— man new—every thing, every object, and every creature shall be in harmony with the new-born creation which the coming of the Lord will usher in.

But not only are our days "few," they are "*evil.*" "Few and evil have the days of the years of my pilgrimage been." This is the solemn conviction and testimony of a man of God—of a man who knew his own heart, who as he threw back his glance on his one hundred and thirty years, could trace nothing in them all that he could speak of as being righteous and holy and good. If we take the interpretation of the word simply as referring to trials, adversities, and sorrows, what an instructive life, in that point of light, was the life of the good old patriarch! His life seemed one continuous trial, one series of vicissitudes, calamities, and sorrows. Look at him, a fugitive from the parental home while yet a youth; look at him fleeing from the wrath of his incensed brother; think of his fourteen years of labor in Laban's house; think of his crushing, domestic affliction in Shechem. Then came the supposed death of his son Joseph—then the biting famine—and then the series of trials growing out of that famine. Ah! well might he say, "Few and *evil* have the days of the years of my pilgrimage been; my life has been a life chequered and changeful and sad. Few and evil have my days been."

But this, more or less, is a picture of the Christian, find him where you may. It is through much tribulation he is to enter the kingdom. Trial is the allotment of the believer here. It is his Father's will, it is the portion of Christ's pilgrims, that affliction should trace their road hence to the eternal blessed city. Has God thus led you, beloved, or is He thus leading you now? Oh, be not discouraged or cast down! The Lord is not dealing strangely with you, but as He deals with all His saints in all ages of the world; therefore do not write hard and bitter things against yourself, and infer that you cannot be a child of God, a Christian pilgrim, one whom God loves, because the Lord afflicts you and permits you to be tempted in many stages of your Christian journey.

But, oh, what veiled blessings are these "evils!" Exempted from them, you would be exempt from the choicest lessons of the Christian school, from the most fruitful seasons of spiritual growth, from the most authentic seals of divine adoption, from some of the most tender, winning, precious unfoldings of Jesus. Oh, they are not "evil" in the sense of a judicial correction, for there is no curse, no wrath, no frown in a believer's afflictions—they are covenant blessings wearing a disciplinary garb.

But was there no allusion in these words of Jacob to the *sins* that had traced all his chequered history—to the outbreak of spiritual evil dwelling in his heart—to his ten thousand times ten thousand backslidings, declensions, and stumblings? Do you think that he did not remember how often he had erred from God, like a wandering sheep, sinning against Him who loved him so? Do you think he did not remember how much ingratitude, unbelief, and disobedience, failure and flaw, had traced the whole of his pilgrimage, from the moment that, by fraud and falsehood, he had obtained the birthright, down to the moment when, in unbelief and despondency, he pronounced against God's dealings, and exclaimed, "All these things are against me!"

Oh yes! this would be his testimony to the heathen king of Egypt: "I am but a poor sinner. My life, as a man who professedly feared God, has been shaded and defiled, tinted and tainted, with many a sinful blot, departure, and fall. I have been a disobedient, wayward, foolish child, murmuring, rebellious, and restless beneath the yoke, and many a sad memory now lays me in the dust of self-abasement before my covenant God. Behold, I am vile, and abhor myself in dust and in ashes. *Few* and *evil* have the days of my pilgrimage been."

Such will be our humiliating acknowledgment when life's pilgrimage draws near its close. "Unclean, unclean, evil and sinful have been the days of my life. I enter heaven with the publican's petition—'God be merciful to me a sinner.' I rest now my hopes of acceptance with the Holy One, not upon a long life, a useful life, an active life, a religious life; for all, *all* is stained, and sullied, and darkened with sins countless as the sands, sins as scarlet and as crimson; but I rest in the spotless righteousness, in the atoning blood, in the one sacrifice, of my Lord and Savior Jesus Christ. This is all my salvation, all my desire, and all my plea—the blood of Jesus has washed them all away."

"How old art thou?" A solemn question to ask ourselves. How old are you in nature? how old in grace? how old in sin? Sit down and ask yourself the question. Let there be a solemn pause between time and eternity—the busy whirl of life and its final account. Oh, drive not your worldly pursuits, and gains, and pleasures into the *last stages* of life! Set apart from it a season of self-examination, solemn reflection, of faithful dealing with your soul. Let your petition to God be, "Oh, spare me, that I may recover strength, before I go hence and be no more!" Let not the solemn summons to eternity surprise you. Let it not find you immersed in the cares and pursuits and gains of this world. Look well to your religion; look well to your foundation; look well to your hope! Aged pilgrim! how old are you? Nearing the end of the journey? Entering upon its last, its closing stage? Have you reached the verdant, sunlit slopes of Jordan's bank? Do its waves murmur at your feet? Do you see

"Sweet fields beyond the swelling flood?"

Oh, rejoice that you are *so near* the end of sin and sorrow, *so near* the end of the weary pilgrimage, *so near* to heaven, to Christ, to the spirits of just men made perfect.

"Shudder not to cross the stream;
Venture all your trust in Him;
Not one object of His care
Ever suffered shipwreck there."

"And Jacob blessed Pharaoh." It is a touching, an exquisitely beautiful feature this in our picture—Jacob blessing the king. Pharaoh had never been so blessed of man before! Here was a great saint blessing a great monarch. This was no empty compliment, no fawning, flattering act of the aged man of God. That the blessing of Jacob was a real blessing, there cannot be a doubt. The blessing of a man of God is one of the sweetest blessings God gives us. The prayers of a man of God, the best wishes of a believer in Jesus, are not to be despised. Jacob was a man of prayer— a man *mighty* in prayer. He wrestled all night with the Angel of the Covenant, and he was a successful petitioner with God. Now, for the king of Egypt to have had his prayers and his blessing, oh! all the riches of his kingdom were as nothing in comparison!

If God lays you on the heart of a Christian man, if God gives you a place in his prayers, his sympathies, his Christian desires, count that, my reader, among your most precious treasures. The intercessions of a godly man, the blessing of a man of prayer, of an aged pilgrim, of a departing father, of a dying mother, oh, treasure them up in the deepest cell of your memory, in the warmest nook of your heart, as among life's sweetest, holiest, costliest privileges. But, above all, seek the blessing of the God of Jacob, for the God of Jacob is yours, and it is infinitely better to have the blessing of the God of Jacob than even the blessing of Jacob himself. "I will *bless* thee, and thou shalt be *a blessing*." This is the divine order—first, *blessed of God*, and then *a blessing* to man.

Aged saint! the God of Jacob is your covenant God! And what was Jacob's testimony of God? "The God which fed me all my life long unto this day, the Angel which redeemed me from all evil." And still His promise and His presence are with you, your rod and your staff in old age, the strength of your heart and your portion forever, when your flesh and your heart fail. Does your trembling faith still cry, "Cast me not off in the time of old age; forsake me not when my strength faileth"? Again the divine promise responds, "Hearken unto me, O house of Jacob;…even to your *old age* I am he; and even to *hoar hairs* will I carry you."

Enclosed within such Almighty arms, borne upon such a Divine bosom, you have nothing to fear, and nothing to do, but in faith, hope, and calmness, to exclaim to the loved ones clustering around your dying bed, "Behold, I die! but God shall be with you." Ah! who could fill the vacant place your departure hence will create but God himself? He has promised to fill it, and will fulfill His promise. "Leave thy fatherless children, I will preserve them alive; and let thy widows trust in me."

Dying pilgrim! your Joseph is with you! Your Jesus is at your side! His blood has washed away all your sins. "I have blotted out, as a thick cloud, thy transgressions, and as a cloud, thy sins." Salvation is finished—the great debt is paid—the covenant of grace is unchangeable—and Jesus has gone before to give you an abundant entrance and a loving welcome into the everlasting kingdom. And now, you have but calmly and patiently to wait until Jesus gently closes your eyes in death, and unseals them again in heaven's glory, bliss, and immortality. "In thy presence is fulness of joy, at thy right hand there are pleasures for evermore."

"ABSENT FROM THE BODY—PRESENT WITH THE LORD."

"Absent from flesh! O blissful thought!
    What unknown joys this moment brings!
Freed from the mischiefs sin has wrought,
    From pains and fears, and all their springs.

"Absent from flesh! illustrious day!
    Surprising scene! triumphant stroke
That rends the prison of my clay,
    And I can feel my fetters broke.

"Absent from flesh! then rise my soul
    Where feet or wings could never climb,
Beyond the heavens, where planets roll,
    Measuring the cares and joys of time.

"I go where God and glory shine,
    His presence makes eternal day;
My all that's mortal I resign,
    For angels wait and point my way."

THE END

Printed in the United States
80453LV00007B/1-99